A FIELD GUIDE TO
THE LARGER MAMMALS
OF AFRICA

A FIELD GUIDE TO

The Larger Mammals
of Africa

Jean Dorst and Pierre Dandelot

with 44 colour plates

COLLINS
Grafton Street, London

First Edition 1970
Second Edition 1972
Reprinted 1976
Reprinted 1980
Reprinted 1983
Reprinted 1984
Reprinted 1986
Reprinted 1987
Reprinted 1988
Reprinted 1990

TO OUR WIVES

ISBN 0 00 219294 2

© in the text, Jean Dorst 1970
© in the colour plates, Pierre Dandelot 1970

Printed in Hong Kong by
South China Printing Co

CONTENTS

Preface	*page* 9
How to use this book	11
HEDGEHOGS: *Erinaceidae*	17
ELEPHANT SHREWS: *Macroscelididae*	18
OTTER SHREWS: *Potamogalidae*	18
HARES AND RABBITS: *Leporidae*	20
SQUIRRELS: *Sciuridae*	23
SPRING HARE: *Pedetidae*	29
LARGE RATS: *Cricetidae*	30
PORCUPINES: *Hystricidae*	34
PANGOLINS: *Manidae*	35
POTTOS and GALAGOS: *Lorisidae, Galagidae*	38
MONKEYS: *Cercopithecidae*	43
MANGABEYS, GUENONS and PATAS: *Cercopithecidae*	51
COLOBUS MONKEYS: *Colobidae*	74
CHIMPANZEE, GORILLA: *Pongidae*	83
JACKALS, FOXES, WILD DOG: *Canidae*	91
ZORILLAS, RATEL and OTTERS: *Mustelidae*	102
CIVET, GENETS and MONGOOSES: *Viverridae*	109
HYAENAS and AARDWOLF: *Hyaenidae*	128
CATS, LION, LEOPARD and CHEETAH: *Felidae*	135
DUGONG: *Dugongidae*	147
MANATEE: *Trichechidae*	148
AARDVARK: *Orycteropodidae*	150
HYRAX or DASSIES: *Procaviidae*	152
ELEPHANTS: *Elephantidae*	155
ASS and ZEBRA: *Equidae*	159
RHINOCEROSES: *Rhinocerotidae*	166
HIPPOPOTAMUS: *Hippopotamidae*	171

WILD PIGS: *Suidae*   173

CHEVROTAIN: *Tragulidae*   179

GIRAFFE and OKAPI: *Giraffidae*   182

ANTELOPES, GAZELLES, BUFFALO and allies: *Bovidae*   186

ELAND, KUDU, NYALA and BUSHBUCK: *Tragelaphinae*   186

ADDAX, ORYX, ROAN and SABLE ANTELOPES: *Hippotraginae*   200

WATERBUCK, KOB, LECHWE and REEDBUCK: *Reduncinae*   206

TOPI and allies, HARTEBEEST and WILDEBEEST: *Alcelaphinae*   218

GAZELLE, IMPALA and allies: *Antilopinae*   232

DUIKERS: *Cephalophinae*   249

PYGMY ANTELOPES, ORIBI, KLIPSPRINGER, GRYSBOK: *Neotraginae*   260

BEIRA, DIK-DIK: *Madoquinae*   267

IBEX and SHEEP: *Caprinae*   270

BUFFALO: *Bovinae*   274

Bibliography   278

Index   280

COLOUR PLATES

1	Hedgehogs, Shrews, Pangolins	*facing page* 32
2	Squirrels	33
3	Flying Squirrels	48
4	Rodents	49
5	Galago, Potto	52
6	Baboons	53
7	Patas, Mangabey	60
8	Guenons i	61
9	Guenons ii	64
10	Colobus	65
11	Chimpanzee, Gorilla	80
12	Jackals, Foxes	81
13	Foxes	84
14	Civet, Ratel, Otters	85
15	Genets and allies	92
16	Genets	93
17	Larger Mongooses	96
18	Smaller Mongooses	97
19	Small Mongooses, Zorilla	112
20	Hyaenas, Wild Dog	113
21	Smaller Cats	132
22	Medium-sized Cats	133
23	Big Cats	140
24	Wild Ass, Zebra	141
25	Rhino, Hippo	160
26	Wild Pig	161
27	Giraffe, Okapi	176
28	Eland, Bongo	177
29	Kudu, Nyala	180
30	Sitatunga, Bushbuck	181
31	Addax, Oryx	188
32	Kob	189
33	Lechwe	192

34	Reedbuck	193
35	Hartebeest	208
36	Topi, Sassaby, Bontebok	209
37	Wildebeest, Gnu, Dassie	224
38	Larger Gazelle	225
39	Smaller Gazelle	240
40	Duiker i	241
41	Duiker ii	256
42	Pygmy Antelope, Chevrotain, Dik-Dik	257
43	Grysbok, Oribi and allies	272
44	Ibex, Sheep, Buffalo	273

PREFACE

Many books have been published on African mammals. Some are purely technical, such as checklists of species found within a particular area, with their scientific names and range; others deal with only one of the African countries. They are of invaluable help for the scientist, but less useful for the layman.

However, there has been no Field Guide to the mammals of the whole continent south of the Sahara, and the need for one has often struck us while walking or driving through different regions of Africa. Hence this book. We felt that such a book would be useful at a time when more and more people are interested in African wildlife and travel, and when there is so much concern over the fate of African mammals, the last great community of large animals in the world. So we started work with enthusiasm.

But we soon found that we had seriously underestimated the task. So little is known about large animals apparently familiar to man for decades and even centuries. The systematics of many antelope and primates need to be thoroughly revised. The status and distribution of many other groups, such as the small carnivores, are largely a matter of guesswork. Large areas of Africa have still to be investigated thoroughly, particularly in Ethiopia and West Africa. And in spite of all the information gathered by hunters and travellers, and all the biological research of recent years, relatively little is known about the habits of most African mammals.

This book is not a work of systematics. We have tried to follow the modern trends of classification—but not too rigidly: ease of identification sometimes seemed to require a modified order. Nor is it a work of bio-geography. The maps are mere sketches to show the broad lines of distribution as known today. And it is certainly not a comprehensive book on mammals, with full descriptions of the animals, their coat, horns, skull and teeth, their ecology and behaviour. We have limited its scope to species which a mammal watcher can identify in the field, south of Tropic of Cancer. We have ignored all those smaller mammals which are difficult to observe and impossible to identify—except by specialists holding a specimen in the hand or through an examination of the skull and teeth.

It is meant primarily as a practical book for recognition. We have concentrated on game, carnivores and primates, adding some species frequently seen, like big diurnal rodents, squirrels, a few shrews, and oddities like pangolins, aardvark and manatee. All the species described are illustrated in colour.

We received constant co-operation from many well-known scientists.

Several sets of rough drafts were circulated for comments and we are most grateful here to Mr. W. F. H. Ansell, Dr. R. Bigalke, Prof. F. Bourlière, Mr. L. H. Brown, Mr. C. G. Coetzee, Dr. K. Curry-Lindahl, Mr. R. W. Hayman, Dr. X. Misonne, Mr. R. Rosevear, Mr. N. Simon and Dr. L. M. Talbot. They made many most useful comments, suggestions and criticisms. Mr. C. W. Benson, Mr. J. H. Blower, Dr. A. Kortlandt, Dr. V. de Pienaar, Dr. U. Rahm and Mr. D. R. M. Stewart were also particularly helpful, as was Prof. Th. Haltenorth in collecting German names.

For specimen material in addition to that kept at the Museum of Paris, we made use of the extensive collections at the British Museum (Natural History), London, the Institut Royal des Sciences naturelles, Brussels, and the Musée Royal de l'Afrique Centrale, Tervuren. Dr. G. B. Corbet, Mr. R. W. Hayman, the late Dr. S. Frechkop, Dr. X. Misonne, Dr. M. Poll and their staffs have been most helpful.

We called on the help of many zoos. Professor J. Nouvel and his staff at the Parc Zoologique de Vincennes and the Ménagerie du Jardin des Plantes were exceptionally kind. We are also much indebted to the London and Antwerp Zoological Gardens. Their directors, Dr. L. Harrison Matthews, and Dr. W. van den Bergh, and their staffs all helped us in every possible way. It would be impossible to list here all the directors and staffs of National Parks, Game Reserves and other areas throughout Africa, who kindly helped us in our travels and observations in the field. In preparing the illustrations we benefited greatly from numerous unpublished pictures taken by various photographers; we are particularly indebted to Mr. M. Langer who supplied so many documents to us.

Rowland Ward Ltd. and its director, Mr. Gerald A. Best, kindly allowed us to make use of material published in Rowland Ward's *Records of Big Game.*

Mr. W. F. H. Ansell checked many maps and very generously provided us with certain first hand and unpublished information. Mr. F. Edmond-Blanc contributed with many records, particularly from Portuguese Africa. Mr. F. Roux did the same for the Senegal. Dr. F. Petter and Mr. J. Roche contributed valuable information. Mrs. Jean Dorst drew the distribution maps and improved them to a large extent. Mr. J. Brouillet drew the geographic and vegetation maps, while Miss Odile Jachiet coped nobly with typing and re-typing the manuscript.

We would like to express our deep gratitude to all of them. This book owes a great deal to their wide knowledge and generous assistance.

J.D. and P.D.

HOW TO USE THIS BOOK

This book is primarily intended to be used for identification of mammals in the wild. Many are nocturnal and secretive in their habits, particularly carnivores and smaller mammals—such as most rodents. Most primates are diurnal, but as they live in close habitats, their recognition often is quite difficult. So are many forest dwellers, even among larger mammals, like duikers and forest antelopes. Plains game is easier to observe, and many larger carnivores like big cats, jackals, and hyaenas are seen by day.

We have listed only characters which can be noted in the field; if characterisation sometimes seems vague, it is because these mammals do not show obvious field marks; two species can look much alike and differ mainly by internal characters (skull, teeth etc.).

Recognition

Those not yet well acquainted with the mammals should first study the plates. This will at least determine the group to which the mammal in question belongs, and in most cases the illustrations and the short captions given opposite will suffice for identification (most illustrations are drawn from live animals, photographs or field notes; but for a few species no documents are available and we have had to imagine what they would be like when alive). Species are illustrated by an adult male, unless specified by the signs ♂ (male) and ♀ (female). When several well-characterised subspecies can be recognised, the name of the subspecies illustrated is indicated between brackets on the opposite page.

From the plates you can turn to the descriptions in the main text and read the characters listed. Take note not only of the pattern, colour contrasts and coloration, but also of the general features, the shape of the body, paying particular attention to the field marks indicated by bars on the plates. The distribution maps will help in showing which species are to be found in your area. The characters given under *Similar species* will draw your attention to the species showing superficially the same characters. Finally the data given under *Habitat* and eventually *Habits* (particularly social behaviour, gait etc.) should help you to recognise the animal.

Do not forget that identifying mammals can also be a matter of elimination.

One must be particularly careful in identifying young or subadults. Shape and development of horns are especially misleading in the case of antelopes; the horns of young animals may seem quite odd compared with the final stage reached in the adult, and can sometimes resemble those of a very different species.

11

The geographical variation within the range of a species must be taken into account. Most of the species are illustrated by one animal only, showing the average type; other populations belonging to the same species can be markedly different, particularly among monkeys. Such points are treated in the text under the heading *Intraspecific variation.*

Measurements

The most useful measurement to estimate the size of larger mammals is the height at shoulder. This is given for most species, except for the long-bodied ones, like genet, mongoose and rodents, and for the monkeys; the length of body is given for those. In the text, the words 'large' or 'small' must be understood as *proportionately* large or small, in relation to the size of the animal or its general features.

The given measurements (in inches, rarely in feet) and weights (in pounds, rarely in tons) are average figures for the species. They may vary to a wide extent individually and according to sex, age, race and season (weight). They should be considered as rough indications only.

The animals on each plate are illustrated to the same scale, though it was impossible to keep to the same scale throughout the book, owing to the great differences in size. The measurement given in the text will assist the reader.

For horn lengths, two figures are given: the first is the length of an approximate or average good head of the species (and not of any particular subspecies), the second the maximum possible length known or record length as given by Rowland Ward's *Records of Big Game*, XI edn., 1962 (with two addendum lists). Thus for Grant's Gazelle: '22; 31¾' means 'good average horns measure about 22 inches; the record is 31¾ inches'. For the method of measuring trophies, the reader should also refer to that classic work.

Similar Species

Under this heading the most similar species are listed with their main distinctive field marks. These species are not always closely related, but may superficially show the same features. Only those animals occurring in the same habitat are listed. Cross-references are given.

Habitat

The type of habitat can be an important aid to identification. Many animals are closely linked to a particular type of habitat, while others do not show very precise ecological preferences and are therefore widespread through a wide range of habitats. The information given is only approximate.

The vegetation map on p. 15 is based largely on the *Vegetation Map o, Africa* published on behalf of l'Association pour l'Etude taxonomique de la Flore d'Afrique Tropicale by Oxford University Press (1959), but is considerably simplified. It shows the main types of vegetation in Africa,

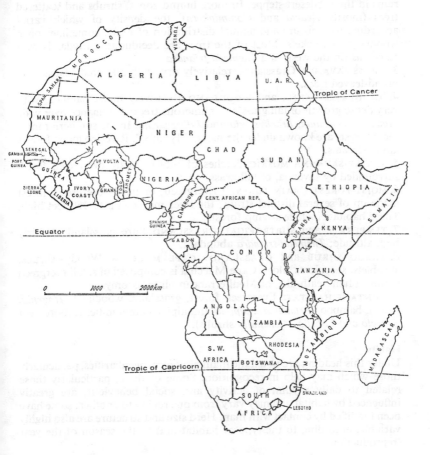

AFRICA: POLITICAL BOUNDARIES AND RIVERS

so that the reader may compare distribution maps with the vegetation belts.

The main vegetation types shown on the map are as follows:

1. DESERT An area with widely scattered plants, often almost entirely devoid of vegetation, owing to the very low rainfall.

2. SUBDESERT STEPPE, 'SUDAN' SAVANNA, WOODED STEPPE Low perennial plants widely spaced, and grasses, generally low, which flourish after the rains in the subdesert steppe. In more humid zones, shrubs and scattered trees (mostly *Acacia* and *Commiphora*), the density of which varies according to moisture and annual distribution of rains; sometimes open woodland or thickets. Most of the trees are deciduous. Grasslands with *Cenchrus* (in the west) and *Themeda triandra*.

3. GRASS SAVANNA Grasslands, relatively dry, with scattered acacias and broad-leaved trees.

4. 'GUINEA' SAVANNA and WOODLAND Relatively moist habitats, with very dense growth of tall grass and numerous trees; dominance over wide areas of *Isoberlinia*, *Brachystegia* and *Julbernardia*. In the southern range, these forests are known under the name 'Myombo'. Riverine moist forests along streams.

5. FOREST-SAVANNA MOSAIC Patches of moist, partly evergreen, forest surrounded by savanna, of tall grass.

6. MOIST FOREST ('RAIN FOREST') Evergreen, or partly evergreen, forest made up of several distinct strata; the trees may be up to 180 feet high. These habitats include swamp forests.

7. TEMPERATE and SUBTROPICAL GRASSLAND Pure grassland at fairly high altitude; *Themeda triandra* abundant.

8. KAROO SHRUB and GRASSLAND: CAPE MACCHIA Woody shrubs, shrublets, succulents, aloes. Cape Macchia is composed of small evergreen shrubs, often heath-like, of Mediterranean physiognomy.

9. MONTANE HABITATS Evergreen forest, grassland, woodland (*Hagenia*, *Erica*), bamboo (*Arundinaria alpina*) and alpine communities (arborescent *Senecio* and *Lobelia*, *Alchemilla* shrubs).

Habits

Under this heading are noted the main biological peculiarities, particularly those which may help in recognition. Some of these, particularly those related to daily rhythm of activity and social behaviour, are greatly influenced by habitat and may vary from one region to another; some have been modified by contact with man. Herd size and structure are also highly variable, according to the type of habitat and to the season of the year (reproduction).

Distribution Maps

The black parts of the maps represent the approximate areas within which the species may be found. This does not mean that it will be found over the

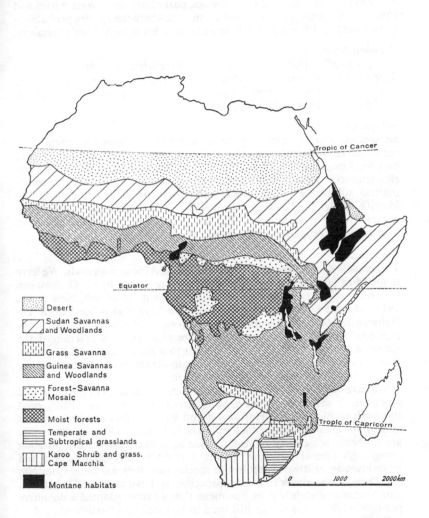

Tropic of Cancer

Equator

Tropic of Capricorn

Desert

Sudan Savannas
and Woodlands

Grass Savanna

Guinea Savannas
and Woodlands

Forest-Savanna
Mosaic

Moist forests

Temperate and
Subtropical grasslands

Karoo Shrub and grass.
Cape Macchia

Montane habitats

0   1000   2000km

AFRICA: VEGETATION ZONES

entire range, but only where suitable habitat exists, and where man has not suppressed local populations. Former distribution has not been taken into account. The boundaries are only approximate, for we are still not aware of the exact distribution of most species, particularly over West Africa and Ethiopia. A question mark indicates an area where the species probably is to be found, but from which it has not yet been recorded with certainty.

Common Names

There is no official list of vernacular names for African mammals. We have adopted the most commonly used, but they may change from one country to another, and have added French (F), German (G), Kiswahili (K) and Afrikaans (A) names where appropriate.

Subspecies

Subspecies, which within the geographic range of a species represent races recognisable by morphological characters, variations in coloration, size and development of horns, are usually not recognisable in the field. Their characteristics are mostly apparent in museum series. We have therefore omitted subspecies unless some well-marked races are fairly easy to identify. Under the heading *Intraspecific variation* we have indicated the general trends of variation within the species and listed the local races which can be recognised in the field.

Systematics

This book is not concerned with systematics of African mammals. We have followed as far as possible the classification proposed by G. G. Simpson (*Principles of Classification and a Classification of Mammals*, New York, 1945) adopted by most mammalogists. We have also made use of Th. Haltenorth (*Die Klassification der Saügetiere: Artiodactyla*, 1963) for even-toed ungulates. But for practical reasons we have rearranged the sequence adopted by most mammalogists to make the book easier to use. Within each group, we go from the larger to the smaller member as a rule, except when the animals look quite different.

We have had a hard time with some groups. Systematics of the genet and mongoose is still in its infancy. Many groups of 'Ungulates' badly need thorough revision. Bubal Hartebeest and Red Colobus can be split into several well defined forms, which might be full species. Dibatag and impala are probably not closely related to gazelle. Duiker constitute a puzzling group with several 'problem' forms. Dik-dik need re-examination and probably may be divided into more species than they are here. Common and Defassa Waterbuck may be conspecific, as Bubal and Red Hartebeest. Our treatment certainly does not mean that we have adopted a definitive position on questions which still need to be carefully investigated.

We have given the main external characteristics of each group of mammals within the scope of this book, but we have ignored the anatomical and structural characters as useless for identification in the field.

ORDER Insectivora

Small mammals, primitive in structure, usually with short limbs, a long, narrow snout and numerous teeth, the cheek-teeth with cusps arranged in a V or W (an adaptation for grasping and crushing insects and the kinds of hard food on which they feed).

Some of them are tiny creatures (some shrews are the smallest of all mammals), rarely seen, although sometimes very common.

Ubiquitous over the world, except for Australia and most of South America, they are well represented in Africa (Elephant Shrews, Golden Moles, Hedgehogs, Otter Shrews, Shrews).

Most of the species escape the attention of the non-specialist. However, a few are frequently seen, either because they are larger or because, although small, they are diurnal, like the Giant Musk Shrew (*Crocidura occidentalis* and allies), from western Africa (head and body up to 5 in.), which lives in houses. Hedgehogs, Elephant Shrews and Otter Shrews can sometimes be observed in the field.

HEDGEHOGS: Erinaceidae

The members of this family are immediately characterised by their upper-parts being entirely covered by hard, sharp spines, their protection against predators. They are able to roll themselves into a tight ball, thereby protecting their face, short limbs and underparts. The muzzle is pointed and protruding.

Hedgehogs[1] are widespread over Europe, Asia and Africa. In North Africa and in the Saharan zone, they are represented by the Long-eared Hedgehog (*Hemiechinus auritus*), easily recognisable by its very large ears, erect and somewhat pointed (fringes of the desert in north-eastern Africa, and also driest part of western and central Asia); and by the Desert Hedgehog (*Paraechinus aethiopicus*) which also has fairly large ears, rather long legs and a strikingly contrasted pattern on the head, the muzzle being dark brown, the rest of head and neck white; fur of underparts is long and soft (northern Africa to Near East). Farther south are found several forms which resemble each other closely. The Common Hedgehogs of tropical Africa are *Atelerix albiventris* (p. 32), *A. pruneri* and allies, all similar to the European Hedgehog. In southern Africa, *Erinaceus frontalis* is the common species.[2] (p. 32)

Hedgehogs are mainly nocturnal, and hide in holes or in thickets during the day. They feed on various insects, worms, snails, young rodents, bird's eggs, vegetable matter and soft fruits. In cold climates, they hibernate during the winter.

[1] F Hérisson. G Igel. A Krimpvarkie. K Kalunguyeye.
[2] Related to another species, *E. algirus*, from North Africa. Extralimital.

The litter usually numbers 4, but may reach 6–7. The young are born in holes or in nests made in the grass.

ELEPHANT SHREWS: Macroscelididae[1]

Members of this family, indigenous to Africa, vary between the size of a mouse and that of a common rat, occasionally larger. They are recognisable by their elongated and mobile snout, like a little trunk (hence their common name). The hind legs are well developed, slender, and much longer than the fore-legs, giving to the animal the appearance of a miniature kangaroo. (However, their common name of 'Jumping shrews' is inadequate, for their usual form of progress is a run or a walk; they never hop like a Jerboa.) The tail is usually long and the ears fairly large.

Several genera and many species have been described and some cannot be distinguished in the field. Members of the genus *Elephantulus* of the size of a small rat, are found in the Sahara and in the driest savannas, down to South Africa, but as yet are not known from western Africa. Others, belonging to the genera *Macroscelides*, *Nasilio* and *Petrodromus* (p. 32) are spread over eastern and southern Africa, some to the Ubangui basin and the northern bank of the Congo.

The Chequered Elephant Shrews (*Rhynchocyon*) are easily recognised by the bigger size (head and body up to 12 in.), and the chequered pattern on the back (p. 32). Rows of white rectangular spots contrast with the fawn ground colour. Various forms of this attractive animal are spread in forested country from the northern Congo to the Zambesi River.

Several species of Elephant Shrews frequent rocks exclusively; others live among grasses and bushes. Most are found in dry open country, but some, such as members of the genera *Petrodromus* and *Rhynchocyon*, live in forests.

Solitary or living in pairs, they are mostly diurnal, hiding in holes in the ground, in crevices, or under rocks or the roots of large trees. Insectivorous, they feed mostly on ants, and also on grasshoppers and beetles. Apparently they do not drink. They never go too far from their retreat, using recognisable pathways leading to the feeding grounds. Elephant Shrews show alarm by tapping rapidly with their hind feet and utter a shrill but loud squeak. They are preyed on mostly by raptorial birds.

OTTER SHREWS: Potamogalidae

OTTER SHREW *Potamogale velox* Du Chaillu   p. 32
(Giant Water Shrew)
F Potamogale, Parpassa G Otterspitzmaus
Identification: Length (without tail) 12 in. An otter-like giant 'shrew' with a fairly broad, flattened snout, an elongated body, tail thick at its base,

[1] F 'Rat' à trompe. G Rüsselspringer. A Klaasneus. K Sange.

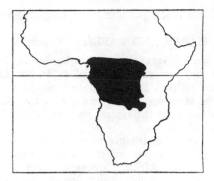

Otter Shrew, p. 18

compressed laterally like a rudder and covered with short hairs. Coat dense and soft, glossy chocolate brown on the upperparts, white on the underparts. Long, stiff vibrissae on the snout.[1]

Habitat: Rivers and swamps in forested areas, including mountainous regions. Map, p. 19.

Habits: Aquatic, the Otter Shrew hides among reeds and aquatic plants or in burrows, the entrances of which are below water level. It swims very well, the tail serving as a rudder. It feeds on aquatic insects, crustaceans, molluscs, fish and amphibians.

The litter apparently consists of two young.

---

[1] Two related species, one from Mt Nimba, Guinea (*Micropotamogale lamottet*), the other from Ruwenzori, Congo (*M. ruwenzorii*), have been described; both are much smaller and more shrew-like.

ORDER Duplicidentata (Lagomorpha)

HARES AND RABBITS: Leporidae

This order was formerly regarded as a suborder of the Rodentia, but there are several very important points of difference. Lagomorphs have two upper incisors on each side, a minute second incisor being located directly behind the large first one. There are many other characteristics which separate them from the typical rodents, which is also shown by palaeontological evidence.

Lagomorphs are widely distributed over both the Old and New Worlds. The best known are the rabbits and the hares, the only members of this order occurring in tropical Africa.[1] Externally, hares[2] are characterised by their long ears, short and woolly tail and long slender limbs. The hind legs are especially long and well adapted to jump and to run at high speed. Their coat is soft and woolly. Many of them have a white spot on forehead. Most live in open habitats. Several species are found in Africa south of the Sahara; they are very difficult to identify, even in the hand, as the most important specific characters are found in the morphology and anatomy of the teeth and skull.[3] The systematic status of some forms is still doubtful.

One rabbit occurs in central Africa.

CRAWSHAY'S HARE *Lepus crawshayi* De Winton[4] p. 49
A smaller hare with short ears, not unlike a rabbit in some of its features.[5] Face sloping, muzzle projecting beyond the incisors. Generally dark coloured; above bay, grizzled with blackish, neck rufous. Tail moderately long, black above, white laterally and below.
Habitat: Savannas. Map, p. 25.

CAPE HARE *Lepus capensis* L.[6]
A smaller hare with moderately short ears. General colour yellowish grey, especially on the flanks. Nape buffish grey. Distinguished from Crawshay's Hare by its larger, more typically hare-like ears, and its fulvous yellow coloration; from the Scrub Hare by the greyish back of neck instead of

[1] True rabbits (*Oryctolagus*) do not exist south of the Sahara, but are found in North Africa.

[2] F: Lièvre. G: Hase. A: Haas. K: Sungura.

[3] The enamel folds of the upper incisors are among the most important characters. We follow here the classification proposed for the African hares by Petter; see *Mammalia*, **23**, 1958; *ibid.*, **27**, 1963: and *Zeitschr. Saugetierkunde*, **26**, 1961.

[4] Crawshay's Hare is considered as possibly conspecific with the Indian Hare, *L. nigricollis*, from south-eastern Asia.

[5] In some parts of its habitat it is called 'rabbit' by Europeans.

[6] Cape Hare should be considered as conspecific with the European Hare, *L. europaeus*, from Europe and northern Asia.

pale rufous and by the relatively shorter ears; no white spot on forehead. Tail black above, white laterally and below (or entirely white, *L. c. starcki*, Ethiopia).
Habitat: Open grassy flats, with scattered scrub. Map, p. 25.

SOUTHERN BUSH or SCRUB HARE *Lepus saxatilis* F. Cuvier
A large hare with enormous ears and a proportionately long tail. General colour grey, with no rufous on flanks and limbs. Usually a rufous patch on nape. Tail black above, white laterally and below.
Habitat: Scrub and dry forest. Map, p. 25.

ABYSSINIAN HARE *Lepus habessinicus* Hemprich and Ehrenberg
A puzzling species, very variable in size and coloration (upland specimens are larger and have longer ears than those from lowlands). General coloration from greyish ochraceous and even isabelline to tawny brown. Where its range overlaps with Cape Hare, it may be distinguished by the coloration of the back of ears on which there is only a small distal black or grey spot instead of a broad black patch.
Habitat: From desert lowlands up to 8000 feet.[1] Map, p. 25.

RED ROCK HARE *Pronolagus crassicaudatus* (I. Geoffroy) (and allies)
A hare with short ears, shorter legs and feet, more rabbit-like in its features, and a very bushy tail, which is entirely reddish or brown, never black and white as in the true hares of the genus *Lepus*. General colour reddish brown, especially on limbs, paler below. In contrast with other Leporids, Red Hares are noisy and utter loud screams.
Habitat: Rocky country or fringe of forest. They use rocky blocks as observation posts and shelter under boulders rather than in 'forms' like the ordinary hares. Map p. 25.

BUSHMAN HARE *Bunolagus monticularis* (Thomas)
A hare with rather long ears, very short and woolly feet and a thick, rounded tail. Fur soft and fine, but not woolly. General colour above grizzled drab-grey, with no rufous suffusion; sides dark drab. A patch of rich deep fulvous on nape, in strong contrast with the general coloration. Chin yellowish white, separated from the cheeks by a blackish line; throat pinkish buff; belly yellowish brown. Tail vinaceous brown, with a black tip.
Habitat: Scrub along the eroded dongas. Map, p. 25.

[1] We do not list some particular forms of hares, like *L. whytei* (Tanzania, Malawi, Rhodesia), the status of which is still uncertain.

Habits of hares: Hares are confined to open and even desert habitats with the ecological preferences recorded above. They live singly or in pairs. Nocturnal, they spend the day in a 'form', a smooth patch under tufts of grass on bushes, where they lie flat with the ears laid back over the back, except the South African Red Hares which usually shelter under rocks. They never excavate burrows like rabbits.

They are very fast runners owing to their long and powerful hind-legs. Speed is their only means of escape from their enemies, among which are birds of prey, most of the smaller carnivores and the cheetah.

They feed almost entirely on grass.

Young, one per litter, sometimes 2–4, are born in an unlined 'form'. Well haired at birth, they are very soon able to look after themselves, though the mother feeds them until they are about a quarter grown.

AFRICAN RABBIT   *Poelagus marjorita* (St. Leger)   p. 49
A rabbit, smaller and stouter than the hares, with short ears and rather short, harsh fur. Above drab grey, with a rufous spot on the neck. Flanks lighter. Underparts white. Tail short, brownish above, sides and below, white.

Habitat: Woodlands and clearings in forest. Map, p. 39.

Habits: Unlike hares, this rabbit lives in burrows, where the young are born naked.

ORDER Rodentia

Because it includes such a large number of forms which play a dominant role in the mammalian world, the order Rodentia is the most important group of mammals. The many species are very different from each other in size, appearance and habits. However, rodents are remarkably uniform in their structural characters, and particularly in the possession of curved, large and powerful gnawing front teeth (incisors) in both the upper and lower jaws (one on each side). These teeth grow throughout life and are constantly worn off by gnawing. Canines are invariably absent, and the incisors are separated from the grinding cheek-teeth (often three, rarely less, sometimes up to five) by a wide gap (diastema). These features oblige the rodents to take their food in a very peculiar manner. They gnaw and then grind their food—mainly vegetable matter, sometimes insects or small animals—in a way that is unique among mammals.

Most of the rodents are small, not exceeding the size of a rat or a house mouse, and many are nocturnal. They are thus very difficult to observe and to identify in the field. Their identification may be difficult even when they are in hand, as the distinction between species is based on anatomical characters, principally the teeth.

This very successful group of mammals is spread all over the world. It is well represented in Africa south of the Sahara, where the number of species probably exceeds several hundred. They will not be described here in detail.

A few species, owing to their size, coloration, diurnal activity, or familiarity with man, may, however, be observed and even recognised in the field.

Such are the Flying Squirrels, Squirrels, Spring Hares, some large Rats and the Porcupines. Their main characters are listed below.

SQUIRRELS: Sciuridae

Africa is inhabited by a large number of squirrels[1] belonging to a dozen genera with numerous species. These well-known rodents are easily recognised by their general features, their elongated body, short legs, small ears lying close to the head, and their furry, even bushy, tail. It is quite impossible to give a list and description of all the species, most of which are not recognisable from each other in the field. We shall only indicate the main types, for each of which a number of species are distributed over Africa.

Squirrels may easily be divided into two groups according to their mode of life, arboreal or terrestrial.

Tree Squirrels

These squirrels, arboreal in habits, characterised by their soft fur, and curved and sharp claws, are found only in wooded country or in dense

[1] F Ecureuil. G (Eich)hörnchen. A Eckhorinkie. K Kindi, kidiri.

forest, to which many species are confined. Several types can be distinguished.

GIANT FOREST SQUIRREL (*Protoxerus stangeri*) (p. 33). Large size (head and body up to 14 in.); big head; long very bushy tail (over 12 in.), with white and black rings; rather harsh, speckled coat, olive-brown to blackish, greyer on the head; underparts thinly haired, almost naked, the fur stopping abruptly along the sides. High forest, and penetrating the Guinean savannas in the riverine forests (from Sierra Leone to Kenya, Tanzania and Angola). Its great size and strength make it able to crush hard foods (oil-palm nuts) which are too tough for smaller species.

PALM SQUIRREL (*Epixerus ebii*) (p. 33). Large size (head and body 10–12 in.); upperparts speckled, rufous and black, becoming bright rufous on limbs; underparts almost naked; tail well haired, black and white. High forest from Sierra Leone to Ghana. A related species (*wilsoni*) is found in Gabon and in the Cameroons.

STRIPED SQUIRRELS (*Funisciurus*). Small or medium sized (head and body 6–8 in.; fur very soft, marked by at least one conspicuous longitudinal stripe on the upperparts; tail moderately long, not very bushy, sometimes shorter than head and body, carried arched over the back in an S shape. A dozen species are distributed over Africa, through high forests and woodlands. Some are dark coloured, with a striking pattern of olive green tinged with greyish on back, chestnut red on head and limbs, and pure white on underparts. Red-footed Squirrel, *F. pyrrhopus* (Guinean and Congolese forests) (p. 33); White-spotted Squirrel, *F. leucostigma* (high forests from Ivory Coast to the Cameroons). Others are lighter coloured, mostly olive green (*F. congicus*). The two Four-striped Squirrels, *F. lemniscatus* (p. 33) and *F. isabella*, have a striking pattern of four black stripes down the back, in strong contrast with the brownish or olive green ground colour (high forest from Nigeria to Gabon). Both species may be found in the same locality and with almost the same pattern and coloration, they cannot be distinguished in the field.

SUN SQUIRRELS (*Heliosciurus*). Medium sized (head and body up to 10 in.); uniform in colour on the upperparts, which are finely speckled with black, brown, reddish and whitish, the general effect varying from grey to greenish and brown, according to the species or races. No lateral stripes. Underparts and limbs sometimes in strong contrast with the upperparts. Tail long (as long as head and body or even longer), the same colour as back, generally annulated. About ten species distributed through high forests and woodlands. The Gambian Sun Squirrel *H. gambianus* (p. 33) (savanna from Senegal to Angola and Mozambique) is often very pale grey or light brown above, and white below; the only typical tree squirrel found in savannas. The Small Forest-squirrels, *H. punctatus* and allies (light, secondary and gallery forests from Upper Guinea to eastern Africa) are darker coloured, brown, or dark grey on the upper-parts, without the warm colours present in other species. The

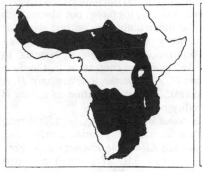

Crawshay's Hare, p. 20

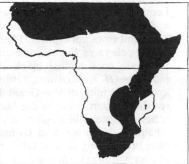

Cape Hare, p. 20

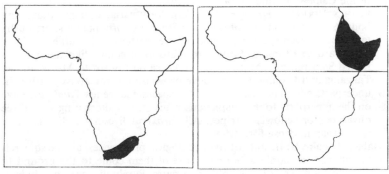

Scrub Hare, p. 21

Abyssinian Hare, p. 21

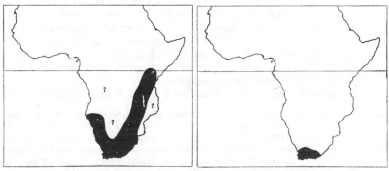

Red Rock Hare, p. 21

Bushman Hare, p. 21

Red-legged Sun Squirrel, *H. rufobrachium* (p. 33) (high forest from Sierra Leone to Kenya and Angola), is very variable in colour, but always with a deep red or orange tinge on the inner limbs, in contrast with the blackish brown upperparts. The intensity of coloration varies from relatively pale races (Isabelline Sun Squirrel, *H. r. isabellinus*, Nigeria) to very dark ones, almost black above, in strong contrast with the deep red limbs (*H. r. maculatus*, Guinea; *H. r. undulatus*, Kilimanjaro; *H. r. nyanzae*, vicinity of the Great Lakes). The intensification of colour is roughly proportionate to the humidity of climate.[1]

Several species belonging to the genus *Aethosciurus* (Green Squirrels) inhabit the Guinean and Congolese forests (*Ae. poensis*, smaller size, olive brown, long slender tail) or eastern Africa (*Ae. ruwenzorii, lucifer*).

PYGMY SQUIRREL (*Myosciurus pumilio*) (p. 33). Very small size (the smallest squirrel in the world; head and body 3 in.); upperparts buffy green tinged with rufous; underparts whitish; tail narrow. High forest of the Cameroons and Gabon.

BUSH SQUIRRELS (*Paraxerus*) (p. 33). Very variable in size (head and body 6–10 in.) and in coloration, with a proportionately short bushy tail. About seven species distributed over eastern and southern Africa, northward to Ethiopia. Some are uniform in colour like the Yellow-footed Squirrel, *P. cepapi* (southern Africa northward to Mozambique, Tanzania and Katanga); dark olive brownish or grey above, with light underparts and yellowish feet. Other species (subgenus *Tamiscus*) have on the upperparts four conspicuous black stripes alternating with three olivaceous or yellowish stripes. All *Paraxerus* live in wooded savanna rather than in dense forest.[2]

Habits of squirrels: In spite of their ecological preferences, all the squirrels listed above are mainly arboreal; some of them come to the ground to search for food. They live singly or in pairs. Purely diurnal, they hide at dusk in holes in trees or sometimes among dense vegetation. Some, like the Four-striped Squirrels, build a nest of leaves and plant fibres.

Squirrels have a very varied diet; many fruits, even very hard ones, like nuts or oil-palm nuts, are consumed, also leaves and young shoots. A part of their diet is carnivorous: eggs, young birds, lizards, insects. They grind very hard material, even ivory, probably to wear down their teeth. They often invade farms, cocoa or oil-palm plantations and may cause much damage, even becoming pests.

Some squirrels, like the Gambian Sun Squirrel, living in countries with

[1] All the sun-squirrels listed above belong perhaps to one species or super-species. See Ingoldby, *Proc. Zool. Soc. London* 1927, p. 471.

[2] The American Grey Squirrel (*Sciurus carolinensis*), recognisable by its greyish colour and bushy tail bordered with white-tipped hairs, was introduced around 1900 from eastern North America into South Africa. It spread over an area of a few hundred square miles in the south-western Cape Province, to the limits of suitable environments (conifer plantations).

a seasonally variable climate, seem to store food for use during the dry season.

Ground Squirrels

These squirrels are readily distinguished from their arboreal congeners by their coarse, bristly and scanty pelage with little underfur, the belly being almost naked. Their claws are long and stout, only slightly curved, and the ears are very short. They are purely terrestrial, seldom climbing trees, and are fossorial in habits. All African Ground Squirrels belong to the genus *Xerus*[1] and several species may be recognised. Some have a conspicuous stripe along the flank. The most widely distributed is the Striped Ground Squirrel, *X. erythropus* (p. 33), a large squirrel (head and body 9–12 in.), with the upperparts varying from pale sandy to reddish and dark brown (according to the humidity of the environment), a white lateral stripe and whitish underparts. The very bushy tail is as long as the head and body, covered by long black and white hairs forming alternating rings (savanna, from Mauritania to Ethiopia, Kenya and Uganda); the only ground squirrel in West Africa.[2]

In southern Africa are found two related species, both brownish with a pronounced white stripe along the flanks: the Cape Ground Squirrel, *X. inauris*, distributed from South-West Africa to northern Cape Province; and the Kaokoveld Ground Squirrel, *X. princeps*, from Southern Angola and South-West Africa, distinguished by three blackish bands on the long hairs of the tail, instead of two, and yellow, instead of white, incisors.

The Pallid Ground Squirrel, *X. rutilus* (p. 33), distributed in eastern Africa from Ethiopia and Somalia to Kenya and Uganda, has the same coloration, but lacks the white lateral stripe.[3]

All these squirrels are purely terrestrial and live in open habitats. They are strictly diurnal and in spite of being wary, they make little effort to conceal themselves. Very sociable, they live in colonies, sometimes with meerkats and smaller rodents. They excavate burrows, sometimes simply straight tunnels, others veritable warrens from 4 to 6 feet in length with several entrances where the squirrels may be seen sitting up on their haunches. They move with a peculiar jumping gait, the tail arched behind.

Ground Squirrels feed on various types of vegetable matter, particularly roots and bulbs, but also on fallen fruit. They seem to store food to enable them to withstand the dry season. They may cause much damage to crops, especially to maize, ground nuts, yam, cassava. They have even followed man into the high forest where they have settled in cultivated areas. They are considered as pests in some areas.

[1] Including the genus *Geosciurus*.

[2] It is called 'Rat palmiste' by the French, a regrettable mistake for it is not a rat and it does not live in palm trees, being purely terrestrial.

[3] In North Africa another ground squirrel, *Atlantoxerus getulus*, is distributed throughout Morocco, in the Grand Atlas to the Middle Atlas and Algerian Sahara.

Young, 3 to 4 in a litter, are born in burrows.

In some districts, Africans consider the Ground Squirrels to be poison-ous and believe that a bite may result in death. Their salivary glands are indeed full of streptobacillae, which are responsible for septicemia. So this belief may have some basis in fact.

SCALY-TAILED or FLYING SQUIRRELS: Anomaluridae

In spite of some superficial resemblances with the true Flying Squirrels from south-eastern Asia and North America, due to adaptations to the same environment and to parallel development, these mammals are not really squirrels. The family Anomaluridae constitutes a peculiar group of rodents, the only living remnants of a family now extinct except in tropical Africa.

These animals, the size of large squirrels, slenderly built and with a very long and rather bushy tail, are easily recognised by their gliding membrane, a flap of furred skin stretched along the side of the body from wrist to ankle, and from ankle to base of tail (except in one species). The fur is dense, long and very soft. On the underside of the tail near the base are two rows of sharp-pointed scales, with the edge directed backwards, hence the name of 'Scaly-tailed Flying Squirrels'.[1]

Several species are distinguished.

BEECROFT'S FLYING SQUIRREL (*Anomalurops beecrofti*) (p. 48). Large size (head and body 12–16 in.). Olive green above, orange to reddish below. High and dry forest from Casamance to north-east Congo.

FRASER'S FLYING SQUIRREL (*Anomalurus derbianus*) (p. 48). Large size (head and body 12–16 in.). Above dusky grey, mixed with yellowish; below white. Forest from Sierra Leone to the Congo, Angola, Zambia, Tanzania and Mozambique.

PEL'S FLYING SQUIRREL (*A. peli*) (p. 48). Large size (head and body 17 in.). Above black and white below. Tail white. High forest from Liberia, Ivory Coast and Ghana.

RED FLYING SQUIRREL (*A. fulgens*) (p. 48). Large size (head and body 14 in.). All rufous, paler on the underside. High forest of Gabon.

RED-BACKED FLYING SQUIRREL (*A. erythronotus*) (p. 48). Large size (head and body 14 in.). Head grey with sides blackish; neck and back dark chestnut; gliding membranes blackish grey; below white. High forest from the Cameroons to the Congo.

LESSER FLYING SQUIRREL (*A. pusillus*) (p. 48). Smaller size (head and body 8–10 in.). Above olive brown, below yellowish. High forest from the Cameroons to the Congo.

PYGMY FLYING SQUIRREL (*Idiurus*) (p. 48). These animals, of which there are several species distributed through the high forest from Sierra Leone to the eastern Congo, are miniatures of the species listed above

[1] F Anomalure. Ecureuil-volant. G Dornschwanzhörnchen.

head and body 3–5 in.). Brownish or greyish above, lighter, even whitish below. Tail covered with hairs arranged in a unique way: above long soft hairs; below, on each side, a line of short stiff hairs.

FLIGHTLESS SCALY-TAILED SQUIRREL (*Zenkerella insignis*) (p. 48). Small size (head and body 8 in.). The only member of the family not provided with a lateral gliding membrane and therefore unable to 'fly'. Sharp-pointed scales present on underside of tail. Brownish grey above, lighter below. Tail black with long stiff hairs. Not unlike a dormouse but the scales distinguish it easily when in the hand. High forest from the Cameroons to the Congo.

Habits of flying squirrels: Flying Squirrels are as a whole confined to forests and dense woodland. They are nocturnal (except the Flightless Scaly-tailed Squirrel), hiding during the day in hollow trees or in dense foliage. They show numerous adaptations to arboreal life, the most obvious of which is their lateral membrane.

Although incapable of true flight, they glide from tree to tree over distances of up to 100 yards. They launch themselves into the air, spreading out their legs, thus using the lateral membranes as a parachute and steering with the tail. The loss of height may not be very great. They generally land on a vertical trunk, stalling head up, tail down, with all four feet together. The scales grip the trunk and prevent the animal from slipping backwards.

The membranes are also used to conceal the animal when lying on a branch; coming in close contact with the branch, they prevent any shadow which may reveal its presence.

The larger Flying Squirrels live singly or in pairs. But the Pygmy Flying Squirrel is gregarious and lives in colonies, up to a dozen massed in a hollow tree or under bark, sometimes in company with bats or dormice.

They feed on fruits (even oil-palm nuts), leaves, flowers, and probably also insects, larvae and grubs.

Probably one, sometimes two, young are born at a time.

SPRING HARE: Pedetidae

SPRING HARE *Pedetes capensis* (Forster) (=*cafer*) p. 49
F Lièvre sauteur A Springhaas G Springhase K Kamendegere
Identification: Length (without tail) up to 17 in.; weight up to 8 lb. An odd, large rodent with a kangaroo-like appearance, the forelegs being short and the hind legs extremely long and powerful. Head short, with fairly long pointed ears, and large eyes. Fur long and rather soft. Upperparts cinnamon-buff, with a black tinge on head and back. Underparts buffish white. Tail as long as the head and body or longer, very bushy, of the same colour as the base of the back and with a wide dark-brown or black tuft at the tip.
Habitat: Open dry country, mostly on sandy soils. Map. p. 39.

Habits: Nocturnal, occasionally active by day, the Spring Hare spends the day in burrows, which consist of an open tunnel with several openings, generally blocked from inside. It emerges at dusk, often jumping into the air apparently to avoid enemies which may be expecting it at the entrance of the burrow. It moves very rapidly, usually jumping on the hind legs like a kangaroo. It is said to be able to hop up to 9 yards. It can travel several miles at night, sometimes up to 20 miles when water is scarce. Entirely vegetarian, it feeds on bulbs and roots, also on grain and young shoots of plants, eventually on insects. It may be destructive to crops (maize, ground nuts).

Young—one at a time, sometimes two—are born in the burrows.

LARGE RATS: Cricetidae

GIANT RATS *Cricetomys* spp. p. 49

F Rat de Gambie   A Reuserot   G Hamsterratte   K Buku

Identification: Length (with tail) up to 18 in.; weight up to 2 lb. Very big rats, the largest of the true rats, with slender limbs, large conspicuous ears, and a long naked tail, the terminal half white, in strong contrast with the dark proximal part. Fur short and thin, relatively sleek. (*C. emini*) or long and harsh (*C. gambianus*). Upper-parts from dusky grey (*C. gambianus*) to brown (*C. emini*), with a vinaceous tinge, lighter on flanks; underparts white, sometimes sharply defined from the darker upperparts. Very large cheek pouches.

Habitat: From Gambia eastwards to the Sudan and Kenya, southwards to north Transvaal. (*C. gambianus*: grass woodlands: *C. emini*: dense forest). Commensal with man.

Habits: The Giant Rat often lives in cultivated areas and in gardens, though it rarely enters houses. Mostly nocturnal, it digs a burrow in the shape of a long deep gallery, often with several entrances; the terminal chamber is provided with a bed of vegetable matter; several lateral chambers are used to store food and also odd stolen materials like coins and small brilliant objects, transported inside the cheekpouches.

Its diet is purely vegetarian (roots, bulbs, young shoots, fruits). Males often live singly, but females and their young live all together in groups of up to 30 in the same burrow. The period of gestation is 42 days and the litter usually consists of from 2 to 4 young.

Very docile and becoming tame in captivity, the Giant Rat makes a charming pet. It is much prized as food by Africans.

MANED RAT *Lophiomys imhausi* Milne-Edwards p. 49

G Mähnenratte

Identification: Length (without tail) 10–14 in. A rodent about the size of a guinea-pig, which it resembles in some ways (shape of the head) with very long, dense, soft fur all over the body, which gives it the appearance of having a proportionately very small head. Very short ears. Head mostly blackish with a broad white frontal band. Along neck, spine and basal part of tail, a prominent erectile mane of coarser hairs. From behind the ears to the rump, on each side, a narrow band covered with shorter and harsher whitish fur, forming a furrow in the fur, just below the mane (glandular area). Underparts grey to black. Limbs short, entirely black. Tail long and very bushy, blackish with a conspicuous white tip.

This very peculiar rodent is spread in thick forests from the Sudan, Ethiopia and Somalia to Kenya. Nocturnal, it lives in burrows excavated under roots, but climbs trees very easily (toes well developed, big toe partially opposable). It feeds on leaves and young shoots. The voice is a snort followed by a growl.

CANE RATS: Thryonomyidae

CANE RATS   *Thryonomys* spp.   p. 49
F Aulacode   A Rietmuis   G Bambusratte   K Ndezi
Cane Rats are large rodents measuring up to 24 in. (head and body), and weighing up to 16 lb., heavily built, with short stocky legs, a short rat-like tail, clothed with coarse, bristly and even spiny hairs, looking like short soft quills. General coloration speckled brown or buffy above, paler on flanks, greyish or whitish below.

They belong to two different types:
LARGER CANE RAT (*swinderianus*). Greater size (head and body from 20 to 24 in.); a rather long tail. Spread from Senegal to South Africa.
LESSER CANE RATS (*gregorianus* and allies). Smaller size (head and body from 16 to 18 in.); a shorter tail. A more limited distribution from Chad and the Sudan, southward to Rhodesia.
Generally solitary or in pairs, more rarely in small parties, Cane Rats live among reedbeds and thickets along marshes or lakes, occasionally among bushes or rocks and sometimes even in dry habitat. They swim easily. They dig burrows and use Aardvark or Porcupine's holes or hide among dense scrub. They generally remain hidden during daylight.

Entirely vegetarian, they feed on roots, coarse grasses, shrubs, bark of trees and fruits, and may become a pest to crops. They often grind hard materials, limestone, bones or even ivory (probably to wear down their incisors).

Young are born in dense scrub or in burrows, the number in a litter varying from two to four; at birth they are covered with hair, have their eyes open and are able to walk.

Cane Rats are prized by Africans and Europeans (these rodents are called 'edible rats' in some parts of Africa[1]). Leopards prey on them, as do snakes.

[1] They are sometimes called 'agoutis' by the Europeans, a mistake and a confusion with these rodents confined to the Tropics of the western hemisphere.

Plate 1   HEDGEHOGS, SHREWS, PANGOLINS

1. **TROPICAL AFRICAN HEDGEHOG**   *Atelerix albiventris page* 17
   Head and underparts white.

2. **SOUTHERN AFRICAN HEDGEHOG**   *Erinaceus
   frontalis*   17
   Muzzle and underparts blackish.

3. **FOUR-TOED ELEPHANT-SHREW**   *Petrodromus
   tetradactylus*   18
   Long snout; long legs, particularly hind legs; uniform
   fawn, lighter below.

4. **CHEQUERED ELEPHANT-SHREW**   *Rhynchocyon cirnei*   18
   Larger; chequered pattern, rows of white spots in contrast with fawn ground colour.

5. **OTTER SHREW**   *Potamogale velox*   18
   Broad snout; long body; compressed tail; glossy chocolate
   brown.

6. **LONG-TAILED PANGOLIN**   *Manis tetradactyla*   36
   Small; scales broad, less numerous; dark brown; underparts blackish; tail very long.

7. **TREE PANGOLIN**   *Manis tricuspis*   36
   Small; scales small and numerous; light fawn; underparts
   whitish; tail long.

8. **GIANT PANGOLIN**   *Manis gigantea*   35
   Large and massive; scales broad and rounded; proportionately short tail, pointed at tip.

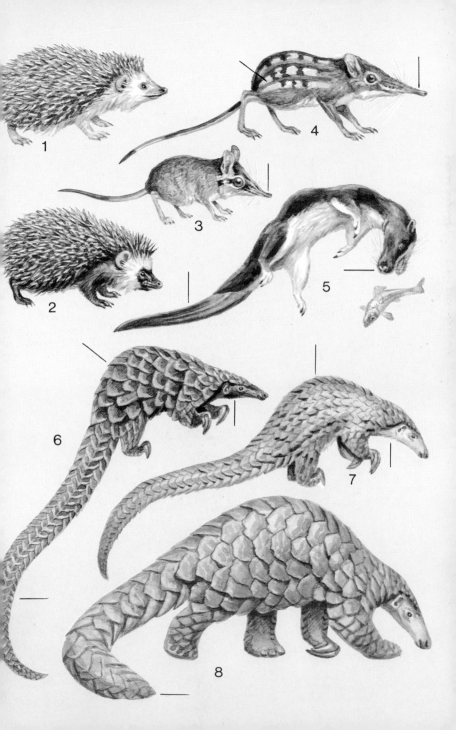

SQUIRRELS

Plate 2

1. **RED-FOOTED SQUIRREL** *Funisciurus pyrrhopus* *page* 24
Greenish above, white below; head and limbs bright chestnut red.

2. **FOUR-STRIPED SQUIRREL** *Funisciurus lemniscatus* 24
Four black stripes on back.

3. **PYGMY SQUIRREL** *Myosciurus pumilio* 26
Very small; brownish above, whitish below.

4. **GIANT FOREST SQUIRREL** *Protoxerus stangeri* 24
Large; dark olive-brown above, lighter below; long,
bushy tail, with black and white rings.

5. **GAMBIAN SUN-SQUIRREL** *Heliosciurus gambianus* 24
Conspicuously speckled, pale or greyish brown above;
whitish below; tail long, annulated.

6. **RED-LEGGED SUN-SQUIRREL** *Heliosciurus
rufobrachium* 26
Dark brown above (including head); limbs deep red; long
tail.

7. **PALM SQUIRREL** *Epixerus ebii* 24
Large; olive-brown above, lighter below; reddish
limbs; long, bushy tail, mixed black and white.

8. **BUSH SQUIRREL** *Paraxerus palliatus* 26
Back olive brownish; head, limbs, underparts and tail
bright cinnamon.

9. **PALLID GROUND SQUIRREL** *Xerus rutilus* 27
Fulvous to reddish above; no white stripe along flanks;
tail mixed black and white.

10. **STRIPED GROUND SQUIRREL** *Xerus erythropus* 27
Sandy to dark fulvous above; white stripe along flanks;
tail mixed black and white.

PORCUPINES: Hystricidae

Porcupines are large rodents, the Crested Porcupine being the largest and the heaviest African rodent, with upperparts thickly covered with long quills, up to 1 foot long, cylindrical, stout and very sharp. The animal is capable of raising them when annoyed or attacked, which gives it a crested appearance. It vibrates them so that the quills produce a characteristic rattle, also audible when the animal walks (a warning sound, added to grunting noises often uttered during periods of activity). The porcupine charges backwards, its hindquarters being heavily armed, with the quills directed to the rear. These are lightly rooted and easily become detached from the body when they come into contact with anything solid. The animal cannot 'shoot' them. When lodged in the flesh, the quills can cause wounds which may be fatal to predators. This unusual covering does protect porcupines very effectively.

African porcupines belong to two well-defined types:

The CRESTED PORCUPINES (*Hystrix*),[1] with three species distributed all over tropical Africa, from Senegal to the Cape, all recognisable by their large size (head and body up to 33 in.; weight up to 45 lb.), stout body and long legs; on the head and neck, an upstanding crest of long, thin, backward-curved bristles; back, rump and tail covered with long black, brown and white banded quills. Tail short and hidden amongst the quills (p. 49).

The BRUSH-TAILED PORCUPINES (*Atherurus*),[2] with several species distributed through Africa, recognisable by their smaller size (head and body less than 20 in.), elongated body and short legs. Coat almost entirely spiny, the spines of the middle back the longest, intermixed with a few thick quills. Tail long, covered with spines at its base, then scaly with at its extremity a conspicuous thick brush of odd bristles, looking like little bands of parchment (p. 49).

Porcupines are nocturnal, sheltering in daylight in burrows made by themselves or by aardvark, or in caves or crevices under rocky boulders. They live in pairs or in groups, especially the Brush-tailed Porcupines (up to eight individuals have been observed in the same shelter). The Brush-tailed Porcupines climb trees very well.

They are exclusively vegetarian, feeding in bulbs and roots, scratched out of the ground, on bark, berries and fruits. They may do much damage to cultivated fields, being wasteful feeders. Young—two, sometimes up to four in a litter—are born in crevices or burrows. They do not leave their hide before the quills are strong and hard, after about two weeks.

---

[1] F: Porc-épic. G: Stachelschwein. A: Ystervark. K: Nungu.
[2] F: Athérure. G: Quastenstachler.

ORDER Pholidota

PANGOLINS: Manidae

Pangolins (or Scaly Anteaters),[1] an order on their own, with a single family and a single genus, are among the strangest mammals in the world. They are not unlike reptiles, having large overlapping, armour-plated scales of dermic origin (resembling those of a pine cone) which cover the entire upperparts and the underside of tail. They are elongated in shape, with a small, narrow, earless head. They have no teeth, but a long and narrow protractile tongue, sticky with saliva, to which adhere the insects (termites, ants) on which they feed.

These strong animals move very slowly, often walking on their hind legs (better developed than the forelegs) and using the tail as a counter balance, with the forelegs off the ground. The claws are well developed and recurved.

They are able to roll themselves up into a ball with only the scales on the outside. This passive attitude is their only defence. However, the cutting action of the scales, worked by powerful muscles, can inflict serious wounds on an enemy getting its fingers or snout between them.

The sense of sight is very limited, but the senses of smell, taste and hearing are very acute.

They are solitary animals and pairs remain together only during a short mating season. Young are born singly. The scales harden two days after birth. The mother carries its young at the base of its tail, and protects them by wrapping her body round them.

Four species, belonging to two well defined groups, one terrestrial, the other arboreal, are found through the forests and forested savannas of Africa; other species occur in tropical Asia.

GIANT PANGOLIN   *Manis (Smutsia) gigantea* Illiger   p. 32
F Pangolin géant   G Riesen-Schuppentier
Identification: Total length up to 60 in. A large, strongly built pangolin, with only three well developed claws (toes 1 and 5 much reduced). Scales rounded and broad (up to 4–5 in.), uniformly grey-brown. Belly and inner surface of the limbs bare. A proportionately short tail, shorter than head and body, thick at its base but pointed at its tip, entirely covered below with scales; about 15–19 lateral scales on each side.
Habitat: Forests and savannas. Map, p. 39.
Habits: Terrestrial, it never climbs trees. It sometimes moves on its hind feet only, with the help of the tail. It lives among rocky boulders where it digs burrows with its powerful claws, spending the day sleeping. It seeks its food at night, digging termite mounts and feeding also on ants.

---

[1] They are sometimes erroneously called Armadillos, which are completely different animals found only in tropical America (Edentata, Dasypodidae).

CAPE PANGOLIN Manis (Smutsia) temmincki Smuts

F Pangolin terrestre du Cap   A Ietermagog   G Steppen-Schuppentier
K Kakakuona

Identification: Total length 40 in.; weight up to 18 lb. A smaller, but strongly built pangolin, only three well developed claws (toes 1 and 5 much reduced). Scales broad and rounded. A proportionately short tail, shorter than head and body, but very broad at its base, rounded at its tip, and entirely covered with scales below; about 11-13 lateral scales on each side.
Habitat: Dry bush country, preferring sandy soils. Map, p. 39.
Habits: Nocturnal, though partly diurnal, it usually spends the day in burrows or under dense thickets. Terrestrial, it lives on ants, its principal diet, and on termites.

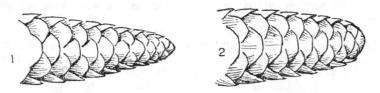

1. Tip of tail of the Giant Pangolin (*Manis gigantea*) (1) and of the Cape Pangolin (*M. temmincki*) (2)

TREE PANGOLIN Manis (Phataginus) tricuspis Rafinesque   p. 32

F Pangolin à écailles triscuspides   G Weissbauch-Schuppentier
Identification: Total length 30 in. A rather small pangolin with a fairly long tail, but less than one and a half times longer than head and body. Scales smaller and numerous, with three little points at their edge, brownish coloured. Underparts covered with whitish hairs ('White-bellied Pangolin'). Eyes relatively large.
Habitat: High forest. Map, p. 39.
Habits: Arboreal, this pangolin is a very accomplished climber, using its long prehensile tail as an aid. It may even hang only by the tip of its tail.

Due to its lesser strength, it can only tear open the soft nests of arboreal termites; it feeds also on tree ants walking in files, a much easier prey and perhaps the most commonly used. It eats on the average 5-7 ounces of insects per night.

LONG-TAILED PANGOLIN Manis (Uromanis) tetradactyla L.
(=longicaudata)   p. 32

F Pangolin à longue queue   G Langschwanz-Schuppentier
Identification: Length (with tail) 36 in. A smaller pangolin with a very long tail, often twice as long as head and body. Scales of large size, less numer-

ous, rounded at the edge, dark brown with a yellow tinge on the outer edge. Underparts covered with dark brown hairs ('Black-bellied Pangolin'). Eyes relatively small.

Habitat: High forest. Map, p. 39.

Habits: This pangolin is arboreal, and shows a series of adaptations to life in trees, such as the long prehensile tail. Nocturnal and to some extent diurnal, it spends a part of the day in burrows or in holes in tree trunks. Its diet is the same as that of the preceding species.

ORDER Primates

POTTOS and GALAGOS: Prosimians—Lorisidae, Galagidae

Lower primates with a number of characteristic anatomical features, among which are a pointed snout, a wet muzzle and sharp teeth, not unlike those of Insectivora. Spread over the warmer regions of the Old World, and particularly well represented in Madagascar where the higher primates do not occur.

The African Prosimians, all quite small, are easily divided into two groups.

Pottos belong to the family Lorisidae also well represented in Asia. They show some relationship with the Asian Loris. They are little bear-like animals, with no or much reduced tail, a rounded head, small ears, and limbs subequal in length. They move very slowly and climb by means of a hand-over-hand action.

Galagos or Bush-babies constitute a family by themselves (Galagidae), and are confined to Africa. They have large ears, greatly elongated hind-limbs and a very long, sometimes bushy, tail. They progress by leaping and are very active, moving very fast.

Pottos and Galagos are nocturnal and arboreal, rarely coming down to the ground; they are confined to forests and woodlands.

BOSMAN'S POTTO *Perodicticus potto* (P. L. S. Müller)　　　p. 52
F Potto de Bosman　G Potto
Identification: Length (without tail) 13–16 in. A potto the size of a small cat, heavily and robustly built, with a rounded head, a short broad muzzle, a small mouth and short, stout limbs. On the neck, the cervical vertebrae protrude and form a row of blunt spikes just under the bare skin. A very short tail visible beyond fur.[1] Fur thick and woolly, from rich reddish and brown to blackish, mixed with long bristly hairs. Underparts paler, often greyish. Colour and size vary considerably in individuals as well as with race, sex and age.
Habitat: High forest. Map, p. 45.
Habits: Purely nocturnal, this potto sleeps all day rolled up with its head between its legs, generally sitting upright in a hollow tree or in dense foliage, gripping so powerfully that it is impossible to remove it. In this posture, the elongated processes of the cervical vertebrate protrude, and perhaps protect the animal from being seized by a predator on which it may inflict serious wounds (the Palm Civet seems its commonest enemy). The potto will in fact use its spines for striking at potential enemies, as well as biting them severely. At night it begins to move, with very slow movements. It rarely comes down to the ground, preferring to climb from tree to tree.

[1] This potto is called 'half a tail' by some Africans speaking pidgin-English.

38

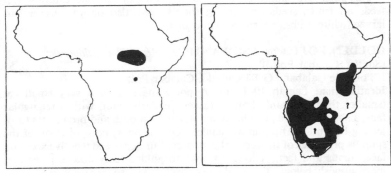

African Rabbit, p. 22

Spring Hare, p. 29

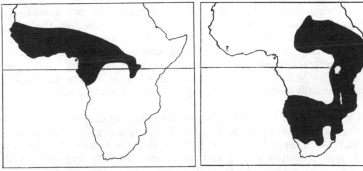

Giant Pangolin, p. 35

Cape Pangolin, p. 36

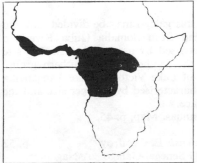

Tree Pangolin, p. 36

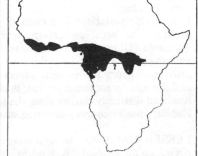

Long-tailed Pangolin, p. 36

This potto lives singly, even the pairing being of very short duration. It feeds on fruits, seeds and young shoots, and also on various insects, larvae (white grubs, caterpillars) and snails.

GOLDEN POTTO or ANGWANTIBO *Arctocebus calabarensis*
(Smith) (Calabar Potto)   p. 52
F Potto de Calabar   G Bärenmaki, Calabar-Potto
Identification: Length 10–12 in. A potto the size of a very small cat (smaller than Bosman's Potto), rather slenderly built, with a triangular face, a sharper, more prominent snout, a wide mouth and broad ears (projecting beyond the fur; limbs slender). On the neck, no projection of the spinous processes of the cervical vertebrae. Fur dense and woolly except on face, hands and feet, yellowish-brown to golden-rusty above, paler and more greyish below. Young darker, becoming progressively paler with age. Tail absent or entirely hidden in the fur.
Habitat: High deciduous forest. Map, p. 45.
Habits: Purely nocturnal and arboreal. Rarely seen, this rare potto sleeps all day, suspended from a horizontal branch by all four feet, the hands grasping the branch behind the feet, the arms between the legs and the head bent forward on the chest. The limbs seem to be entirely disconnected from the central nervous system, showing no signs of feeling.

It feeds on vegetable matter and on soft bodied insects, grubs, and worms. The calls include 'whimpering wails' and throaty cries.

THICK-TAILED GALAGO *Galago crassicaudatus* E. Geoffroy   p. 52
F Galago à queue épaisse   K Komba   G Riesengalago   A Bosnagaap
Identification: Length (without tail) 14 in. A large galago, the size of a rabbit, with a relatively long and robust muzzle, very large ears, with rounded distal margin. Upperparts from silvery grey to red-brown; underparts white. Tail longer than head and body, thick and bushy, of the same colour as the back or whitish below, or entirely white; often carried above the back.
Intraspecific variation: The races of this galago may be divided into two groups. The northern group, spread from Somalia (Juba River) to Tanzania (Uluguru Mts.), is characterised by a somewhat smaller size and the face similar in colour to the forehead. The southern group, distributed from the eastern shores of Lake Victoria, Lake Tanganyika and Angola to southern Africa, is characterised by a larger size and the forehead distinctly darker than the face.
Habitat: Bushy country and tree savannas. Map, p. 45.

LESSER GALAGO *Galago senegalensis* E. Geoffroy   p. 52
F Galago du Sénégal   K Komba   G Senegal-Galago   A Nagapie
Identification: Length (without tail) 7–8 in. A small galago, with a shortened face, very large ears with an angle at the summit of the conch,

and elongated hind legs terminated by short fingers. Coat soft and woolly, grey suffused with yellow, never with reddish. Tail long and thin, covered with short hairs, sometimes darker than the body, especially at its tip. **Intraspecific variation:** Systematists have divided this species into a number of local races. The northern race (*senegalensis*, from Senegal to Ethiopia) is grey without any brownish suffusion. Others, like *braccatus* (Yellow-thighed Galago; highlands of Kenya and Tanzania), *gallarum* (Somalia and Gallaland), have distinctly yellow limbs contrasting with the grey body. The eastern races (*zanzibaricus*, Zanzibar and the opposite mainland; *granti*, Mozambique) are strongly washed with cinnamon or brownish, while the southern African race (*moholi*) is more like the typical *senegalensis*, with the lower back washed with otter-brown.
Habitat: Bushy country and tree savannas. Map, p. 45.

ALLEN'S GALAGO *Galago alleni* Waterhouse   p. 52
F Galago d'Allen   G Allens Galago
Identification: Length (without tail) 8–9 in. A small, dark-coloured galago (the darkest of all the galagos) with an elongated snout and long fingers. A black mask over face. Upperparts dark reddish brown. Limbs rusty red. Underparts grey suffused with yellowish, sometimes a rufous bar across the chest. Tail long, slightly bushy, almost black.
Habitat: High deciduous forest; also secondary growth and cultivated land. Map, p. 45.

NEEDLE-CLAWED GALAGO[1] *Euoticus elegantulus* (Le Conte) p. 52
F Galago élégant, Galago mignon   G Kielnagel-Galago
Identification: Length (without tail) 9 in. A small galago with a rounded head, enormous eyes, relatively short ears, and a shortened and broadened muzzle. Fur very dense, soft and woolly. Upperparts cinnamon; underparts grey, suffused with cinnamon. Tail very long and thick, uniformly fluffy, similar in colour to the upperparts.
Intraspecific variation: The southern race (*elegantulus*; lower Guinea, between the Sanaga, Ubangui and Congo Rivers and the Gulf of Guinea, is darker (orange cinnamon) and has a white tip at its tail. The northern race (*pallidus*, upper Guinea to the Sanaga River; Fernando Po) is paler (dull cinnamon-grey) and has no white tip at its tail.[2]
Habitat: High forest. Map, p. 45.

_____

[1] The name derives from a raised keel, prolonged distally into a sharp point, projecting beyond the edge of most of the nails. This character is peculiar to the species.
[2] Another species has been described from the hills west of Lake Albert, Congo: *E. inustus* (Schwartz), distinguished from *elegantulus* by its brown coloration and a thinner tail. Its status seems still hypothetical.

DWARF GALAGO *Galagoides demidovi* (Fischer)
(Demidoff's Galago) p. 52
F Galago de Demidoff G Zwerg-Galago

Identification: Length 6–8 in. A very small galago, the smallest of all, not bigger than a rat, with a broad head, a shortened muzzle, enormous eyes and very short ears, conical and naked. Upperparts brownish; underparts and limbs yellow, often very bright.[1] Tail very long, longer than body, not very bushy, of the same colour as upperparts.

Intraspecific variation: A large number of races have been described, distinguished from each other mainly by size and intensity of coloration. Most of them are not clearly defined and their characters overlap. The only distinct race is *thomasi* (north-east Congo, eastwards to Lake Victoria).

Habitat: High forest; also montane forest. Upper storey of the canopy, whereas other galagos prefer the lower. Map, p. 55.

Habits of Galagos:

In spite of some differences in the habits of the various species, it seems better to consider the habits of galagos altogether.

Galagos are very active animals, completely different from the pottos in this respect, well adapted to an arboreal life (Demidoff's Galago is the most active and the swiftest). Their feet are well adapted to grasp branches and the tail is used as a balancing organ. They leap from place to place in the trees in a frog-like fashion, using their hind limbs to give the initial push. They sometimes also come down to the ground occasionally where they progress in an erect or semi-erect posture, leaping on the hind legs like a little kangaroo. Smaller species, like the Lesser Galago, are able to jump distances of up to 10 ft. The large galagos are more quadrupedal, and also more sluggish. The forelimbs are used for capturing prey and for carrying the food to the mouth.

Most of the galagos are nocturnal ('Night-apes'; the large size of the eyes seems to be related to this fact), though some may be active in daylight (especially the Dwarf and Needle-clawed Galagos). The Dwarf Galago is said to be more diurnal than its relatives. They spend the day asleep in hollow trees or in nests made by themselves, or in disused squirrels' nests, often several individuals together (pairs or families).

Galagos have a fairly large vocabulary. The Lesser Galago has at least eight different calls, including an alarm-note and a piercing noise, with two pitches, high and low, maintained for periods of up to an hour or more. Some calls are rather musical, others resemble those of a crying baby.

Galagos feed largely on insects (moths, crickets, winged termites) and spiders; the larger species also prey on small birds and lizards and plunder birds' nests. They also eat various vegetable matter, mostly fruits, and also leaves, young shoots, gum of mimosa tree and bark.

The period of gestation is 4 months, probably longer in the larger

[1] These bright colours fade after death.

forms. The young—sometimes one, usually two in a litter—are born in a shelter where the mother builds a nest. The young are not carried by the mother on her nocturnal wanderings. In captivity they are nursed for 3½ months.

Galagos may be easily raised in captivity and may be fed with fruit and milk, with the addition of insects.

MONKEYS: Cercopithecidae
BABOONS, MANDRILL and DRILL

Large primates with a very characteristic dog-like head, a naked protruding muzzle with the nostrils at its very tip (except in Gelada) and long sharp canines. Shoulders higher than the rump. Hairs of neck and shoulders well developed, sometimes forming a mane or a cape around the head and anterior part of body. Tail proportionately short, sometimes reduced to a mere stump, never reaching to the ground. Callosities well developed on buttocks, which are naked to a wide extent. Females are much smaller than males, weighing about half (30 lb. against 75 lb. on the average).

All are largely terrestrial, though they may climb trees.

True baboons are confined to savannas and even semi-desert country; some are rock-dwellers. Mandrill and Drill are confined to high forest.

HAMADRYAS *Papio hamadryas* (L.)   p. 53
F Hamadryas   G Hamadryas
Identification: Length (without tail) up to 30 in. A smaller baboon, with massive features, sloping of back much pronounced. A well developed shaggy cape or mane on shoulders and back (the animal looks like a French poodle). Head pink, with a very long muzzle, in the same line as the braincase. Whiskers dense and long. Coat of male ashy grey, slightly washed with brownish. Tail curved gently backwards, never 'broken' near the base. Callosities very much developed, bright reddish pink.

Female and young fulvous brown, without mane.
Habitat: Dry rocky country. Also in Arabia. It was the sacred monkey of the ancient Egyptians. Map, p. 55.

WESTERN BABOON *Papio papio* (Desmarest)   p. 53
F Babouin de Guinée   G Sphinx-Pavian
Identification: Length (without tail) up to 30 in. A smaller baboon, with massive features; sloping of back much pronounced; a well developed cape or mane on shoulders and back, in strong contrast with the short coat on rump and limbs. Muzzle forming a distinct angle with the braincase. Whiskers very thick and dense. General colour speckled olive rufous. Tail rather short, never 'broken' near the base, carried gently curved. Callosities broad and purplish (adults).
Habitat: Savannas, mostly in broken rocky areas. Map, p. 55.

ANUBIS BABOON *Papio anubis* (J. P. Fischer) (=*doguera*)   p. 53
F Babouin doguera   K Nyani   G Anubis-Pavian
Identification: Length (without tail) up to 40 in. A large baboon, very heavily built; back sloping gently backwards. A moderately developed mantle over the shoulders, not markedly different from the rest of coat. Braincase and muzzle almost in the same line; nostrils protruding beyond upper lip. Whiskers thick, giving a rounded outline to the head. General colour speckled olive brown. Hands and feet blackish. Tail 'broken', first curving upwards, then downwards, with a sharp angle. Callosities broad, purplish grey (adults).
Habitat: Savannas. Map, p. 55.

YELLOW BABOON *Papio cynocephalus* (L.)   p. 53
F Babouin jaune   G Bärenpavian
Identification: Length (without tail) up to 40 in. A generally large baboon, slenderly built (except old males), back sloping gently backwards, almost horizontal; legs thin and slender. No well defined cape over shoulders. General coloration light; upperparts yellowish buff to greyish; whiskers and underparts creamy white. Tail long and thin, carried 'broken' near the base. Callosities broad, purplish grey (adults).
Habitat: Savannas and woodlands. Map, p. 55.

CHACMA BABOON *Papio ursinus* (Kerr)   p. 53
F Chacma   A Bobbejaan   G Tschakma-Pavian
Identification: Length (without tail) up to 40 in.; weight up to 90 lb. A large baboon, slender and rather lightly built; back sloping gently backwards. Head with a well marked angle between braincase and muzzle. Whiskers poorly developed. General coloration more or less dark olive green; underparts lighter, almost naked. Hands blackish. Tail carried 'broken' near the base, with a very sharp angle, blackish on its terminal part. Callosities small and narrow, not extending upwards on each side of tail, slaty grey.
Habitat: Savannas, mostly in broken rocky areas, near kopjes. Map, p. 55.

Habits of Baboons:
All baboons share the same way of life and live in open habitat, ranging from sub-desert to light woodland; they are also to be found in galleries and on lava plains in high altitude. They are large, terrestrial and highly sociable monkeys.

They live in troops numbering from 10 to about 200, on the average from 40 to 80; size of troops varies according to food supply and social behaviour, and shows a tendency to grow where vegetation becomes denser. These troops which may temporarily split into smaller ones, constitute very stable and permanent units, with well defined structure. When a troop is resting or feeding, the most dominant males occupy the

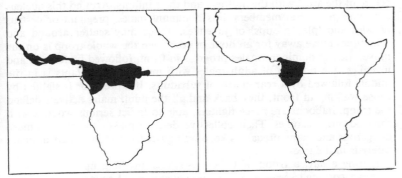

Bosman's Potto, p. 38

Golden Potto, p. 40

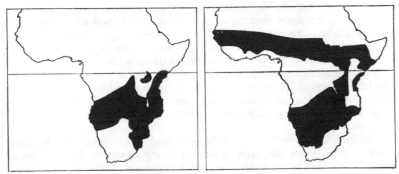

Thick-tailed Galago, p. 40

Lesser Galago, p. 40

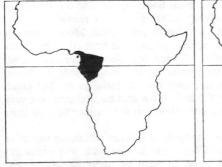

Allen's Galago, p. 41

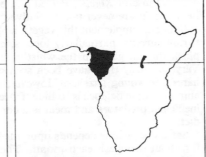

Needle-clawed Galago, p. 41

centre of the area, with the mothers and their infants. Around this nucleus are more peripheral members, less dominant males, pregnant or oestrus females and 'play groups' of juveniles. These may scatter around and sometimes move away for an hour or so. When the whole troop is on the move, the less dominant males progress in front, followed by females and juveniles; the nucleus of adult males with mothers and infants is in the middle followed by a rear guard of subadults. If a predator is sighted by those walking in front, they bark and all the adult males actively defend the troop. Baboons are fierce fighters, able to inflict serious wounds with their powerful canines. Their collective defence makes them much more dangerous and many predators keep well away from them. Their ultimate safety is in the trees.

During a day, a troop of baboons travels anything up to 7 miles. It moves according to season over an area averaging 15 square miles in open savannas, much less in woodland. The home ranges of different troops may overlap, but the districts more frequently used—the 'core area', where are located the sleeping trees, the water and food sources and the resting places—are rarely invaded by another troop. During the dry season, different troops may cluster around water holes, without any conflict. No part of the home range seems defended as a territory.

Baboons feed intensively for 2 or 3 hours in the morning, then again in the late afternoon. They rest in the shade during the heat of the day, and retire at night to sleeping trees, mainly acacias. In more open country, they take refuge in rocky eminences, particularly Hamadryas and Anubis Baboon.

The bulk of the diet is vegetable food, and grass constitutes the main part of it. They eat the seeds as well as young shoots or the juicy lower stems at the base of the culm; during the dry season they dig up rhizomes and tuberous roots. Baboons also feed on various bushes, flowering plants and acacia trees (buds, flowers, seed-pods, sap); fruits, particularly figs as well as those of *Kigelia*, *Parkia* and even Baobab, are also an important item; leaves are never taken. Native cultivations may be raided.

Baboons supplement this vegetarian diet by some animal food. They eat various insects, particularly locusts, caterpillars and ants (they regularly pluck the ant galls on the whistling-thorn trees, *Acacia drepanolobium*). Very curiously they have been seen catching and eating fledgling birds, hares and young gazelles. However, they do not stalk game, but catch animals whose defence is to hide 'frozen' on the ground. Baboons are very inefficient predators and meat is a consistent but very minor part of their diet.

Sexual behaviour depends upon the cycle of females which are receptive for about one week each month. They mate at first with less dominant males, then with the dominant ones, 'presenting' their callosities and naked parts of the hindquarters. A female may form a consort pair with a male but the duration of such an association does not exceed a few days.

There is no family nor harem among baboons and sexual behaviour does not play as important a role in social structure as in most other mammals.

The period of gestation varies between 154 and 193 days according to the species. One, rarely two young are born at a time. Infants are at first carried by the mother under her belly; then they ride on her back in a peculiar manner. They are carefully nursed and learn a great deal of social behaviour very early in life.

Baboons are preyed on by Leopard, Lion and many big carnivores.

GELADA BABOON   *Papio (Theropithecus) gelada* (Rüppell)   p. 53
F Gelada   G Dschelada

Identification: Length (without tail) up to 30 in.; weight up to 45 lb. Unmistakable. A baboon with a very characteristic head, rounded with an upturned face, marked with large ridges running from below the outer side of the eyes to the nose; nostrils projecting upwards, located well behind the muzzle and swollen lips. Face dark brown, with wrinkles. Very long whiskers, forming falciform tufts of light coloured hairs projecting backwards and upwards on the sides of head. Three bare red areas: one median, crescentic, on throat; two symmetrical, triangular, on chest. A mane over the neck and a cape over the shoulders, reaching almost to the ground in old males when sitting, varying from light to dark brown. Rest of body lighter, greyish brown. Tail long, brownish with a tuft of long hairs, lion-like, at its tip. Callosities divided into four rounded areas, purplish grey in colour.

Female much smaller, about half the size of the male; mane much less developed.

Habitat: Rocky highlands; up to alpine pastures. Map, p. 59.

Habits: Gelada favour particularly rims and steep slopes of precipices and gorges, their distribution being therefore linear along the escarpments. They retreat to them when alarmed. When feeding, the females and young tend to remain near the cliffs, with the males scattered out around them.

They form troops of up to 400 individuals, divided into smaller groups. The social unit is a one-male group, with a large mature male, females with their babies and juveniles. Males may collect into small units. Groups intermingle within herds, except when on the move. Aggressive behaviour of the male occurs only in relation to his harem. The social structure resembles that of the Hamadryas and differs markedly from that of multimale troops of other baboons.

Gelada wander freely, their range exceeding four miles a day. They move out and up from the cliffs in the morning and settle for the day on meadows, where they feed. At dusk they go down and retire to small ledges and rock crevices; they do not return each night to the same sleeping place but move along for several days before returning. Distance over

Plate 3   FLYING SQUIRRELS

1. **FRASER'S FLYING SQUIRREL** *Anomalurus derbianus*
   Dusky grey above; white below.
   28

2. **RED-BACKED FLYING SQUIRREL** *Anomalurus erythronotus*
   Upper back chestnut; gliding membranes blackish; white below.
   28

3. **PEL'S FLYING SQUIRREL** *Anomalurus peli*
   Black above; fringe of membrane white; white below; white tail.
   28

4. **BEECROFT'S FLYING SQUIRREL** *Anomalurops beecrofti*
   Green above; reddish below.
   28

5. **LESSER FLYING SQUIRREL** *Anomalurus pusillus*
   Small; olive brown above; yellowish below.
   28

6. **RED FLYING SQUIRREL** *Anomalurus fulgens*
   Rufous above; paler below.
   28

7. **PYGMY FLYING SQUIRREL** *Idiurus zenkeri*
   Very small; tail with a row of short stiff hairs on each side.
   28

8. **FLIGHTLESS SCALY-TAILED SQUIRREL** *Zenkerella insignis*
   Small; no gliding membrane; brownish grey above, lighter below.
   29

RODENTS

Plate 4

1. **AFRICAN RABBIT** *Poelagus marjorita*   *page* 22
Short ears, short legs; drab grey above, white below; tail
short.

2. **CRAWSHAY'S HARE** *Lepus crawshayi*   20
Long ears, long legs; greyish brown; neck rufous; tail
longer.

3. **CANE RAT** *Thryonomys sp.*   31
Stout; head massive; short legs; bristly coat; brownish
above, whitish below; short tail.

4. **GIANT RAT** *Cricetomys emini*   30
Elongated head; large ears; long naked tail; coat short;
brownish above, white below.

5. **MANED RAT** *Lophiomys imhausi*   30
Long coat; mane of coarse hairs along spine; whitish band
along side; tail long and bushy.

6. **BRUSH-TAILED PORCUPINE** *Atherurus sp.*   34
Small; spiny coat, with a few quills on the back; long tail,
with at tip a thick brush of horny bristles.

7. **CRESTED PORCUPINE** *Hystrix sp.*   34
Large; stout; back and short tail covered with long quills.

8. **SPRING HARE** *Pedetes capensis*   29
Hind legs enormous; fore legs very short; tail very long
and bushy; kangaroo-like appearance.

which a troop moves, dispersion and size of herds are to a large extent dictated by the habitat and the food availability.

The voice is very high pitched, and they do not utter the hoarse barks of the other baboons.

Apart from small quantities of animal food, particularly insects, Gelada are entirely vegetarian, foraging for grass, roots, bulbs, seeds and fruits.

MANDRILL *Papio* (*Mandrillus*) *sphinx* (L.) p. 53
F Mandrill G Mandrill
Identification: Length (without tail) up to 38 in.; weight up to 90 lb. Unmistakable. A large baboon, very stoutly built when fully adult, with an elongated face, naked and marked with deep ridges, highly variable in coloration according to sex and age, sometimes conspicuously coloured. In adult males, middle of face, nose and lips bright scarlet; sides of muzzle bright cobalt blue. Young male with only nostrils red and bluish sides of nose; coloration intensifies with age. Adult females, which are much smaller, are duller, with a dusky tinge on the whole face, a reddish flush on the nose and a livid blue on the sides of nose. Ears bright flesh colour. Head and neck densely furred, forming a well developed olive brownish mane all around the head, darker on top of head; beard yellow or orange. Upperparts and flanks olive brown. Underparts lighter, greyish, tinged with yellowish. In adult males, hind parts naked and bright coloured. Circumanal region scarlet, callosities pale pink and violaceous; genitalia pink, lilac and scarlet. In females, the corresponding regions are dark. Tail reduced to a mere stump.
Habitat: High forest. Map, p. 59.

DRILL *Papio* (*Mandrillus*) *leucophaeus* (F. Cuvier) p. 53
F Drill G Drill
Identification: Length (without tail) up to 35 in. A large baboon, somewhat smaller than the Mandrill, stoutly built, with shorter muzzle, a face marked by ridges but not brightly coloured. Face black; in adult males, a transverse crimson band across the lower lip. Ears black with a pinkish spot of naked skin on the back. Around the face, a ring of long dense hairs, whitish like the beard. A mane of long hairs over the shoulders. Coat brownish grey, tinged with olive. Underparts lighter, greyish to whitish. In adult males, hind parts naked and bright coloured. Circumanal region black; confluent callosities pink; below an extensive Tyndall-blue area, with peripheral region deep mauve; male genitalia with scarlet patches. In females, the corresponding region is slaty black. Tail reduced to a mere stump.
Habitat: High forest. Map, p. 59.
Habits: Mandrill and Drill live mostly in primary rain forest, where the ground is sufficiently clear of undergrowth for easy walking. Mandrill favour open, rocky places. They are terrestrial and feed on the ground,

climbing trees only to look for fruit, in case of danger, or to rest at night. They live in troops of up to 50 individuals, wandering within a limited perimeter. They are very noisy: they growl, grunt, roar, bark, and utter shrill calls.

Omnivorous, they feed on seeds, nuts and fallen fruits of various trees, apparently on fungus, also digging up roots and bulbs. They also eat insects, spiders, grubs, snails, worms, and small vertebrates. They may raid native cultivations, particularly cassava, causing much damage just as Bushpigs do.

They are preyed on by leopard.

MANGABEYS, GUENONS and PATAS

Primates of medium or smaller size with a rather rounded head and naked face. Forelimbs with five digits. Tail long and non-prehensile as a rule, carried differently according to the species. Female similar to the male, but much smaller.

These monkeys are distributed all over Africa. Most of them are arboreal and live in forested country. The subfamily to which they belong is represented in tropical Asia by other genera.

The African representatives may be split into three different groups:

MANGABEYS (*Cercocebus*). Tall, with an elongated and slender body; muzzle rather long; back horizontal. Tail proportionately long, sometimes covered with long coarse hairs, sometimes carried almost erect or curved forward over the body, with a sharp angle at its base. Coloration generally dull and not contrasted. Live in forests.

GUENONS or CERCOPITHECID MONKEYS (*Cercopithecus, Allenopithecus, Miopithecus*). Smaller than the mangabeys; generally back sloping forwards. Tail long, never held over the back with a sharp angle at its base. Coloration very variable, often bright and contrasted. Live generally in forests, sometimes in savannas.

PATAS (*Erythrocebus*). Larger than the guenons and slenderly built; back horizontal; legs proportionately very long. Coloration uniform, mostly bright rufous. Live in savannas and open country: the most terrestrial of all African Cercopithecinae.[1]

---

[1] In view of their appearance and coat pattern, it might be supposed that the different species of arboreal monkeys would be immediately distinguishable from each other. This is certainly the case when they are seen in good light or at close quarters, but often they present only a short glimpse among dense vegetation or a dark silhouette against the sky. Then great care has to be taken and other characters, like outline, general features and carriage of the tail must be taken into account.

Plate 5   GALAGO, POTTO

1. **ALLEN'S GALAGO**   *Galago alleni*   *page* 41
   Small; dark; black mask over face; tail black.

2. **LESSER GALAGO**   *Galago senegalensis*   40
   Small; greyish; limbs often yellowish; tail thin at base,
   then bushy.

3. **THICK-TAILED GALAGO**   *Galago crassicaudatus*   40
   Large; silvery grey to red brown; tail long and very bushy.

4. **NEEDLE-CLAWED GALAGO**   *Euoticus elegantulus*   41
   Medium-sized; upperparts cinnamon, sharply contrasting
   with grey underparts; tail bushy.

5. **DWARF GALAGO**   *Galagoides demidovi*   42
   Very small; brownish above; underparts and limbs
   yellow; tail long, not bushy.

6. **GOLDEN POTTO**   *Arctocebus calabarensis*   40
   Slenderly built; gracile limbs; pointed head; no tail.

7. **BOSMAN'S POTTO**   *Perodicticus potto*   38
   Robustly built; stout limbs; rounded head; very short
   tail.

BABOONS

Plate 6

1. WESTERN BABOON *Papio papio*   *page* 43
Smaller; mane well developed; olive rufous.

2. GELADA BABOON *Papio gelada*   47
Upturned face, with nostrils projecting upwards well
behind muzzle; very long whiskers; red bare areas on chest.
well developed mane over shoulder; tail with terminal
tuft.

3. DRILL *Papio leucophaeus*   50
Face black, except crimson band across lower lip (male);
callosities bright blue, violaceous and scarlet (male); tail
very short.

4. MANDRILL *Papio sphinx*   50
Face with deep ridges, bright scarlet and blue (male);
orange beard; buttocks bright scarlet and violaceous; tail
very short.

5. HAMADRYAS *Papio hamadryas*   43
Smaller; mane well developed; ashy grey (male); head
and callosities bright pink.

6. ANUBIS BABOON *Papio anubis*   44
Large; nostrils protruding beyond upper lip; mane moderately developed; tail carried 'broken'; olive brown.

7. YELLOW BABOON *Papio cynocephalus*   44
Large; slender; yellowish fawn above. whitish below

8. CHACMA BABOON *Papio ursinus*   44
Large; slender; tail carried 'broken'; dark olive brown
callosities small.

Mangabeys

WHITE-COLLARED MANGABEY   *Cercocebus torquatus* (Kerr)

p. 60

F Cercocèbe à collier blanc   G Rauchgraue Mangabe (*atys*), Weiss-scheitelmangabe (*lunulatus*), Halbbandmangabe (*torquatus*)

Identification: Length (without tail) 26 in.; weight up to 25 lb. A large monkey, slender but robustly built, with long legs, tail moderately long, stiff, held with a sharp angle at its base. Coat rather short. Head and upper-parts smoky grey. Underparts of the same colour or white (see below).

Intraspecific variation: This species is divided into three well-defined races which may be recognised in the field:

    atys (=*fuliginosus*) (from Guinea to the Sassandra River, Ivory Coast), entirely grey, slightly lighter below; whiskers with a dark border.

    lunulatus (from Sassandra River to Ghana), upperparts smoky grey with a white crescent on nape, underparts pure white.

    torquatus (from Nigeria to the Congo River), dark smoky grey above, crown bright chestnut, contrasting with the rest of the head; nape pure white; underparts white, tail grey with a white tip.

Habitat: High forest; also clearings. Map, p. 59.

CRESTED MANGABEY   *Cercocebus galeritus* Peters   p. 60

F Cercocèbe agile   G Hutmangabe

Identification: Length (without tail) 26 in. A larger monkey, slender but robustly built, with long legs, tail moderately long, stiff, held with a sharp angle at base. General colour dull yellowish brown, tinged with olive; no mark on crown, sometimes with a whirl forming a fringe of hairs on fore-head. Underparts whitish or yellowish.

Intraspecific variation: Several well defined races may be distinguished.

    galeritus (Lower Tana River, Kenya[1]), whitish underparts, a fringe of hairs on forehead.

    agilis (from Gabon to eastern Congo), somewhat darker.

    chrysogaster (southern and central Congo), no fringe of hairs on fore-head; whiskers and underparts golden yellow.

Habitat: High forest and galleries. Map, p. 59.

BLACK MANGABEY   *Cercocebus aterrimus* (Oudemans)   p. 60

F Cercocèbe noir   G Schopfmangabe

Identification: Length (without tail) 28 in. A larger monkey, slender and elegantly built, with long legs and long, lithe and mobile tail, covered with long coarse hairs, thus with a penicillated appearance. A median crest on top of head. Face slaty black. General colour pure black; coat coarse and glossy.

---

[1] This subspecies is badly threatened through the destruction of its habitat by heavy cultivation.

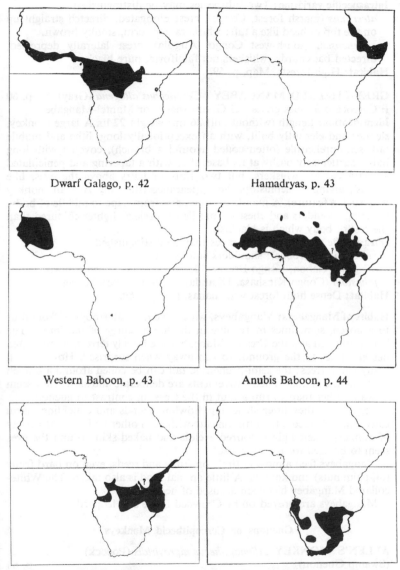

Dwarf Galago, p. 42

Hamadryas, p. 43

Western Baboon, p. 43

Anubis Baboon, p. 44

Yellow Baboon, p. 44

Chacma Baboon, p. 44

Intraspecific variation: Two subspecies may be distinguished:

aterrimus (marsh forest, Congo), crest elongated, directed straight up on the top of head like a tuft; whiskers falciform, smoky brown.

opdenboschi (south-west Congo, Angola), crest laterally depressed, directed backwards; whiskers not falciform, pure black.

Habitat: High forests. Map, p. 59.

GREY-CHEEKED MANGABEY   *Cercocebus albigena* (Gray)   p. 60
F Cercocèbe à joues grises   G Grauwangen- or Mantel-Mangabe
Identification: Length (without tail) 26 in.; weight 22 lb. A large monkey, slender and elegantly built, with an exceptionally long, lithe and mobile tail, semi-prehensile (often coiled around a branch), covered with long hairs, particularly bushy at its base, thus with a tapering and penicillated appearance. No whiskers, but two tufts of hairs above the eyes, like 'horns', giving a mephistophelic appearance (the only African monkey with such a feature). A mantle of long hairs from nape to middle of body, covering shoulders and chest to middle of forelegs, lighter coloured than the rest of body which is blackish.

Intraspecific variation: Three races may be distinguished:

zenkeri (Cameroons): shoulders smoky grey.

albigena (Gabon, Congo Brazzaville): shoulders brownish fawn.

johnstoni (Congo Kinshasa, Uganda): shoulders dark brown.

Habitat: Dense high forest with lianas. Map, p. 69.

Habits of Mangabeys: Mangabeys, which live in small troops of from four to a dozen, sometimes more, live in the lower storey of the forest. The White-collared and the Crested Mangabey are largely terrestrial and often descend trees to the ground, to run away when surprised. However, all easily climb trees; the semi-prehensile tail can be coiled around a branch to steady the animal. Their movements are deliberate and slow; they seem to walk rather than to run about in the trees, in contrast to guenons.

Very noisy, they utter shrieking, howling sounds and chuckling alarm calls. They also seem to communicate with each other with a great variety of mimicry; their light coloured eyelids and naked skin around the eyes seem to be used for this purpose.

Mangabeys feed almost entirely on fruits and seeds, even on hard fruits (oil-palm nuts) and kernels. A little animal food is also taken. The White-collared Mangabey has been accused of necrophagy.

Mangabeys are preyed on by Crowned Eagle and leopard.

Guenons or Cercopithecid Monkeys

ALLEN'S MONKEY   *Allenopithecus nigroviridis* (Pocock)
(Swamp Guenon)   p. 64
F Cercopithèque noir et vert   G Sumpfmeerkatze
Identification: Length (without tail) 18–20 in   A medium-sized monkey,

not unlike a macaque in its features, heavily and stockily built, with a rounded head, and prominent muzzle, relatively short limbs, a proportionately short tail, thickened at base and stiff. Face slaty purplish. Whiskers projecting backwards, grey, with a black line near their edges. Upperparts dark olive green. Underparts from chin to belly dirty white, tinged with pinkish on belly. Outer sides of limbs like the back. A red patch of bare skin under the tail. Tail like the upperparts above, whitish below.

Habitat: Swamp forest. Map, p. 69.

Habits: Almost nothing is known of the habits of this monkey which shares the same habitat with the Talapoin and Brazza's Monkey.

It lives in bands and probably has a specialised vegetarian diet, as shown by some anatomical peculiarities of the stomach. However, small fish, shrimps, snails and other aquatic animals are included in its diet in addition to fruits, seeds and insects.

TALAPOIN *Miopithecus talapoin* (Schreber) p. 61
F Talapoin G Zwergmeerkatze

Identification: Length (without tail) 14 in.; weight up to 3 lb. A very small monkey (the smallest of all African monkeys), not bigger than a large squirrel, slenderly built, with a large rounded head, very large rounded ears and the back conspicuously sloping forwards. Face salmon pinkish, with the muzzle partly covered with blackish hairs. Whiskers golden yellow, well developed from ear to temple. Upperparts yellowish olive green; limbs brighter. Underparts creamy white. Tail long, greyish fawn, darkening at tip, yellower below.

Intraspecific variation: Several subspecies have been described, not recognisable in the field.

Habitat: Lowland swamp forest; coastal and estuarine mangrove swamps. Map, p. 69.

Habits: Talapoin live in bands of up to 60–80 individuals, but usually much less, probably composed of family units. They are fully arboreal and diurnal, retiring at night in dense cover, more often in inundated forest. They are extremely agile and lively, in spite of their natural timidity. Relatively silent, they utter whistling notes when alarmed.

Talapoin feed on various fruits and seeds, palm-nuts, leaves and flowers; they are extremely fond of cultivated fruits like paw-paw. They probably also eat insects and even small vertebrates.

The most striking feature of their reproductive physiology is the ocurrence of a genital swelling in the female, according to a cycle of 27 to 43 days, with a seasonal cessation of sexual activity, at least in captivity.

MOUSTACHED MONKEY *Cercopithecus cephus* (L.) p. 61
F Moustac G Blaumaul, Schnurrbartaffe

Identification: Length (without tail) 19–22 in.; weight 9–11 lb. A medium-sized monkey. Face blue, with a conspicuous white chevron on the upper lip, immediately below the nose; no nose patch. Whiskers bushy, but simple, directed downwards and backwards, bright yellow. A large triangular black patch on each side of muzzle, separating the whiskers from ashy grey throat. Often a conspicuous yellowish fringe of hairs on ears. Upperparts rufous brown, with a faint olive tinge. Underparts ashy grey.

Intraspecific variation: The true *cephus* (from the Cameroons to Congo River, except south-west Gabon) has the greater part of the tail red; *cephodes* (south-west Gabon) has a greyish tail.

Habitat: Forests and galleries. Map, p. 69.

RED-EARED NOSE-SPOTTED MONKEY *Cercopithecus erythrotis* (Waterhouse)   p. 61
F Moustac à oreilles rousses   G Rotohr Meerkatze

Identification: Length (without tail) 14–20 in. A rather small monkey. Face largely blue, becoming pink on the muzzle; no white chevron on the upper lip, but a conspicuous triangular spot on the nose, brick red or white tinged with ochraceous. Whiskers simple, directed backwards, yellow except for a black temporal stripe and a large triangular black patch on each side of the muzzle. Upperparts dark olive green, with a reddish tinge posteriorly. Underparts ashy grey. Tail bright red, at least basally.

Intraspecific variation: The true *erythrotis* (Fernando Po) has the nose spot brick red to orange, like *camerunensis* (north-west Cameroons), which is lighter coloured on the upperparts; tail entirely red; *sclateri* (Nigeria) has the nose spot white tinged with ochraceous; tail red, then whitish.

Habitat: Forest and galleries. Map, p. 69.

RED-BELLIED MONKEY *Cercopithecus erythrogaster* Gray[1]   p. 61
F Cercopithèque à ventre rouge   G Rotbauch

entification: Length (without tail) 18 in. A medium-sized monkey. Face very dark, bluish grey, with a spot on nose, sometimes white as in *C. nictitans*, but often jet black, contrasting with the face. A black temporal band from forehead to sides of head and nape, broadening posteriorly and meeting its fellow on the nape. Whiskers projecting backwards, speckled black and white near the face, then pure white. No black stripe across the cheek, but a black triangular spot on each side of the mouth, not reaching the ear. Crown bright lemon yellow, speckled with black, in sharp contrast with black temporal and nuchal band. Upperparts uniform olive brown. Underparts rufous or grey. Tail olive green above, darkening towards tip, white below.

Habitat: Secondary high forest. Map, p. 69.

[1] An apparently rare and puzzling monkey, owing to the very variable coloration of face and hair, known only from a few skins.

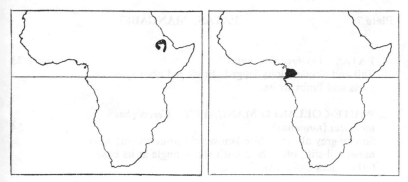

Gelada Baboon, p. 47

Mandrill, p. 50

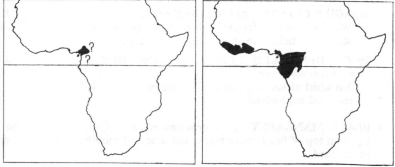

Drill, p. 50

White-collared Mangabey, p. 54

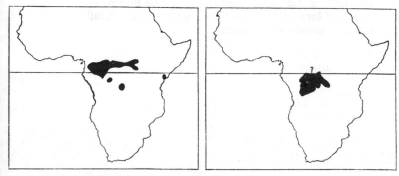

Crested Mangabey, p. 54

Black Mangabey, p. 54

Plate 7   PATAS, MANGABEY

1. **PATAS**   *Erythrocebus patas*   *page* 73
   Tall and slender; long legged; brick red above; underparts and limbs white.

2. **WHITE-COLLARED MANGABEY**   *Cercocebus*
   torquatus (*torquatus*)   54
   Smoky-grey above, white below; chestnut crown; white
   nape; tail stiff, often held with sharp angle at its base
   (other races different).

3. **CRESTED MANGABEY**   *Cercocebus galeritus*   54
   Yellowish brown above, lighter below.

   3a. **AGILE CRESTED MANGABEY**   *C. g. agilis*   54
       Whirl of hairs on forehead; dirty white below; tail
       stiff, often held with sharp angle at its base.

   3b. **GOLDEN-BELLIED CRESTED MANGABEY**   54
       C. g. chrysogaster
       No whirl of hairs; golden yellow below; tail carried
       recurved backwards.

4. **BLACK MANGABEY**   *Cercocebus aterrimus*   54
   Crest on top of head; pure black; tail lithe and mobile,
   penicillated.

5. **GREY-CHEEKED MANGABEY**   *Cercocebus albigena*   56
   Two tufts of stiff hairs above eyes; blackish brown;
   mantle of long hairs on shoulder, lighter coloured; tail
   lithe and mobile, penicillated.

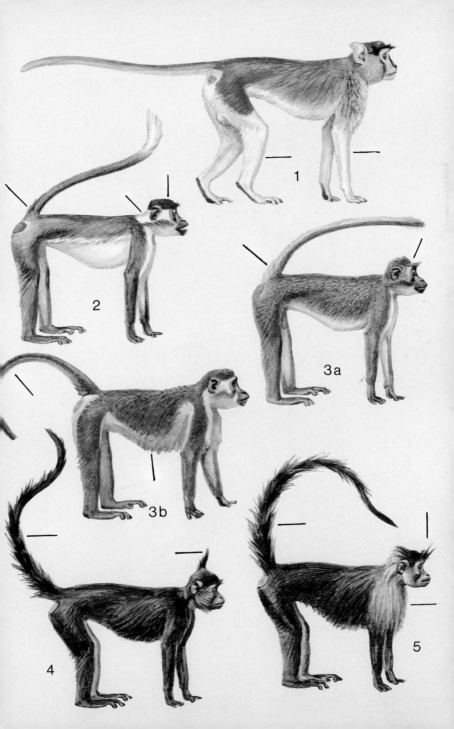

GUENONS i   Plate 8

1. **GREATER WHITE-NOSED MONKEY** *Cercopithecus*
   nictitans (*nictitans*)   63
   White nose; dark green above, blackish below; in one
   race (*martini*) white chest.

2. **BLACK-CHEEKED WHITE-NOSED MONKEY**
   Cercopithecus ascanius (*ascanius*)   62
   White nose (or buff or black) contrasting with bluish
   face; whitish cheeks with black stripe; white below; tail
   rufous.

3. **LESSER WHITE-NOSED MONKEY** *Cercopithecus*
   petaurista   62
   White nose; white cheeks with temporal black stripe;
   white below; tail dark above, whitish below.

4. **RED-BELLIED MONKEY** *Cercopithecus erythrogaster*   58
   Nose white or black; whiskers pure white, greyish near
   the face; rufous or grey below; tail olive above, white
   below.

5. **MOUSTACHED MONKEY** *Cercopithecus cephus*   57
   Face blue with white chevron on upper lip; cheeks
   yellow; ashy grey below; tail red or greyish.

6. **RED-EARED NOSE-SPOTTED MONKEY**
   Cercopithecus erythrotis   58
   Nose reddish or white; greyish underparts.

   6a. **RED-EARED NOSE-SPOTTED MONKEY**   58
       Cercopithecus e. erythrotis
       Nose reddish; tail red.

   6b. **SCLATER'S MONKEY** *Cercopithecus e. sclateri*   58
       Nose whitish; tail red basally, then whitish.

7. **TALAPOIN** *Miopithecus talapoin*   57
   Very small; blackish muzzle; greenish above, whitish
   below.

BLACK-CHEEKED WHITE-NOSED MONKEY *Cercopithecus ascanius* (Audebert) p. 61

F Cercopithèque ascagne   G Schwarzbackigen Weissnase

Identification: Length (without tail) 16–20 in.; weight up to 14 lb. A medium-sized monkey, with a proportionately long tail carried extended in line with the back, drooping towards the tip when the animal is progressing. Face bluish, with a conspicuous white, buff or black heart-shaped spot on nose. A dark band across forehead from ear to ear. Whiskers with crests and whirls, creamy white with a black stripe across the cheek from corner of mouth to below the ear. Upperparts uniformly dark olive, washed with reddish. Underparts pure white. Forearms, lower parts of legs, hands and feet slaty black. Tail largely bright rufous, except underside near base which is grey or white.

Intraspecific variation: Several races are recognised according to the shape of whiskers, the colour of nose spot, the extent of rufous on back, and the colour of underside of base of tail: *schmidti* (north of the Congo River), *whitesidei* (central Congo), *ascanius* (south-west Congo, Angola), *atrinasus* (north-east Angola), *katangae* (Katanga). They cannot be distinguished in the field.

Similar species: May be confused with *C. cephus*, owing to the red tail, but the latter has no spot on the nose, and shows a conspicuous chevron on upper lip.

Habitat: Forests and galleries. Map, p. 75.

LESSER WHITE-NOSED MONKEY *Cercopithecus petaurista* (Schreiber) (Spot-nosed Monkey) p. 61

F Pétauriste   G Helle Weissnase

Identification: Length (without tail) 14–18 in.; weight 6 lb. A small or medium-sized monkey. Face dark slaty blue to blackish, with a conspicuous oval white patch on nose. A black frontal band from ear to ear. Whiskers well developed, directed backwards, with no crest or whirl; pure white with a black stripe from eye to below the ear. Upperparts dark greenish brown. Underparts white. Lower legs strongly washed with grey. Tail long, bicoloured; above brownish at base, darkening to black on the tip, below whitish.

Intraspecific variation: Two races may be distinguished: *buttikoferi* (from Guinea to Sassandra River, Ivory Coast), no blackish band across nape; and *petaurista* (east of Sassandra River), a blackish band across nape.

Similar species: May be confused with other Cercopithecids with a white patch on the nose. But *C. ascanius* has a red tail, and *C. nictitans* a black tail.

Habitat: Forest, especially secondary growth; also swampy areas, thickets and fringing forest in Guinea savanna. Particularly in the lower strata of the forest canopy. Map, p. 75.

GREATER WHITE-NOSED MONKEY *Cercopithecus nictitans* (L.)
(Putty-nosed Monkey) p. 61
F Hocheur[1] G Dunkle Weissnase
Identification: Length (without tail) 18–26 in.; weight up to 17 lb. A large monkey, stoutly built. Face slaty black with a conspicuous oval white spot on the nose. No frontal band. Whiskers well developed, with no whirl, projecting backwards. Sides of head and upperparts uniform dark olive green. Underparts slaty black, sometimes white on foreparts (*martini*). Limbs black. Tail long and black.
Intraspecific variation: Two races may be distinguished in the field: *martini* (from the Cameroons and Fernando Po westwards), underparts except hinder part of abdomen, white; and *nictitans* (central Africa), darker, underparts slaty black.
Similar species: May be confused with *C. mitis* (*stühlmanni*), but the conspicuous white nose-spot is lacking in the latter; and with *C. petaurista* but nose spot different in shape, no white whiskers, and tail entirely black.
Habitat: Forest (this species can be considered as the western representative of *C. mitis*). Map, p. 75.

BLUE MONKEY *Cercopithecus mitis* Wolff (including the *albogularis* group) (Diademed Monkey) p. 64
F Cercopithèque à diadème G Diademaffe K Kima, Nchima
Identification: Length (without tail) 20–26 in.; weight up to 15 lb. A rather large, stoutly built monkey; back horizontal; a rather long and thick tail carried high in a slight curve, concave downwards, the tip higher than the body line when the animal is walking. Face purplish black, narrow and elongated. No white patch on the nose, but muzzle more or less covered with white hairs. No beard. Whiskers long, dense and projecting backwards. On the forehead, hairs dense and bristly ('diadem') directed forwards, variable in coloration, sometimes contrasting with the crown. Throat or collar white. Coat generally dense and thick, of a very variable coloration (see below). Lower limbs black. Blue Monkeys have a rather quiet trotting gait, unlike the rapid movements of smaller Cercopithecids.
Intraspecific variation: At first, a rather unnatural specific unit, due to the wide range of variation in pattern and coloration. Two natural groups (sometimes considered distinct species) based on coloration and geographical distribution may be considered.
CONGOLESE GROUP (*mitis*). The only Cercopithecids with the shoulders entirely crossed by a black band, the anterior limbs and back of shoulders being black and thus contrasting with the back. Crown pure black (except *opisthostictus* (Katanga and Zambia), which has the crown speckled with buff). Upperparts varying, according to race, from dark

[1] The French name comes from its habit of wagging the head up and down.

Plate 9 GUENONS ii

1. **BLUE MONKEY** *Cercopithecus mitis* (*mitis*)   *page* 63
Diadem of dense hairs on forehead; coloration very
variable (refer to the text).

2. **MONA MONKEY** *Cercopithecus mona* (*mona*)   66
Forehead white; black stripe across temporal region;
white or yellow below.

3. **BRAZZA'S MONKEY** *Cercopithecus neglectus*   67
Broad reddish diadem on forehead; white beard; white
stripe across thigh.

4. **L'HOEST'S MONKEY** *Cercopithecus l'hoesti*   68
Dark; back reddish; white or greyish cheeks in strong
contrast with body; tail semi-prehensile, carried with
hooked tip.

5. **DIANA MONKEY** *Cercopithecus diana* (*roloway*)   67
Chest and forelimbs pure white; white beard; rump bright
chestnut; white stripe across thigh; buttocks bright
rufous to creamy white.

6. **OWL-FACED MONKEY** *Cercopithecus hamlyni*   68
Dark; face rounded and massive, blackish with white
vertical band on nose.

7. **GREEN MONKEY** *Cercopithecus aethiops* (*johnstoni*)   71
Greenish or yellowish above, white below; face black;
white cheeks; generally white band on forehead.

8. **ALLEN'S MONKEY** *Allenopithecus nigroviridis*   56
Proportionately short tail; dark olive above, whitish
below.

2

3

4

5

6a

6b

7

1. WESTERN BLACK-AND-WHITE COLOBUS
Colobus polykomos   76
Black; whiskers and foreparts greyish; tail not bushy,
entirely white.

2. BLACK COLOBUS   *C. satanas*   78
Entirely black.

3. ABYSSINIAN BLACK-AND-WHITE COLOBUS   *C.*
abyssinicus   77
Black; white mantle around upperparts; tail black, with
a white, bushy terminal part.

4. ANGOLAN BLACK-AND-WHITE COLOBUS   *C.*
angolensis   76
Black; long white hairs on shoulders; no mantle around
upperparts; tail pure black to white, may be bushy.

5. WESTERN RED COLOBUS   *C. badius*   78
Dark above, reddish below; nose turned up above
swollen lip.

6. RED COLOBUS   *C. pennanti*   78
Reddish to brown above, washed with black on shoulders.

a. OUSTALET'S RED COLOBUS   *C. p. oustaleti*   79
A whorl of hairs above the ear.

b. ZANZIBAR RED COLOBUS   *C. p. kirki*   97
Tufts of long white hairs on forehead.

7. OLIVE COLOBUS   *C. verus*   82
Two grey patches on forehead; greenish brown above,
grey below.

grey to bluish and greenish, exceptionally reddish. Underparts dark, grey to black. Hindlegs darker than body. Several races may be recognised: *mitis* (Angola), grey above, a conspicuous white band across forehead; *stuhlmanni* (from eastern Congo to western Kenya), silvery bluish grey, washed with olive above, underparts ashy grey; *kandti* (Kivu; bamboo and Hagenia forests at high altitude), golden rufous to olive green above, rusty below (other races: *maesi, schoutedeni*, Congo; *dogetti*, Rwanda, Burundi, southern Uganda; *boutourlini*, Ethiopia). ORIENTAL GROUP (east of the Rift Valley) ('Sykes Monkeys'; *albogularis*). No black on crown, nape and shoulders. Forelimbs black. Throat extensively and sharply contrasted ('White-throated Guenons') white. Upperparts from greenish to reddish, often showing some red on the back. Underparts light coloured. Several races may be distinguished in the field: *zammaranoi* (Somalia), smaller, back uniform olive green; *kolbi* (Kenya highlands), *albotorquatus* (Kenya lowlands), *albogularis* (Zanzibar) and *moloneyi* (Tanzania), general colour deep reddish, throat and collar broadly white; *nyasae* (south of Lake Nyasa), greener on upperparts; *erythrarchus* (Mozambique), light greenish grey on upperparts, root of tail bright rufous; *labiatus* (Samango Monkey; South Africa, from Zululand to eastern Cape Province), dark green, underparts dirty white.

Habitat: High forest, galleries; also wooded savanna; from sea level up to 10,000 feet of altitude. Map, p. 75.

MONA MONKEY *Cercopithecus mona* (Schreber) and allies[1] p. 64
F Mone   G Monameerkatze

Identification: Length (without tail) 18–22 in.; weight 6–14 lb. A medium-sized monkey, robustly built, with a tail moderate to very long, often recurved towards the back. Face above slaty blue, contrasting with the flesh coloured muzzle. A white or whitish band on the forehead, contrasting with the dark crown. Whiskers densely furred, with a black band from eye to ear. Crown and shoulders olive greenish or yellowish (speckled yellow and black), outer side of forelimbs black. Upperparts generally brightly coloured, the hinderparts darker than remainder of back. Underparts light. Coloration of upperparts varying from grey to reddish (see below). Tail always dark above, white or yellow below.

Intraspecific variation: A wide range of variation occurs among this group of monkeys. A number of subspecies may be recognised in the field.

THE *mona* GROUP is recognisable by the absence of crest on crown. *Campbelli* (from Senegal to Sassandra River, Ivory Coast) and *lowei* (from Sassandra River to Ghana) have the head and the shoulders

---

[1] This group of monkeys has been split into several species by recent authors. This systematic treatment seems sound and based on morphological differences; moreover the ranges of several forms apparently overlap. We prefer to consider them as one species for practical reasons.

yellowish, the back being grey or blackish, the former being lighter coloured than the latter; *mona* (from Ghana to the Cameroons) has the back bright chestnut and two conspicuous white spots at the root of the tail, a unique feature in Cercopithecid monkeys.

THE *wolfi* GROUP is characterised by the absence of crest on crown, and a white frontal diadem; the colour of belly invades the flank, with a sharp line between it and the back. *Wolfi* (marsh forest of the Congo) back reddish with a well defined black line along the flank, belly washed with orange, hind legs rufous fawn; *pyrogaster* (Kasai, south Congo), like *wolfi*, but deeper coloured; *denti* (north-east Congo), back dark brown, belly creamy white, hindlegs brownish fulvous.

THE *pogonias* GROUP is characterised by a frontal crest on crown ('Crowned Guenons'), a white frontal chevron and golden yellow underparts; *grayi* (Cameroons to north-east Gabon and the Ubangi River), back bright rufous, hind legs fulvous; *nigripes* (west Gabon) back reddish, legs iron grey; *pogonias* (Fernando Po, Cameroons), back dark grey with a wide black band; legs fulvous.

Habitat: High forest and galleries. Preferably lower and middle strata. Map, p. 75.

DIANA MONKEY *Cercopithecus diana* (L.) p. 64
F Cercopithèque diane   G Dianameerkatze

Identification: Length (without tail) 16–21 in. A medium-sized monkey, elegantly built, with back curving forwards, the tail often carried recurved upwards with the tip turned back. A very striking pattern. Face black; a narrow, but conspicuous white band across forehead. A pointed white beard. Sides of head, chin, throat, chest and inner face of forelimbs pure white, sharply defined from the rest of body. Crown almost black, upper back and flanks speckled grey, becoming darker towards the belly which is entirely black. From the middle of back to root of tail, a wide triangular patch of bright chestnut. Limbs otherwise black; a conspicuous white oblique stripe across the thigh. Buttocks and inner sides of hind limbs bright rufous to creamy white. Tail entirely black.

Intraspecific variation: Two well defined races may be distinguished: *diana* (west from Sassandra River, Ivory Coast), beard shorter, inner sides of hindlegs deep bright rufous; *roloway* (east from Sassandra River), beard very long, inner sides of hindlegs from yellowish to creamy white. The alleged race *dryas*, from Sankuru, Congo, known only from the type specimen, is highly questionable.

Habitat: Dense high forest, mainly in the upper strata. Map, p. 75.

BRAZZA'S MONKEY *Cercopithecus neglectus* Schlegel p. 64
F Cercopithèque de Brazza   G Brazza-Meerkatze

Identification: Length (without tail) 16–24 in.; weight up to 18 lb. A medium-sized monkey, stoutly and heavily built with a dumpy appear-

ance. Back sloping forwards (the rump seems distinctly higher than the shoulders). A proportionately short but thickened tail, carried in a drooping arch or hanging downwards when the animal is walking. Forehead with a broad conspicuous bright reddish ochraceous diadem, surmounted by a jet black transverse band. A well developed pure white beard. Whiskers, upperparts and flanks speckled olive grey. Underparts blackish (whitish in young). Forelimbs black distally; a conspicuous oblique white stripe across the thigh. Buttocks white. Tail black.
Habitat: Marshy and riverside forest; lower strata. Map, p. 87.

L'HOEST'S MONKEY *Cercopithecus l'hoesti* Sclater   p. 64
F Cercopithèque de l'Hoest   G Vollbartmeerkatze
Identification: Length (without tail) 18–22 in. A medium-sized monkey, slenderly and elegantly built, dark coloured, with back sloping forwards, and with a very mobile tail, semi-prehensile (the only African guenon showing this feature) carried high above the back, with the tip turned abruptly in a hook. Face pinkish or greyish, with a blackish muzzle. No frontal band. Whiskers well developed, fluffy, projecting backwards all around the face, pure white or grey, contrasting strikingly with the dark coloration of body. Upperparts speckled dark grey with a conspicuous oval (not triangular, as in *C. diana*) rusty patch from shoulders to root of tail. Underparts dark slaty black. Limbs black. Tail like the body at base, terminal part black.
Intraspecific variation: The typical race (eastern Congo) has the face pinkish, and the whiskers pure white, while *preussi* (Mount Cameroon, Fernando Po) has the face grey, grey whiskers contrasting with the white throat, and the dorsal patch red mahogany.
Habitat: Montane forest. Map, p. 87.

OWL-FACED MONKEY *Cercopithecus hamlyni* Pocock   p. 64
F Cercopithèque à tête de hibou   G Eulenkopfaffe
Identification: Length (without tail) 22 in. A medium-sized monkey densely furred, very dark in colour, with a very peculiar head, giving it an owl-like appearance. Face rounded and flattened, very massive, with very large eyes surrounded by circular wrinkles; purplish black, with a very conspicuous narrow vertical white band from forehead to upper lip. Forehead with a pale yellow band. All around the face, a compact hood over crown, cheeks and throat, of long, dense, dark green hairs, completely concealing the ears. Upperparts dark olive green. Underparts and limbs black. Naked skin around callosities bright sky blue. Tail short, thick and conical at its base, ashy grey, with a thick terminal black tassel.
Habitat: Dense forest, up to 14,000 ft; supposed to be nocturnal. Map, p. 87.

Habits of forest-dwelling Cercopithecids: Guenons of the genus *Cercopithecus* form a fairly homogeneous group of quadrupedal, arboreal (as a rule

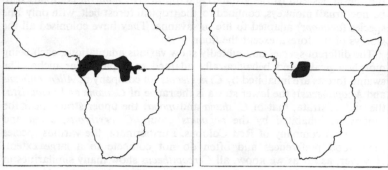

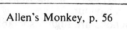

Grey-cheeked Mangabey, p. 56

Allen's Monkey, p. 56

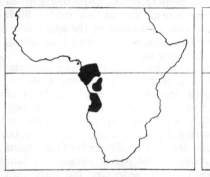

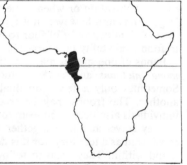

Talapoin, p. 57

Moustached Monkey, p. 57

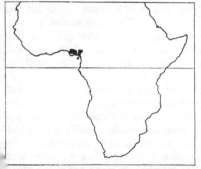

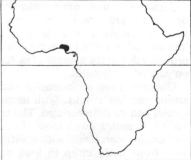

Red-eared Nose-spotted Monkey,
p. 58

Red-bellied Monkey, p. 58

they never descend to the ground) and diurnal (*C. hamlyni* is supposed to be nocturnal) monkeys, confined to the tropical forest belt, with only one species (*aethiops*) adapted to life in savanna. They have colonised all the storeys of the forest, except the floor.

The different species undoubtedly show various adaptations, each being morphologically and behaviourally adapted to a particular niche. The swamp forests are inhabited by *C. neglectus* (in company of *Allenopithecus* and *Miopithecus*); the lower strata is the range of *C. mona* and *petaurista*; the middle strata, that of *C. diana* and *mona*; the upper strata, near the canopy, is inhabited by the *pogonias* group, *C. erythrotis*, *diana* and *nictitans*, in company of Red Colobus. Furthermore, the various species show food preferences and often do not compete to a large extent. However, as far as we know, all *Cercopithecus* show many similarities in their behaviour.

Guenons are highly sociable and live in bands numbering up to 40–50 individuals and troops of 200 have been recorded, particularly when raiding cultivation or when some trees provide a great food supply. Such large bands are, however, not typical and are formed by the aggregation of small family groups of four to five monkeys, which assemble according to food availability into larger bands during the day.

Bands of one species may associate with those of another (for example, *mona*, *nictitans* and *cephus*), and even with Mangabey and Colobus. Sometimes only a few individuals of one species mix with a band of another. The troops may be escorted by hornbills or parrots. Solitary individuals also occur and seem to form a constant part of the population.

They travel and feed together within a particular area which can be considered as a territory, for it is defended by the individuals of the groups found within. They seem to follow well defined routes, usually at about the same hour of the day. They are generally sedentary, but sometimes wander according to the availability of food and ripening of the fruits they favour.

Each family unit seems under the dominance of a master male but the dominance gradient shows a very slow slope. The only social activity between members of a band is mutual grooming; the gestures like 'presenting', so often observed in baboons, are not found in guenons, probably due to the absence of external sexual manifestations, like swelling, on part of the females.

Guenons have an extensive vocabulary and generally emit different grunts and low croaks. With much experience the voices of the various species can be differentiated. The cry of *C. diana* has been described as a yelling, in contrast with those of *C. ascanius* and *mona*, which are bird-like twitterings interspersed with whistling notes. Warning or threatening calls vary from sharp chirp to loud bark. Some species, like *C. mitis* and *neglectus* are rather silent, while smaller species like *mona* are much more noisy.

They have also a great variety of mimicry and gestures (lowering of eyebrows, raising and jerking the head, threat display with mouth wide open, etc.) to communicate with each other.

Vision is very acute, and probably colour vision is good. Hearing is excellent. The sense of smell is not much developed; but it serves at close quarters to test the quality of food, as well as gustation.

Guenons show much activity after sunrise, then later in the morning, and a third peak is observed in the late afternoon. At night they retire to particular places—individual trees, dense foliage—which are used for long periods. The large bands split into the family units referred to above, each one having its own dormitory, though several groups can settle to sleep in the same tree.

Guenons feed primarily on a large variety of vegetable matter: leaves of trees (particularly *C. petaurista*), young shoots, flowers and seeds; fruits (such as *Markhamia, Ficus, Cyanometra, Irvingia, Pachylobus, Musanga*) form an important part of the diet, including those of the oil-palm (*C. cephus* is particularly fond of these fruits and occurs frequently in old oil-palm plantations). This vegetable matter is supplemented to some extent by animal food, particularly insects (ants) and occasionally but very seldom small vertebrates and birds' eggs. Guenons often raid crops, particularly maize, banana, cassava and sweet potato. Drinking is apparently not known to occur, except in some dry habitats.

Breeding seems continuous all the year round. There is no prelude to mating, which occurs mostly at night. The period of gestation is about six months, perhaps a little longer. A single young is born at a time, but twins have been occasionally recorded. It is carried by the mother who nurses it jealously. When she moves, the young clings to her firmly. The natal coat is conspicuously different from the juvenile pelage. The view of an infant in such coat in possession of a man or a predator produces a violent reaction from the adults, particularly from the dominant male which comes close to the intruder with threatening attitudes and vocalisations. This natal coat seems to serve the function of stimulating all adults to rescue the young; as soon as the infant grows its juvenile coat, which differs only in minor respects from that of the adult, this stimulus disappears. Potential longevity exceeds 20 years and may extend to 30 years.

Guenons have few predators, except some large birds of prey, particularly the Crowned Eagle (*Stephanoaetus coronatus*). Large snakes, like pythons, may kill some; Leopard occasionally catch them by surprise.

VERVET and GRIVET MONKEY   *Cercopithecus aethiops* (L.)
(and allies) (Green Monkeys)   p. 64
F Vervet, Grivet   K Tumbili; Ngedere   G Grünmeerkatze A Blauaap
Identification: Length (without tail) 18–26 in.; weight 10 lb. or more. A medium-sized or large monkey; back horizontal; a moderately long, stiff

tail, carried obliquely above the line of the back and arched at the tip when the animal is walking. Face generally entirely black (the only Cercopithecid with black face, except *C. diana*, which is otherwise quite different). General colour light greyish or yellowish olive, sometimes washed with russet. On forehead, generally a white or light coloured band. Whiskers more or less developed, projecting backwards and upwards, generally white. Underparts whitish.

Intraspecific variation: This species is split into several well-defined groups, which represent probably full species. We keep them together in the same specific unit for practical reasons. They can be recognised in the field, as well as some of the subspecies into which they have been divided.

CALLITRIX. No white band on forehead; whiskers yellowish; a whirl on the temporal area, directed forwards. Upperparts strongly washed with yellowish. Tip of tail yellow. *Sabaeus* (Senegal to Ghana).

TANTALUS MONKEY. White band on forehead very conspicuous, separated from the cheeks by a black stripe. Whiskers white, sharply demarcated in colour from the crown. A tuft of white hairs at root of tail. Perineal area orange. Tip of tail whitish. *Tantalus* (Ghana to Central African Rep.); *marrensis* (Jebel Marra, Sudan), *budgetti* (east Congo to Uganda).

GRIVETS. Whiskers pure white, falciform, long and fluffy, in strong contrast with crown. An ill-defined white band on forehead, not separated from whiskers by a black stripe. A tuft of white hairs at the base of tail. Tip of tail whitish. *Aethiops* (Sudan, north Ethiopia), ashy grey tinged with green above; *hilgerti* (south, south-east Ethiopia), darker; *ellenbecki* (south-west Ethiopia), tinged with reddish.

VERVETS. White band on forehead conspicuous, blending on the sides with the whiskers, which are short and not sharply demarcated in colour from the crown. Feet conspicuously black. A tuft of reddish hair under the root of tail. Tip of tail black. Various races from extreme south Ethiopia and Somalia to South Africa, among which: *johnstoni* (Kenya, Tanzania), pale-coloured; *rufoviridis* (Mozambique), reddish green; *pygerythrus* (southern Africa), dark green.

MALBROUCK. The only green monkey with a pale face, fleshy coloured with dark spots. A well defined band on forehead; whiskers dirty white. A tuft of reddish hairs at root of tail. Tip of tail black. *Cynosurus* (from the southern edge of forest in the Congo and Angola to north-western Rhodesia).

Habitat: Woodland and savannas; fringing forests and high bush. Never in rain forest or in semi-desert. Map, p. 87.

Habits: Grivets and Vervets, a widely distributed and very common species, due to its high degree of adaptability, differ notably from other guenons by the fact that they are living in much more open country, which has affected their ecology as much as their behaviour. They favour gallery forests and dense bush as refuge and sleeping quarters; but to

2. Head of Green Monkeys (*Cercopithecus aethiops*)
   1 Callitrix (*sabaeus*)   2 Tantalus (*tantalus*)   3 Grivet (*aethiops*)
   4 Vervet (*pygerythrus*)   5 Malbrouck (*cynosurus*)

forage, they venture into open savanna, travelling long distances, up to
500 yards, with a characteristic cursorial gait.

They live in bands of from 6 to 20, averaging a dozen individuals, but
large aggregations of up to a hundred have been recorded. Mixed troops
with *C. mitis* are unusual. They are rather silent; males utter a harsh
kek-kek-kek.

They are mainly vegetarian and eat mostly leaves and young shoots
besides bark, flowers, fruits, bulbs, roots and grass seeds. This diet is
supplemented by insects, grubs, caterpillars, spiders, eggs and nestlings of
ground-nesting birds, occasionally by larger prey (rodents, hares). They
can be very harmful to crops and orchards. Drinking is extremely rare.

They are preyed on by leopard, caracal, serval and the larger raptorial
birds.

Patas

PATAS or **RED MONKEY**   *Erythrocebus patas* (Schreber)   p. 60
F Patas, Singe rouge   G Husarenaffe
Identification: Length (without tail) 20–23 in.; weight up to 22 lb. A large
and tall monkey, very slenderly and gauntly built, high on the feet (the
'greyhound' of monkeys), with the back horizontal and a short harsh coat.
Face pale pinkish or blackish. A black band across forehead. Whiskers
yellowish. Upperparts brick-red, brighter on top of head, sometimes with
a grey tinge on shoulders (adult males). Underparts white. Lower legs
white, tinged with yellowish in young and females. Tail long, carried

arched upwards above the line of the back when in motion, rufous fawn, lighter distally.

Female like the male, but much smaller (half the weight).

Intraspecific variation: Two subspecies may be recognised. The true *patas*, from Senegal to Chad, has a pinkish face and a black patch on the nose; and the Nisnas, *pyrrhonotus*, from the Sudan to Tanzania, has a grey face and a white patch on the nose.

Habitat: Patas occur in very dry savannas, even to the north of the limits of baboons and grivets; in Air, within the Sahara, they frequent rocky country, unlike their normal habitat. Only on the fringes of forest and thicket, avoiding denser cover. Map, p. 87.

Habits: Very shy and elusive, they are well adapted to terrestrial life, though able to climb easily into trees. They are definitely the fastest of all primates, running at speeds up to 35 m.p.h. When alerted, they stand up on their hindlegs, with the body fully upright.

Very sociable, they live in bands of from 9 to 30 individuals, with an average of 15; in western Africa, at least sometimes, they gather into large aggregations of more than 100. Each unit consists of an adult male which plays the part of watchdog, and up to about 12 females with their young. The male stays with his harem throughout the year. The home range of each group is very wide (up to 20 square miles) and much wandering is observed. They never mix with other monkeys.

Communication within the group is mainly carried out by means of gestures and mimics. The vocabulary is as diversified as that of baboons, and includes harsh and moaning sounds; but the calls are rarely uttered. The barking of the adult male, higher pitched than that of the baboon, is only heard when the animal, stationed in a tree, is warning the approach of another group of patas.

The daily pattern of activity comprises two main feeding periods, with a rest time during the heat of the day. At dusk, the group, which rarely occupies the same areas on successive nights, disperses into several different trees. Patas feed on grass, fruits, beans (like those of the Tamarind) and seeds, supplemented with some animal matter, insects, rarely small vertebrates like lizards. Drinking is very infrequent.

There is a pronounced local birth season and probably the same occurs for mating; the period of gestation is 160 days.

Patas show pronounced differences in adaptation with baboons which share the same habitat. The latter live in larger groups with several adult males, and are much more noisy and aggressive.

COLOBUS MONKEYS: Colobidae

Large primates, slender but robustly built, with a clumsy and 'pot-bellied' silhouette. Only four fingers on the hand, the pollex (thumb) being either vestigial or absent. Tail long and non-prehensile. Rump callosities large.

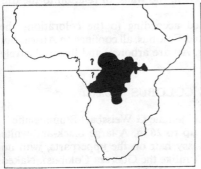

Black-cheeked White-nosed Monkey, p. 62

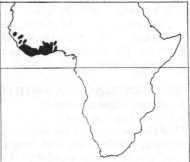

Lesser White-nosed Monkey, p. 62

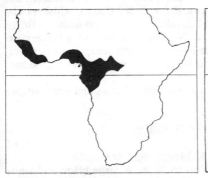

Greater White-nosed Monkey, p. 63

Blue Monkey, p. 63

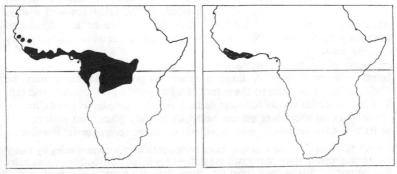

Mona Monkey, p. 66

Diana Monkey, p. 67

Stomach large, with folds and pockets in the walls, in relation to the die which mostly comprises leaves.

Two groups may be distinguished according to the coloration; the Black-and-White Colobus and the Red Colobus, all confined to Africa, but related to the Asiatic *Semnopithecus*. All are arboreal and live exclusively in forested areas.

WESTERN BLACK-AND-WHITE COLOBUS *Colobus polykomos* (Zimmermann)[1]
p. 65

F Colobe blanc et noir d'Afrique occidentale G Weissbart Stummelaffe

Identification: Length (without tail) up to 26 in. A large black-and-white monkey, heavily built, with long glossy hair on the upperparts, with no long haired mantle around the back (unlike the Guereza Colobus). Naked face slaty black. General colour jet black. Whiskers pure white or greyish. Tail entirely white with no terminal tuft.

Intraspecific variation: Two well defined races may be distinguished: *polykomos* (from Senegal to Sassandra River, Ivory Coast), whiskers and around the head greyish, foreparts of shoulders greyish, no white on thigh; *vellerosus* (from Bandama River to Nigeria), beard and whiskers extensively developed, pure white; greater part of thigh conspicuously white; *dollmani* (between the Sassandra and Bandama Rivers) is an intermediate form.

Habitat: High forest, Guinea savanna along river banks and even patches of dry forest. Map, p. 99.

ANGOLAN BLACK-AND-WHITE COLOBUS *Colobus angolensis* P. L. Sclater
p. 65

F Colobe blanc et noir d'Angola   K Mbega   G Mantelaffe

Identification: Length (without tail) up to 30 in. A large black-and-white monkey, heavily built, with long white hairs on the shoulders, but no mantle around the back (unlike the Guereza Colobus). General colour jet black. Whiskers generally well developed, fluffy, falciform and always white. Shoulders covered by long white hairs, more or less developed according to the races. Tail distally white on a variable length, rarely entirely white.

Young white, becoming darker with age.

Intraspecific variation: A large number of geographic races may be distinguished according to the extent of white marks on shoulders and tail. The major trends are as follows: *cottoni*, *cordieri*, *prigoginei* (east Congo), white hairs on shoulders scarce, buttocks entirely black, tail with no tuft at its tip, dark (*cottoni*), grey (*cordieri*) or white (*prigoginei*); *angolensis*,

[1] All Black-and-White Colobus have been considered as one species by many former authors, in spite of the striking differences in the distribution of long hairs and pattern. Actually they constitute three natural groups which may be distinguished specifically.

3. Head of Black and White Colobus
1 Western Colobus (*C. pol. polykomos*)   2 Western Colobus (*C. pol. vellerosus*)   3 Angolan Colobus (*C. ang. angolensis*)   4 Abyssinian Colobus (*C. ab. abyssinicus*)

palliatus (=*sharpei*) (from south of the Congo River to Angola and Tanzania), white hairs on shoulders well developed, a white band on buttocks, the distal half of the tail bushy and white; *adolfi-frederici* (=*ruwenzorii*), Rwanda), coat very long, a wide whitish patch on buttocks, tail black, not bushy.
Habitat: Forest, galleries. Map, p. 99.

ABYSSINIAN BLACK-AND-WHITE COLOBUS or GUEREZA
Colobus abyssinicus (Oken)   p. 65
F Colobe Guereza   K Mbega   G Guereza
Identification: Length (without tail) up to 30 in. A large black-and-white monkey, heavily built. Whiskers and beard white. General colour jet black. A conspicuous and well developed pure white mantle, extending on the sides from shoulders to root of tail around the upperparts. On the buttocks, a broad ring of white hairs around the callosities. Thigh with an ill-defined white patch. Tail pure black or grizzled on its base, then white, very bushy to a variable extent. Young white, becoming darker with age.
Intraspecific variation: A wide range of variations occurs among this species and a number of subspecies may be recognised according to the development of mantle and coloration of tail. The major trends are as follows: *abyssinicus* (south-east Ethiopia), mantle well developed, dark section of tail mixed black and white, tail bushy on half its length; *gallarum* (east Ethiopia), like the preceding race, but basal section of tail pure black; *matschiei* (Kenya, west of Rift Valley), basal half of tail black, terminal section white; *kikuyensis* (Kenya, east of Rift Valley), *caudatus* (Kilimanjaro), mantle as in *abyssinicus*, but tail very bushy and white almost on all its length; *occidentalis* (from the Cameroons, through Gabon and the Congo, to Uganda), mantle less developed, tail longer, mostly black, with a moderately long white terminal tuft. A small population of entirely white Colobus is to be found near Nanyuki, Mount Kenya.
Habitat: Forests. Map, p. 99.

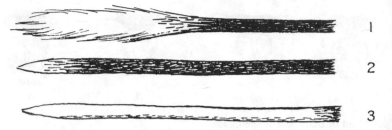

4. Tail of some Angolan Black and White Colobus (*Colobus angolensis*)
1 *C. a. angolensis*   2 *C. a. adolfi-frederici*   3 *C. a. prigoginei*

BLACK COLOBUS *Colobus satanas* Waterhouse   p. 65
F Colobe noir   G Satanaffe, Teufelsaffe
Identification: Length (without tail) up to 30 in.; weight up to 24 lb. A large monkey, heavily built, entirely jet black. Tail not bushy and with no terminal tuft.
Habitat: High forest. Map, p. 99.

WESTERN RED COLOBUS *Colobus* (*Piliocolobus*) *badius* (Kerr)[1]   p. 65
F Colobe bai d'Afrique occidentale   G Westafrikanischer braune Guereza
Identification: Length (without tail) up to 28 in. A large monkey, with back sloping forwards, arched in the middle, a very small head, and proportionately long limbs. Nose broad at its base (narrow in Cercopithecid Monkeys), turned up above a swollen fold on upper lip. Face dark, with conspicuous pinkish 'spectacles' around the eyes. Whiskers bright red, bay or orange. No median crest on crown. Upperparts from crown to root of tail from jet black to smoke grey, in strong contrast with flanks, underparts and limbs, deep bay or orange. On the buttocks, a white triangular patch from callosities to hocks.
Intraspecific variation: Two races may be distinguished: *badius* (Guinea, Ivory Coast to Bandama River), upperparts intensely black; rest of body deep bay; tail blackish red; *temmincki* (Senegal), lighter, grey and orange.
Habitat: High forest. Map, p. 99.

RED COLOBUS *Colobus* (*Piliocolobus*) *pennanti* Waterhouse   p. 65
F Colobe bai   G Braune Guereza, Rotkopf Guereza
Identification: Length (without tail) up to 28 in.; weight up to 24 lb. A large monkey, smaller than Black-and-White Colobus, but heavily built, with the back sloping forward, arched in the middle, a proportionately

[1] The systematics of Red Colobus Monkeys are very complicated and probably the '*badius*' group should be split into several species. For practical reasons, we shall only consider two species, *C. badius* differing by its coloration and shape of the nose.

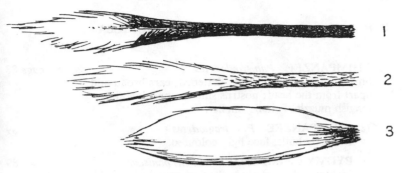

5. Tail of some Abyssinian Black and White Colobus (*Colobus abyssinicus*)
   1 *C. a. occidentalis*   2 *C. a. abyssinicus*   3 *C. a. caudatus*

very small head, with nose 'normal' (not turned up). Face slaty grey, sometimes with pink fleshy patches. Whiskers well developed (except *kirki*). No median crest on crown. General coloration highly variable according to races, but always in the reddish to brown tones, with a blackish tinge on the shoulders. Underparts yellowish rufous to smoky grey or pure white. Tail rather thick, moderately long.

Intraspecific variation: This species is highly variable and perhaps should be split into several species according to coloration, pattern and shape of the whirls on sides of head, apart from anatomical characters: *pennanti* (Fernando Po), whiskers pure white, contrasting with the black crown; *preussi* (Cameroons), middle of back dark brown, flanks orange rufous, underparts creamy white; *oustaleti* (Congo-Brazzaville, north-east Congo), crown of the same colour as the back; whiskers greyish; *tholloni* (marsh forest south of Congo River), entirely bright rufous, somewhat darker on head and shoulders, lighter below; *ellioti* (Ituri, Congo), anterior half of body, including forelimbs, bright reddish, posterior half dark brownish; *foai* (from upper Congo River to Lake Tanganyika), highly variable, with a red frontal crest; *tephrosceles* (from Ruwenzori southwards to south-east of Lake Tanganyika), dark brown above, contrasting with a rufous crown; underparts whitish; *kirki*[1] (Jozani forest, Zanzibar), very distinct; a tricoloured, sharply defined pattern; tufts of pure white long hairs on the forehead; shoulders and forelimbs pure black, back bright chestnut, underparts including inner part of limbs pure white. Other races; *gordonorum*[1] (south-west Tanzania), *rufomitratus*[1] (Lower Tana, Kenya), *waldroni* (Ivory Coast, Ghana), *bouvieri*[1] (southern part of Congo-Brazzaville).

[1] The subspecies *rufomitratus, gordonorum, bouvieri* and *kirki* are seriously threatened by the destruction of the habitat in the restricted areas to which they are confined.

Plate 11   CHIMPANZEE, GORILLA

1. **CHIMPANZEE** *Pan troglodytes*   *page* 88
   Smaller; top of head rather flattened; ears broad and set
   apart from the head; nostrils smaller, opening above a
   longish muzzle. Female smaller.

   1a. **CHIMPANZEE** *P. t. troglodytes*   89
   Robustly built; face light coloured.

   1b. **PYGMY CHIMPANZEE** *P. (t.) paniscus*   89
   Lightly and slenderly built; face very dark.

2. **GORILLA** *Gorilla gorilla*   83
   Larger; top of head elevated; ears small, set close to the
   head; nostrils wide and flaring; line of back concave.
   Female smaller.

   2a. **WESTERN GORILLA** *G. g. gorilla*   86
   Coat moderately developed, browner.

   2b. **EASTERN GORILLA** *G. g. berengei*   86
   Coat well developed, much darker; more massive.

1a

1b

2a

♀

2a

♂

2b

♀

♂

JACKALS, FOXES

Plate 12

1. **SEMIEN FOX**   *Canis simensis*   94
   Large; bright rufous; throat and underparts white with
   two rufous collars; white patch at base of tail.

2. **COMMON JACKAL**   *Canis aureus*   91
   Yellowish, with some blackish on upperparts; black tip
   of tail.

3. **SIDE-STRIPED JACKAL**   *Canis adustus*   91
   Greyish fawn; ill-defined whitish stripe along flank;
   white tip of tail.

4. **BLACK-BACKED JACKAL**   *Canis mesomelas*   94
   Dark back (silvery at a distance) contrasting with rufous
   sides; black tip of tail.

5. **RED FOX**   *Vulpes vulpes*   95
   Back mostly rusty red; white tip of tail.

Habitat: High forest, galleries. Map, p. 79.

Habits of Colobus: Colobus are the most arboreal of all African monkeys and rarely descend to the ground. Black-and-White Colobus live in the middle and upper strata of the forest, and Red Colobus in the upper strata. They climb and jump from tree to tree with great facility; their long hairs and tail are said to act as a parachute when making their prodigious leaps. In spite of their very ornate pattern, they blend very well with their environment. They often remain quiet in trees for hours.

Colobus live in troops of up to 25 individuals, perhaps an aggregation of family units. They utter loud barks when alarmed, and also croaking calls.

They feed almost exclusively on leaves, and are therefore the most specialised feeders of all monkeys though they sometimes eat insects. They are very difficult to keep in captivity.

Their habits are as yet unknown to a large extent. They have been intensively hunted for their coat, highly prized during the last century.

OLIVE COLOBUS *Colobus (Procolobus) verus* Van Beneden   p. 65
F Colobe de Van Beneden

Identification: Length (without tail) 22 in.; weight 12 lb. A medium-sized monkey, the smallest of the Colobus, with back sloping forwards, a small rounded head (not unlike that of an Asiatic *Semnopithecus*); spine of nose straight, and a very dull coloration with no contrasted pattern. Face slaty grey. Whiskers rather long; two whirls on forehead, forming two conspicuous grey patches and a little crest of upright hairs on the middle of crown. Upperparts olive greenish washed with brown on the middle of back, passing to olive on flanks. Underparts ashy grey. Limbs grey washed with olive. Tail like the back, more greyish below.

Female similar to the male but without crest.

Habitat: Thickets in the high forest; river banks, marshy forest and palm swamps. Map, p. 87.

Habits: Olive Colobus live in dense forest where they are strictly confined to dense foliage in the lower strata, exceptionally at a height of more than 20 ft from the ground. They live in small bands from about 6 to 20 individuals, generally from 10 to 15. The leadership by a dominant male is not observable. They are often found feeding in company with other monkeys, particularly *Cercopithecus mona* and *petaurista*, probably a protective adaptation, these more active species being more likely to spot a potential enemy.

Olive Colobus feed almost exclusively on leaves, sometimes on flowers.

The mother carries the young in its mouth for several weeks after birth, behaviour unique among African monkeys.

CHIMPANZEE, GORILLA: Pongidae

The most highly evolved of all the primates, as shown by all their anatomical characters and particularly the development of the brain. Both arboreal and terrestrial, the apes have the forelimbs much better developed than the hind limbs. Tail entirely absent. Growth is slow and sexual maturity reached at quite an advanced age.

Four types of primates are included in this group. Gibbons from south-east Asia are quite separate. The true apes are represented in tropical Africa by two well-known species: the Chimpanzee and the Gorilla; they have a relative in the forests of Malaya, the Orang-utan, with which they form the family Pongidae, primates of heavy proportions, recalling in some ways human beings to which many of their characters converge. All of them occur in forested areas, from the rain forest to savanna woodlands and montane forests.

GORILLA *Gorilla gorilla* Savage and Wyman   p. 80
F Gorille   G Gorilla
Identification: Size and weight of adults varying according to sex. Males have a height up to 5¾ ft and even more, and a weight of 450 lb. Females, smaller and more lightly built, reach a height of 5 ft and a weight of 150–250 lb., exceptionally 300 lb. The largest and the most robust of all primates. The head is particularly massive, with a low forehead and very small ears, set close to the head and almost hidden in the hair. In males, the head is very high, due to a well developed sagittal crest, on which are attached the powerful muscles of the lower jaw. Face rather variable in shape, flat or prognathous, rounded or long, always black, even in the young; nasal region and nostrils always large and flaring. Line of back concave. Limbs very powerful; legs proportionately short, hands short and extremely broad with shortened fingers, always black.

Coat typically black, but length, coloration and distribution of hairs highly variable according to age, sex and environment. Infants sparsely but almost entirely covered with soft, black or brown hair, with a white tuft on the anal area persisting to the age of 4 years. The coat turns black and grey with age. Flanks, sides and abdomen become grey with age until the old animals are almost entirely grey. Males from 10 years of age have a conspicuous grey back ('silverbacked males'). Length of hair varies on different parts of body (a wide range of individual variation also occurs, some Gorillas being woolly looking, others sleek). Hairs of arms relatively long; chest often bare. Hair thicker in colder habitats. Some adults have small ischial callosities ('sitting pads').
Intraspecific variation: Two well defined races of Gorilla have been described, differing mainly in anatomical characters, mostly in the skull.

Plate 13 FOXES

1. **BAT-EARED FOX** *Otocyon megalotis* *page* 101
   Small; enormous ears, broad and oval-shaped; silvery buff.

2. **FENNEC** *Fennecus zerda* 100
   Very small; enormous triangular ears; very pale
   isabelline; tail proportionately short.

3. **SAND FOX** *Vulpes pallida* 98
   Smallish; ears proportionately small; very pale fawn;
   black tip of tail.

4. **RUPPELL'S FOX** *Vulpes rüppelli* 95
   Smallish; ears long; back rufous contrasting with greyish
   flanks; white tip of tail.

5. **CAPE FOX** *Vulpes chama* 100
   Smallish; back silvery grey; black tip of tail.

CIVET, RATEL, OTTERS

Plate 14

1. **CIVET** *Viverra civetta*   *page* 109
   Black spots contrasting with greyish ground colour; two
   black collars on neck.

2. **RATEL** *Mellivora capensis*   105
   Very stout; short tail; upperparts mostly greyish,
   sharply contrasting with black underparts.

3. **SPOTTED-NECKED OTTER** *Lutra maculicollis*   108
   Small; face and foreparts pale buff, mottled by brown
   spots.

4. **CONGO CLAWLESS OTTER** *Aonyx congica*   106
   Large; dark brown; foreparts whitish; no claws (see text).

5. **CAPE CLAWLESS OTTER** *Aonyx capensis*   108
   Large; dark brown; foreparts whitish; no claws (see text).

WESTERN GORILLA.[1] (*gorilla* (Savage and Wyman)). Coat less developed and browner on average. In old males, head lower, due to a smaller sagittal crest. (Cameroons, Gabon, north of the Congo River.)

EASTERN GORILLA. (*beringei* (Matschie)). Coat well developed and more black on average. In old males, head higher, due to better developed sagittal crest. (Eastern Congo, from Lubutu on the north-west, and Lubero on the north-east, to Fizi on the south; Uganda). Threatened by destruction of the habitat by agriculturalists and by the intrusion of cattle.

Habitat: Lowland and montane rain forests, occasionally bamboo forest up to 11,000 feet on the high mountains of Eastern Congo. Not confined to primary forest, but also inhabits secondary growth and plantation. Map, p. 100.

Habits: No African animal has given rise to more legends and tales than the Gorilla, which can be explained by its 'wild man-like' features, enormous size and power, harsh screams and mysterious life amidst the forest. Only recently has a more comprehensive view on the life of this ape been brought to our knowledge.

Gorillas are primarily terrestrial, though they climb around in trees with great caution; they rarely jump from tree to tree, their bulk being correlated with a reduced agility. Juveniles climb trees more often than adults, females more than males. On the ground, they are quadrupedal, the forequarters supported by the middle phalanges of the fingers.

Gorillas live in groups of from 2 to 30 animals; more rarely they are solitary. All groups contain at least one old male, one or more females, a variable number of young or immatures. The old male is the leader of the group and the order of dominance is to a large extent correlated with body size. Each of these groups, which are rather stable, wanders continuously within a home range of about 10–15 square miles, without defending any territory. They intercommunicate by means of a large vocabulary, emitting at least 22 distinct sounds, among which 8 are used frequently. The most intense sounds—the roar of males and the scream of females—are given in response to man. They also beat the chest, an elaborate display which apparently is intended to intimidate. They also make good use of mimicry. They are purely diurnal; they rise between 6 and 8 a.m., feed for two hours, then rest from 10 a.m. to 2 p.m.; they are active again between 2 and 6 p.m., then go to sleep on nests, clustered in an area of half an acre or less. The nests are crude, roughly circular structures made of herbs and shrubs on the ground, or platforms of branches in trees. Old

We prefer the terms 'Western' and 'Eastern' t the more used terms 'Lowland' and 'Mountain', for both forms may be seen at various altitudes, the Eastern Gorilla particularly being found from the lowland rain forest to the moist montane and bamboo forests, up to 11,000 feet.

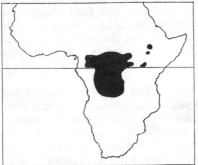

Brazza's Monkey, p. 67

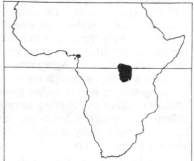

L'Hoest's Monkey, p. 68

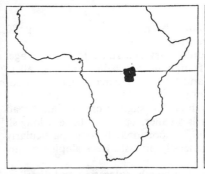

Owl-faced Monkey, p. 68

Vervet and Grivet Monkey, p. 71

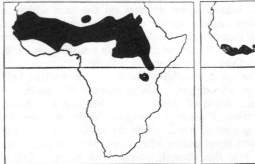

Patas, p. 73

Olive Colobus, p. 82

males rarely nest in trees. Gorillas feed on a wide variety of leaves, bark and fruits (in the eastern Congo, no less than 100 food plants were collected); some of the most abundant plants are not consumed and food preferences vary from place to place. They collect the food manually and the palatable parts of the plant are extracted by ripping and tearing with the hands and teeth. Apparently they never drink in the wild state if vegetation contains enough moisture.

The gestation period varies from 251 to 289 days (in captivity) and females produce an offspring every 4 years. One young is born at a time. Infants are completely dependent on their mothers for food and protection, but they grow rapidly, so that within a period of 6 months they become active youngsters. They begin to eat vegetable matter by the age of 2½ months, but they suckle to the age of 1½ years. Females apparently reach sexual maturity at the age of 6–7 years, males at 9–10 years. Gorillas have reached an age of up to 33 years in captivity but probably can live much longer.

CHIMPANZEE   *Pan troglodytes* Blumenbach   p. 80
F Chimpanzé   K Soko mtu   G Schimpanse
Identification: Size and weight of adults vary according to sex and age. Males standing upright are about 3½ ft high, females being slightly smaller; weight averages 110 lb. for males, and 90 lb. for females. Chimpanzees have a heavy, stout body, but are more lightly built than Gorillas. Top of head rounded, even flattened, never high (no sagittal crest). Ears broad and set apart from the head. Nostrils smaller, opening above a longish prognathous muzzle. Limbs powerful, proportionately long, particularly the arms; hands rather elongated, generally pinkish. Back sloping evenly backwards.

Coat typically black, rather sparse, but length, coloration and distribution of hairs highly variable according to age, sex and environment. Infants covered with black hairs; skin of face pinkish. With increasing age, dark brown and blackish pigmentation appears on the face which is entirely dark in adults; hairs become scarcer on the forehead and top of head, almost bare in some individuals; in addition the coat turns brown and grey, especially on the back. Some old males have a silver-grey back. There is a wide range of individual variation.

Intraspecific variation: The great variability, both in skin and in hair colour, has led mammalogists to describe a large number of 'species' or local races of Chimpanzees. Most of them are not justified and based merely on individual variation. We may also explain in this manner the belief in another distinct species of African Ape called Kulu-Kamba (or Kulu-n'guia) by the Africans from Gabon where this animal is presumed to live; some even think that this animal, intermediate between Chimpanzee and Gorilla, is a hybrid. The animals thus described could be merely old Chimpanzees or, according to recent studies, a particular race (*koolokamba*), restricted to the high level forests of south Cameroons, Gabon and Congo, characterised by smaller ears, nose padded like a gorilla's and dark face.

However, it is possible to recognise four subspecies of Chimpanzees; the fourth represents a well defined form, isolated for a long time and which is probably to be considered as a full species because of its external and anatomical characters.

P. t. verus. Lower face reputed always light coloured; only forehead becoming bare with age; a 'beard' in males (western Africa).

P. t. troglodytes. Face light coloured, darkening only in old individuals; head bare very early; 'beard' reduced in males (from the Cameroons to Congo and Ubangi Rivers).

P. t. schweinfurthi. Face reputed dark; hair very dense (from Ubangui and Congo Rivers to the Great Lakes).

PYGMY CHIMPANZEE, (*P. (t.) paniscus*). A very different Chimpanzee, lightly built with a longish face and long slender limbs. Skin and coat very dark, almost entirely black (left bank of the Congo River), in evergreen rain forest without a dry season.

Habitat: Habitats vary from rain, swamp and montane forests, up to 9,000 feet (on the Ruwenzori) to dry forests, woodlands and savannas with widely scattered trees. Chimpanzees may walk 2 to 3 miles through open grasslands and occur as far north as half-way through the so-called Soudanian vegetation belt (e.g. in the National Park of the Niokolo-Koba in Senegal). The highest population densities are found in forests with a more or less open canopy, including secondary, semi-deciduous and montane forests, and in diversified mountainous landscapes consisting of a mosaic of forests and savanna woodlands, whereas their density is much lower in 'primary' evergreen forest with a closed upper canopy. Map, p. 100.

Habits: Chimpanzee are both terrestrial and arboreal, being much more able at climbing the trees than the Gorilla. However, they spend much of their time on the ground. They are quadrupedal, walking with the fingers half flexed to support the weight of the forequarters on the knuckles, like the Gorilla. In this posture they can move very fast at a kind of loping gallop. They occasionally walk erect for a short distance. Chimpanzee on the move through forest usually progress on the ground, and only rarely from tree to tree. However, they climb trees with consummate agility and may occasionally jump to a nearby or lower tree or to the ground. They move about in irregular bands which may join one another or split up at any moment. No stable groups seem to exist, except for the mother-child relation. A distinction may be made between sexual bands in which the males and females without young predominate, and the nursery bands consisting mainly of mothers with their offspring. The first type of bands vocalises loudly and moves over larger areas, but both types often walk together for some time. Bands may consist of any number from 2 to 50 individuals (youngsters included) and single individuals may also be met with.

They intercommunicate by a very wide vocabulary, emitting a large number of different vocalisations, and are far more communicative than Gorilla, and much more noisy than these or any other wild animal. They also indulge in a great variety of mimicry and gestures. As a whole they are the most expressive of all animals. The use of tools so commonly demonstrated in captive Chimpanzee has also been observed in the wild.

They are primarily diurnal. Like Gorilla their activity begins at dawn, and they move and feed until the middle of the day when they rest. Activity is resumed in the afternoon and evening, when they eat again and then go to sleep at dusk. But they also indulge in a nocturnal activity and may move and even feed during moon-lit nights.

In most areas their nests are always located high up in the trees, from 15 to 120 feet above the ground, but in the eastern Congo ground nests do regularly occur, even in areas inhabited by Leopards. Chimpanzee nests can easily be distinguished from large bird's nests because the branches of the tree have been bent or partly broken and intertwined to form a platform. They generally line the nest cup with twigs, to create a ring round the animal.

Chimpanzee feed on various fruits and nuts, some leaves, young shoots, and bark. Also on eggs and insects. In a savanna area, in Tanzania, they have been observed to kill and eat monkeys, young antelopes and birds; but Chimpanzee in rain forest areas seem never to be carnivorous.

The gestation period averages 236 days. One young is born at a time and nursed by the mother for a long period. Chimpanzee in captivity have reached ages of up to about 40 years. In the wild, individuals have been observed that looked even older.

ORDER Carnivora

JACKALS, FOXES, WILD DOG: Canidae

Small to medium-sized carnivores, with dog-like features, an elongated face, a large number of teeth; legs rather long and slender, without retractile claws. Widely distributed throughout the world, this family is represented in Africa by three different types: the jackals, whose features closely resemble the dogs'; the foxes, smaller and with shorter legs; and the Wild Dog, a very peculiar animal confined to Africa.

They are widespread but do not inhabit dense forest.

COMMON JACKAL *Canis aureus* L.   p. 81
F Chacal commun   G Goldschakal   K Bweha[1]

Identification: Height at shoulder 16 in.: weight 20 lb. A jackal with proportionately large ears, rather plain coloured and with no definite pattern. Back of ears tawny or rufous. General colour dirty yellow with a reddish tinge and mixed with a variable amount of black on the upperparts. Tail reddish fawn, with a black tip, not contrasting strongly with the upper portion.

Habitat: Open and wooded savanna. Also southern Europe and Asia to India and Indochinese peninsula. Map, p. 103.

Habits: Usually nocturnal, the Common Jackal may be often seen by daylight, particularly on cool days. It lives singly or in pairs, sometimes in small packs. The call is a screaming yelp. It feeds on various animals up to the size of a hare or domestic fowl, particularly rodents, and also on insects and vegetable matter (fruits). A scavenger, it eats every kind of garbage and is attracted by kills, helping in the clearance of carcasses. It often adapts to the presence of man and enters villages and even larger cities at night.

SIDE-STRIPED JACKAL *Canis adustus* Sundevall   p. 81
F Chacal à flanks rayés   A Vaaljakkals   G Streifenschakal

Identification: Height at shoulder 16 in.; weight 20 lb. A larger jackal, with rather smaller and shorter ears, and a blunter muzzle, giving a more wolf-like appearance. The back of the ears is dark brown or grey. General colour greyish fawn, darker on upperparts, lighter on sides. Along the flanks, an ill-defined light coloured or whitish line from shoulder to root of tail, bordered sometimes with black at its lower margin. Underparts whitish. Tail bushy, darker than the body, almost blackish, usually with a conspicuous white tip, though some individuals have only a few white hairs at tip of tail.

Habitat: Open savanna; even in mountains. Map, p. 103.

[1] Apparently a name applied to all jackals.

91

Plate 15   **GENETS and allies**

1. **TWO-SPOTTED PALM CIVET**   *Nandinia binotata*   *page* 110
   Stout; rounded head; brownish with small dark spots;
   two light spots on shoulder.

2. **AQUAT C CIVET**   *Osbornictis piscivora*   117
   Almost uniform chestnut; tail thick, black.

3. **AFRICAN LINSANG**   *Poiana richardsoni*   116
   Small; yellowish fawn with rounded blackish spots; tail
   very long, with up to 12 dark rings.

4. **VILLIERS' GENET**   *Genetta villiersi*   115
   Chestnut brown to blackish spots; tail long, with 7-9
   dark rings, the first bright rufous.

5. **ABYSSINIAN GENET**   *Genetta abyssinica*   115
   Black stripes and elongated spots; tail with 6-7 dark
   rings and dark tip.

GENETS Plate 16

1. **COMMON GENET** *Genetta genetta* *page* 114
Spinal crest; medium-sized spots; tail with 9-10 dark
rings and whitish tip.

2. **FOREST GENET** *Genetta pardina* 115
Heavily spotted; spots broad; tail mostly black, with
3-4 narrow light rings and black tip.

3. **SMALL-SPOTTED GENET** *Genetta servalina* 114
Spots numerous and small; tail with 10-12 dark rings.

4. **LARGE-SPOTTED GENET** *Genetta tigrina* 114
Spots brown or chestnut, broad and elongated; tail with
8-9 dark rings and dark tip.

5. **GIANT GENET** *Genetta victoriae* 115
Larger spinal crest; very dense black spots (animal almost
black at a distance); tail bushy, with 6-8 broad dark
rings and black tip.

Habits: The Side-striped Jackal is a shy creature, much more nocturnal than the Black-backed Jackal, and therefore less often seen. It lives singly or in small packs, and is also more silent. The calls are lower pitched, and the commonest is a single yap. Essentially a scavenger, it feeds on carcasses of animals killed by lion and also on small mammals, birds, eggs, reptiles, insects and vegetable matter, but never on larger prey. It does not harm live stock.

The period of gestation averages 2 months. The litter numbers up to 6, born in thicket or in a hole.

BLACK-BACKED JACKAL   *Canis mesomelas* Schreber   p. 81
F Chacal à chabraque   G Schabrackenschakal   A Rooijakkals
Identification: Height at shoulder 16 in.; weight 20–30 lb. A brightly coloured jackal, with a rather fox-like head, and long ears, broad at their base and pointed. Head greyish, tinged sandy particularly on muzzle and cheeks. A broad conspicuous dark mantle on upperparts from neck to tail, sharply defined from and in strong contrast to the rufous sides and limbs, widest over the shoulder, narrowing backwards; this band is black, stippled with white, giving a silvery appearance at a distance. Underparts white or whitish. Tail fairly long, moderately bushy, rufous with a black tip.

Young uniform dusky brown, paler below.
Habitat: Open savanna and light woodland. Map, p. 103.
Habits: Mainly nocturnal, the Black-backed Jackal may often be seen by daylight. It usually lives in pairs or small parties, but is sometimes solitary; up to 30 may be seen together at a carcass. It is a very cunning and resourceful animal. It is very noisy and members of a pack communicate with each other by means of a fairly elaborate vocabulary. The commonest call is a screaming yell followed by yaps; another is a plaintive siren-like howl, uttered when the jackals locate a kill.

It feeds on hares, rodents, birds (guinea-fowl, francolin), reptiles (snakes up to python), insects, eggs, etc.; also on fruits and berries. It also kills young and small antelopes up to the size of a duiker or Thomson's Gazelle, especially dik-dik. As a scavenger it is attracted by kills made by lion or other large carnivores. It stands at a distance when the lions are feeding, then rushes to the carcass when they move away and snatches what it can, in company with vultures and hyaenas. It may be destructive to sheep and small stock, becoming a pest to farmers in some districts (South Africa).

The litter numbers up to 6 pups, even 9, hidden in holes.

SEMIEN FOX   *Canis (Simenia) simensis* Rüppell   p. 81
(Abyssinian Wolf)
F Loup d'Abyssinie   G Abessinischer Fuchs
Identification: Height at shoulder 24 in. A large dog-like carnivore, with a fox-like head, a very long and slender snout, pointed ears, and long legs.

Head rufous fawn, warmer on muzzle and back of ears. Upper lip, chin and throat pure white. Two successive rufous collars across the neck, separated by a whitish transversal band. Lower chest whitish, tinged with rufous. Upperparts bright rufous, somewhat darker on upper back. Underparts whitish washed with rufous. Lower legs whitish. Tail long, very bushy, proximal section rufous on the upperpart, conspicuously white below and on the sides, then blackish.

Habitat: High plateaux. Map, p. 103.

Habits: Active both by day and by night, the Semien Fox lives singly or in pairs, sometimes in small packs. It feeds almost exclusively on rodents, usually caught on the ground but not dug out, also on small game; it rarely preys on sheep.

Two cries are emitted: a high pitched long scream 'weeah-weeah', apparently a call; a bark 'yealp-yealp', uttered when in competition or in alarm.

The Semien Fox has become very rare; it has been accused of killing domestic stock and therefore exterminated in most of its range. The introduction of modern firearms greatly accelerated this process.

RED FOX *Vulpes vulpes* (L.) p. 81
F Renard fauve G Rotfuchs
Identification: Height at shoulder 12 in.; length (without tail) 25 in. A large fox, similar to the European fox, but smaller and lighter coloured. Head rufous; margins of the mouth, chin and interior of the ears white. Back of ears dark blackish brown, contrasting strongly with colour of head and nape. Upperparts greyish yellow with a conspicuous median band of rich rusty red, from the head to the base of the tail; this area is particularly bright on shoulder and upper back. Flanks pale yellowish, tinged with grey. Chin, throat, chest and belly strongly suffused with dark smoky grey, sometimes almost blackish. Limbs rufous, darkening towards the extremities. Tail long, rusty yellowish, strongly suffused with blackish near its base, then lighter and with a white tip.

Intraspecific variation: The North African (*atlantica, barbara*) and Egyptian Red Fox (*aegyptiaca*), almost extralimital, are the African representatives of the Palaearctic species from which they differ very slightly by smaller size, paler coloration and broader ears. The Red Fox has probably erroneously been recorded from Senegal (*dorsalis*).

Habitat: Stony desert, river beds; never sand desert. Also Europe and Asia. Map, p. 103.

Habits: The Red Fox lives in burrows in small family parties. It feeds mostly on rodents. The litter may be up to 7 young.

RÜPPELL'S FOX *Vulpes rüppelli* (Schinz) p. 84
F Renard famélique G Sandfuchs
Identification: Height at shoulder 10 in., length (without tail) 16–20 in.;

96

Plate 17   **LARGER MONGOOSES**

1. **EGYPTIAN MONGOOSE** *Herpestes ichneumon*   *page* 121
   Short legged; brownish grey; long tail, thick at base and
   tapering, with black tassel.

2. **WHITE-TAILED MONGOOSE** *Ichneumia albicauda*   117
   Long legged; shaggy; brownish-grey; tail mostly white.

3. **BLACK-LEGGED MONGOOSE** *Bdeogale nigripes*   117
   Massive, broad head; coat very short, light grey above,
   mostly black below; black limbs.

4. **MELLER'S MONGOOSE** *Rhynchogale melleri*   118
   Uniform fulvous brown; parting of hairs along sides of
   neck; tail very long and bushy, mostly black.

5. **MARSH MONGOOSE** *Atilax paludinosus*   120
   Short-legged; short face; uniform dark brown; tail
   proportionately short.

SMALLER MONGOOSES   Plate 18

1. **RED MEERKAT**   *Cynictis penicillata*   *page* 126
Small; face triangular, large ears; coat thick, tawny
yellowish; tail proportionately short, with white tip.

2. **SELOUS' MONGOOSE**   *Paracynictis selousi*   126
Small; slender; ears low and wide; buffy-brown; tail
long, with white tip.

3. **BANDED MONGOOSE**   *Mungos mungo*   124
Small; stripes on back; short tail.

4. **DARK MONGOOSE**   *Crossarchus obscurus*   123
Small; long snout; short tail; coat shaggy, uniform dark
brown.

5. **GREY MEERKAT or SURICATE**   *Suricata suricatta*   128
Small; bulging forehead; small rounded ears; losange-
patterned netting on back.

6. **LONG-SNOUTED MONGOOSE**   *Herpestes naso*   120
Large; long-legged; long face; almost uniform dark
brown, tail lighter.

7. **BUSHY-TAILED MONGOOSE**   *Bdeogale crassicauda*   118
Rather small; shaggy; blackish; tail very bushy, black.

weight 6 lb. A smaller fox, much smaller and more lightly built than the Red Fox and not unlike a large Fennec, with rather short legs, long broad ears and a light coloured, very soft and dense coat. Middle of muzzle and forehead fawn tinged rusty. A conspicuous dark brown patch on the side of muzzle, extending towards the eye; lips, sides of face and chin white. Ears white inside, with the back deep cinnamon rufous. Along the spine, a deep cinnamon rufous band broadening towards the middle of back, then narrowing backwards. Coat of silvery appearance all over, due to numerous white hairs. Sides greyish buff. Underparts whitish. Limb‑ rufous, more or less suffused with blackish outside; lower parts and fe‹ whitish in front and outside. Soles of feet densely furred. Tail long and very bushy, buff, more or less mixed with black hairs with a very conspicuous pure white tip.

Similar species: May be confused with the Fennec (it is called 'Fennec' in some parts of its range), but is easily distinguished by its larger size, proportionately smaller ears, grey flanks, and white tip of tail.

Habitat: Stony desert. Also Arabia, Iran and Afghanistan. Map, p. 103.

Habits: Almost nothing is known about the specific habits of this fox, which seems rather gregarious (parties of 3–5 have been recorded) and feeds to a large extent on insects.

SAND or **PALE FOX** *Vulpes pallida* (Cretzschmar) p. 84
F Renard pâle, R. blond des sables   G Blassfuchs

Identification: Height at shoulder 10 in.; length (without tail) 18 in.; weight 6 lb. A smaller fox, with proportionately small ears, rounded at their tip, a sharp and pointed muzzle and a very pale coloration. Head pale fawn, with a narrow black eye-ring, extending somewhat forwards to the muzzle. Ears white inside, rufous fawn outside with a distinct white border. Upperparts pale sandy fawn, suffused to a variable extent with blackish; flanks lighter, without any black. Underparts buffy white. Outer limbs more or less rusty, whitish inside. Tail long and bushy, buff, suffused with black on the upper part (sometimes an indistinct blackish spot at base), with a conspicuous black tip.

Similar species: May be confused with the Fennec, but larger and ears very much smaller, higher on legs with a coarser coat. Distinguished from Rüppell's Fox by the smaller ears and the black tip of tail.

Habitat: Sahelian savannas and borders of the Soudanian zone. Map, p. 107.

Habits: Apparently almost nothing is known. The Sand Fox is gregarious and lives in family parties in large burrows; the galleries reach 30–50 ft. in length, and open into small chambers with a lining of dry vegetable material.

It feeds on rodents, small reptiles, birds, eggs, and vegetable matter (wild melons).

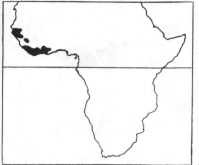

Western Red Colobus, p. 78

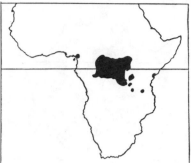

Red Colobus, p. 78

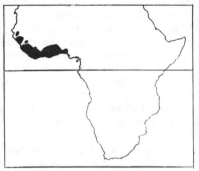

Western Black-and-White Colobus,
p. 76

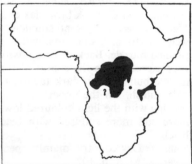

Angolan Black-and-White Colobus,
p. 76

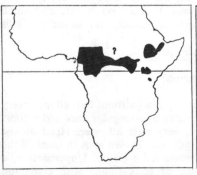

Abyssinian Black-and-White Colobus,
p. 77

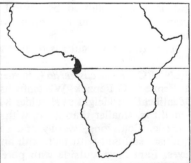

Black Colobus, p. 78

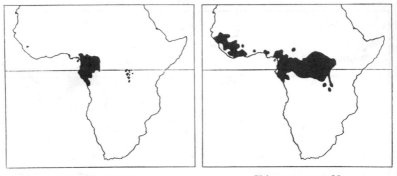

Gorilla, p. 83   Chimpanzee, p. 88

CAPE FOX   *Vulpes chama* (A. Smith)   p. 84
F Renard du Cap   A Silwerjakkals, Draaijakkals   G Kapfuchs, Kama
Identification: Height at shoulder 12 in.; length (without tail) 22 in.; weight 8–10 lb. A small fox, with large pointed ears and a fairly short, but pointed muzzle. Back of ears tawny. Head and upperparts with a silvery grey aspect due to the colour of the hairs, the roots being dark grey, the middle buffish, then dark tawny, with white and black tips. Underparts pale buffish. On the upperparts of hind legs, a dark brown patch, contrasting with the light coloured lower section. Tail very bushy, pale fawn, more and more suffused with black towards its extremity; tip entirely black.
Habitat: Dry country, mainly open plains and karoo veld; also Kalahari savanna. Map, p. 107.
Habits: The Cape Fox is the only true fox found in southern Africa. Mainly nocturnal and very wary, it lives singly or in pairs, remaining hidden in daytime under rocks or in burrows excavated in sandy soil. The call is a yell followed by several yaps. It feeds on insects and small mammals, birds and on various vegetable matter, and sometimes kills lambs.

The litter of 3–5 cubs is born in a burrow.

FENNEC   *Fennecus zerda* (Zimmermann)   p. 84
F Fennec   G Fennek, Wüstenfuchs
Identification: Height at shoulder 8 in.; length (without tail) 16 in. A very small fox, smaller than a cat, with enormous triangular ears and a short muzzle. Coat long, woolly and soft, very pale all over. Head almost whitish, suffused with buff, with an indistinct brown spot in front of the eyes. Ears fawn outside with pure white hairs inside. Upperparts pale isabelline or creamy with the middle of back tinged with cinnamon rufous. Flanks, underparts and limbs almost white. Soles of feet densely

furred. Tail proportionately short, bushy and thick, rufous, often with a blackish patch near the base, and with a conspicuous blackish brown tip.

Habitat: Desert country, mainly in sand dunes. Also Arabia. Map, p. 107.

Habits: The Fennec lives in small groups of up to 10 individuals, sheltering in burrows excavated in the sand. Like most foxes, it is nocturnal. It has a great variety of calls. It feeds mostly on insects (locusts), rodents, lizards, birds and also on vegetable matter (roots). It drinks freely when water is available, but may subsist without water for long periods.

Young are 2–5 per litter.

BAT-EARED FOX   *Otocyon megalotis* (Desmarest)   p. 84
F Otocyon   A Bakoorjakkals; Draaijakkals   G Löffelhund

Identification: Height at shoulder 12 in.; length (without tail) 26 in.; weight up to 11 lb. A small, long-legged fox, not unlike a little jackal, with short muzzle and enormous ears, broad, long and oval-shaped, not unlike those of certain bats, white inside, with the upper edge black. Face blackish. Upperparts grizzled silvery buff. Flanks lighter. Underparts buffish. Limbs darker, black at their extremities. Tail bushy, blackish above and at the tip.

Habitat: A wide range of savanna, even dry open plains. Map, p. 107.

Habits: Mostly nocturnal, the Bat-eared Fox normally spends the day in burrows or in dense bush; but it may quite often be seen in daytime, basking at the entrance to its den. It lives mainly in small parties of up to seven, but sometimes in pairs. It feeds mostly on insects (termites, beetles), scorpions, also on small rodents, nestlings and eggs of ground-nesting birds, lizards, fruits and bulbs.

Its call is a melancholy whine and a thin note.

The period of gestation is of about 2 months. Young, 3–5 per litter, are born in a burrow.

Bat-eared Fox are preyed on by larger raptorial birds.

WILD DOG   *Lycaon pictus* (Temminck)   p. 113
(Hunting Dog)
F Lycaon, Cynhyène, Loup-peint   K Mbwa mwitu   G Hyaenenhund
A Wildehond

Identification: Height at shoulder 30 in.; weight 55–70 lb. Unmistakable. A fairly large carnivore, with the size and features of a big dog, a massive head almost like a hyaena and a slender body. Legs long and thin.[1] Ears very broad and rounded ('bat-like'). Muzzle usually blackish, with a median black line on head; on the nape, often a fawn patch. Coat coarse and short, showing a curious and striking pattern of broad dark brown, black, yellow and white patches. Pattern remarkably variable, no two individuals quite alike, the patches in no way evenly distributed or

[1] The feet have four toes, instead of five as in the true dogs.

symmetrical. Tail reaching beyond the hocks, bushy, fawn at its base then black with a conspicuous white terminal portion.

Habitat: Open or wooded savanna: up to high mountains (summit of Kilimanjaro; on Mount Kenya, above 9,000 ft); never dense forest. Map, p. 107.

Habits: The Wild Dog, a diurnal animal, lives in packs of 6–20, sometimes up to 40 individuals, and is rarely seen alone or in pairs. Packs of over 90 have been recorded. This gregarious species communicate by a large range of vocalisations; the commonest are a short bark of alarm; a rallying howl ('hoooo-hoooo-hoooo'); and a brief 'click' made with the tongue.

The Wild Dogs—the wolves of Africa—hunt in packs in an organised manner, some individuals pressing their quarry closely, which may be anything from a small antelope (duikers) to a Waterbuck; Impala, Gazelle and Reedbuck are favourite prey. The other dogs follow at leisure, and take over the chase when the first begin to tire. When coming within reach of their prey, they bite where they can and snap out portions of flesh until the animal falls. The prey is consumed, sometimes still alive, within a few minutes (an Impala is entirely consumed within about 10 minutes). In the absence of larger game, they may prey on smaller mammals, even rats and birds. They may also cause damage to domestic stock.

These animals could be harmful to game. Nevertheless they play an important role in natural balance, controlling the populations like any other predator. Moreover they wander continuously on a large scale and never stay long in one place.

The period of gestation is about 2 months. The pups are born in a shelter among dense grass or scrub, or in a crevice or Aardvark hole. Communal breeding areas where all the females in a pack bear their young have been reported. The active members of the pack co-operate in bringing food to the dens. The litter may be up to 12 pups, but normally very few survive. Born blind, and coloured black-and-white, they follow their mother after one week and are fed shortly after birth with regurgitated semi-digested meat.

ZORILLAS, RATEL, OTTERS: Mustelidae

Small to medium-sized carnivores, with plantigrade feet, a reduced number of highly specialised teeth, and special scent glands in the perineal region. This family, distributed all over the world, except in Australia and Madagascar, is represented in Africa by three different types of animals[1]: the Zorillas, with weasel- or polecat-features and a striking black and white pattern like the North American Skunks; the Ratel, a stout creature

[1] Moreover the Mustelidae are represented in North Africa by other forms closely related to the corresponding European species: the stoat, *Mustela erminea* (*algirica*), the weasel, *M. nivalis* (*numidica*), the ferret, *M. putorius* (*furo*), and the European Otter, *Lutra lutra* (*angustirostris*). All are extralimital.

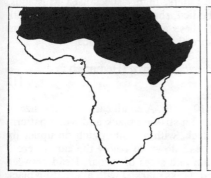

Common Jackal, p. 91

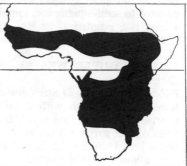

Side-striped Jackal, p. 91

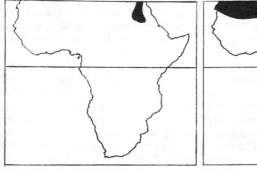

Black-backed Jackal, p. 94

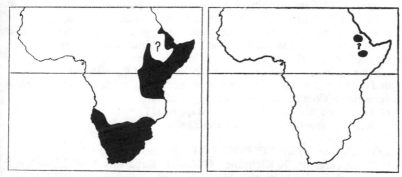

Semien Fox, p. 94

Red Fox, p. 95

Rüppell's Fox, p. 95

like the European badger; and the Otters, highly specialised Mustelids, adapted to semi-aquatic life, long-bodied, short-legged, sleek-furred, with a long tail, pointed at its tip. All these animals occupy very different niches and most of them are widespread throughout Africa.

LIBYAN STRIPED WEASEL *Poecilictis libyca* (Hemprich and Ehrenberg)   p. 112
F Zorille de Libye   G Streifenwiesel
Identification: Length (without tail) 10–12 in. A small carnivore the size of a large weasel, with long soft hair and a striking black and white pattern. Soles of feet partly haired. Head black, with a white patch on upper lip and a broad white band from forehead down to below the ear, where it joins a V-shaped white stripe on chin and sides of throat. Head between the ears black. Nape white. Back and flanks marked with alternating black and white, sometimes buff, stripes (these stripes are not longitudinal but somewhat oblique, forming a lozenge-shaped pattern on the middle of back); white stripes much broader and black stripes partly concealed by long white hairs, giving a whitish effect to upperparts. Underparts and limbs pure black. Tail bushy, short, mostly white, but hairs with a dark ring; often a black tip.
Similar species: May be confused with the Striped Polecat, but size smaller and coat more white; white stripes broader, long white hairs all over the upperparts. Coat softer and with longer hairs.
Habitat: Arid and desert country. Map, p. 111.
Habits: Apparently the same as the Zorilla.

ZORILLA or **STRIPED POLECAT** *Ictonyx striatus* (Perry)   p. 112
F Zorille commun, K Kicheche   G Zorilla, Band-Iltis A Stinkmuishond
Identification: Height at shoulder 4 in.; length (without tail) 12–14 in.; weight 3 lb. A small carnivore, of the size and shape of a polecat with the back slightly hunched as it walks, with short legs, a long soft coat and a strikingly contrasted black and white pattern. Soles of feet naked. Head black with a white spot on forehead between the eyes, and a band on each side of the face, in front of the ear, running backwards. Head between the ears, and nape, white. On the back, from nape to tail, four broad conspicuous white stripes alternating with narrower irregular black stripes (the pattern is broadly similar to the last named species). Underparts and limbs pure black. Tail long and very bushy (hairs coarser), often fluffed out and raised over the back; black at its base, then white.
Intraspecific variation: A number of subspecies have been described. Some authors recognise several species, differing by size and pattern of coloration. The systematics of these animals still need a thorough revision; the different races cannot be recognised in the field.
Habitat: Savanna and open country; even in high mountains. Map, p. 111.
Habits: Nocturnal, though occasionally seen out in daylight, solitary and

terrestrial, the Striped Polecat takes refuge in crevices and burrows, excavated by itself or by some other animal. The alarm call is a high-pitched scream.

It feeds on rodents, up to the size of Cane Rats, hares, reptiles (even larger snakes) and birds, also on insects and birds' eggs. It has two well-developed perineal glands, secreting a nauseating musky matter, ejected with great strength when annoyed, like the American Skunks. When angered, it utters loud high-pitched screams.

The litter is usually 2–3; young, born in burrows, are marked like the adults, but with shorter fur.

WHITE-NAPED WEASEL *Poecilogale albinucha* (Gray)   p. 112
(African Striped Weasel or Snake "Mongoose")
F Poecilogale   A Slangmuishond   G Kappen-Iltis
Identification: Height at shoulder 3 in.; length (without tail) 12 in.; weight 3 lb. A small carnivore, of the size and shape of a large weasel, with very elongated and slender body, short legs, and a striking black and white pattern. Top of head, from forehead to behind the ears, white; thence the white patch narrows on the nape and neck, and divides in two lines which divide again; thus upperparts marked by four well defined longitudinal narrow white or yellowish stripes. Sides, underparts and limbs pure black. Tail long, bushy, entirely white, normally carried in line with the back, but raised and fluffed when the animal is alarmed.

Female similar to the male but smaller and often yellower.
Habitat: Savanna and open country. Map, p. 107.
Habits: The White-naped Weasel—a rather uncommon species—lives singly, in pairs or in small family groups, and is diurnal as well as nocturnal. It is mainly terrestrial, though able to climb fairly well. It often hunts in groups and preys on small mammals, mostly rodents (the Mole-rat (*Cryptomys*) seems to be a favourite prey), sometimes spring-hares, birds (up to guineafowl), reptiles, eggs and insects. It can enter any burrow or hole to hunt its victims. It may be destructive to poultry. Like most weasels, it grasps the throat, and sucks the blood. It kills far more than it needs for food. It has well developed perineal glands, secreting a nauseating oily fluid, not so strong as in the Zorilla. The litter usually numbers two, sometimes three.

It is normally silent. When annoyed, it gives a half growl, half shriek. At mating season, males utter a somewhat rumbling growly call.

RATEL *Mellivora capensis* (Schreber)   p. 85
(Honey badger)
F Ratel   K Nyegere   G Ratel, Honigdachs   A Ratel
Identification: Height at shoulder 10 in.; length (without tail) 27–32 in.; weight up to 25 lb. A stout, stocky animal, the size and shape of the European Badger, with a massive head, small rounded ears, short legs

and powerful claws, and a short bushy tail, often held upright. Coat short and coarse with a strikingly contrasted pattern. Upperparts from crown of head to tail whitish, sometimes washed with grey, buff or brown, particularly on hindquarters, rarely black (see below). This light coloured mantle is sharply defined from pure black sides, underparts and limbs. Tail mostly black.

Young rusty brown above.

Intraspecific variation: The extent of the light mantle is very variable. In some races, it runs from nape to tail; in others, especially those from the dense humid forest, this light 'top' is limited in extent, sometimes to the neck. It may also be completely absent, probably as an individual variation (melanistic form).

Habitat: Every type of habitat, from fairly open dry savanna to dense forest. Also Asia to India. Map, p. 111.

Habits: Nocturnal, but also quite often seen in daylight, the Ratel is capable of digging out deep burrows with its powerful claws. It may also use Aardvark holes. It lives singly or in pairs. Though shy and retiring, it is a courageous and bold animal, that does not know the meaning of fear, capable of charging an intruder and attacking big game (up to a Buffalo, biting the groin and genital organs, the animal then bleeding to death), especially during its breeding season. Omnivorous, it feeds on various small animals, rodents, shrews, snakes, big insects, spiders, occasionally young and smaller antelopes, and also probably eats carrion. In addition, it feeds on roots, bulbs and fruits, and is very fond of honey and the pupae of wild bees, breaking open the nests with its claws; it is protected from the stings by its tough hide and thick subcutaneous fat. It is able to climb trees in order to reach bee-hives in spite of its apparently heavy bulk.

A curious association exists between the Ratel and the Honey Guide (*Indicator indicator*). This little bird finds a bees' nest, attracts the mammal through its particular behaviour and calls and leads it to the hive. The Ratel, which deliberately follows the guiding flights and calls and sometimes provokes the bird, digs out the nest and then both share the feast. But this is not essential to the Ratel, which is able to find the hives without any aid.

The gestation period is about 180 days. The litter usually consists of two, and there may be two litters a year; young are born underground or among rocks.

CONGO CLAWLESS OTTER   *Aonyx (Paraonyx) congica* Lönnberg
p. 85
F Loutre à joues blanches du Congo   G Kongo Weisswangen Otter
Identification: Length (without tail) up to 38 in.; weight 45 lb. A large otter, with no webbing on feet; no claws. General colour uniform dark brown, with a conspicuous silvery gloss (end of hairs white), particularly

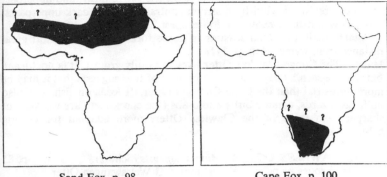

Sand Fox, p. 98

Cape Fox, p. 100

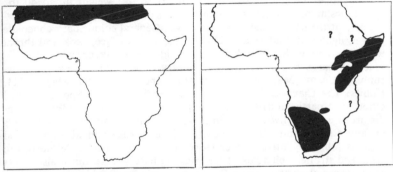

Fennec, p. 100

Bat-eared Fox, p. 101

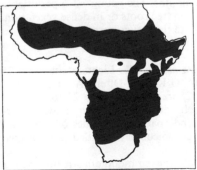

Wild Dog, p. 101

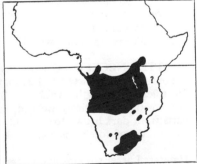

White-naped Weasel, p. 105

on fore parts of body. Sides of face below the eye and ear, and upperpart of chest, greyish or whitish, in strong contrast with the dark upperparts; outlines well defined except on lower chest.

Habitat: Small, torrential streams in dense forest. May be seen at great distance from water. Map, p. 111.

Habits: The Congo Clawless Otter lives in family groups. It is nocturnal, but may be seen by daylight. The structure of toes suggests that it may be more terrestrial than the Cape Clawless Otter. It feeds on fish, but also on frogs, lizards, aquatic birds and crabs (the cheek-teeth are weaker but sharper than those of the Clawless Otter, more adapted for cutting fish).

CAPE CLAWLESS OTTER *Aonyx capensis* (Schinz) p. 85
F Loutre à joues blanches   K Fisi maji   G Weisswangen-Otter
A Groototter

Identification: Length (without tail) up to 36 in.; weight up to 40 lb., sometimes more. A large otter with no webs on feet (only a small connecting skin at the base of the toes); no claws. General colour dark chocolate brown, lighter on underparts. Upper lips, sides of face, neck and throat white, merging with the dark colour on sides. Edge of ears white.

Habitat: Large rivers in savanna country, mostly quiet pools or slow-running streams. May be seen at great distance from water. Map, p. 111.

Habits: The Clawless Otter is far less aquatic than the Spotted-necked Otter. It is partly diurnal and likes to sun on rocks or sandbars in undisturbed areas. It lives singly, in pairs or in small family parties. It feeds on any aquatic animals, particularly on fish, frogs and also crabs and mussels found by turning over stones under water (the cheek-teeth are large and strong, well adapted for crushing hard shells). But it also hunts small mammals such as Cane Rats and aquatic wildfowl in swampy areas and dense thickets near water.

The period of gestation is about 2 months. The young—2-5 per litter—are born in burrows, in hollows between tree roots or in dense vegetation. These otters apparently do not excavate their own burrows.

The voice is a piercing whistle.

SPOTTED-NECKED OTTER *Lutra maculicollis* Lichtenstein p. 85
F Loutre à cou tacheté   K Fisi maji   G Krallen-Otter   A Kleinotter

Identification: Length (without tail) 25 in.; weight up to 20 lb. A small otter, with toes entirely webbed, each with a short, sharp claw. Upperparts from dark brown to chestnut. Underparts paler. Sides of face, chin and inside of forelimbs pale buff, conspicuously mottled with brown spots.

Habitat: Larger streams and rivers, lakes; even mountain streams, with a rapid flow. Map, p. 111.

Habits: The Spotted-necked Otter lives singly, or sometimes in small groups up to 10. Mainly nocturnal, it may be seen by daylight when undisturbed. It is more strictly aquatic than the Clawless Otter, and also shyer and more seldom seen. It feeds mostly on fish captured under water (no direct competition between it and the Clawless Otter), on amphibians and fresh water animals.

CIVET, GENETS, MONGOOSES: Viverridae

Small to medium-sized carnivores, with elongated body and face, a pointed muzzle, short legs, and generally a long and well furred tail. The number of teeth is usually high. Most have scent glands in the anal region, sometimes opening into a pouch outside the anus, secreting a strong smelling or nauseating substance. They are mainly carnivorous although fruits form part of their diet. Spread over the warmer regions of the Old World, they are well represented in tropical Africa where three types may be distinguished. Most of them are forest inhabitants, or live in dense bush.

The Civet is a rather long-legged terrestrial animal with some dog-like features and short, semi-retractile claws.

The Palm Civet and the Genets[1] are small, long-bodied and short-legged animals, with a long annulated tail carried straight out behind when on the move, and prominent ears. The short, soft and dense coat is heavily spotted all over. Terrestrial and arboreal, with short, but curved and retractile claws.

Mongooses are more stockily built, though their face is conical and their body elongated. They have no retractile claws, as might be expected from their terrestrial and fossorial habits. The ears are small and the tail, never annulated, is shorter than in Genets[2].

AFRICAN CIVET *Viverra civetta* (Schreber) p. 85
F Civette K Fungo G Zibetkatze A Siwetkat
Identification: Height at shoulder 16 in.; length (without tail) 35 in.; weight 20–45 lb. A rather large, heavily built, long-bodied and long-legged carnivore. The largest and most dog-like Viverrid. Back usually arched, head carried low. Coat of long, coarse and bristly hairs. Head with a light grey forehead and a white muzzle; both separated across the eyes by an intermediate broad black band circling the face and throat. Ears rather long, rounded, protruding beyond the hair of the head with white edges. Down the spine, from neck to tail, a line of shaggy black hairs

---

[1] The systematics of the genus *Genetta* badly need a thorough revision. Many forms of uncertain status have been described, some very recently (*lehmanni*, Liberia; *deorum*, Somalia; etc.). The present treatment is only tentative.

[2] Two Asiatic species have been introduced: the Indian Civet *Viverricula indica*, in Zanzibar, Pemba and some districts of Tanzania; and the Small Indian Mongoose *Herpestes auropunctatus*, in Mafia Island.

forming an erectile crest. Ground colour greyish or buffy. On the neck, two black bands from behind the ear to lower neck, forming a double collar, the first broadening into a large patch under the neck. On the body, a conspicuous and very variable pattern of black spots more or less disposed in transverse rows on sides and in longitudinal rows on hindquarters. Underparts and lower limbs pure black. Tail bushy at base, then becoming thinner, black except for 3–4 broad whitish rings at its base. Pure black specimens have been observed.

Habitat: All types of savanna; sometimes dense forest. Map, p. 119.

Habits: Solitary and nocturnal, the Civet hides during the day among thickets, in tall grass, or in old Aardvark or Porcupine burrows, purely terrestrial. Omnivorous, it feeds on carrion and on a variety of prey, including rodents, birds, birds' eggs, small game, lizards, frogs, snails, slugs and insects (termites, locusts). It also eats vegetable matter (berries, fruits, young shoots of bushes). It may cause damage to poultry. It often deposits its dung in particular places where the droppings may accumulate in great quantities. The litter is of 2–4 young; cubs are coloured like the adults, but rather darker. Civets have well developed scent glands in the perineal region, secreting a nauseating oily substance used by the Civet for territorial marking. This product is used in perfume manufacture. In West and East Africa, the animals are kept in captivity and the musk collected.

The call is a kind of low-pitched cough and a growl.

TWO-SPOTTED PALM CIVET   *Nandinia binotata* Gray
(Tree Civet)   p. 92
F Nandinie   A Palmsiwet   G Pardelroller

Identification: Length (without tail) 18–22 in.; weight 5 lb. A medium-sized viverrid, not unlike a stout genet, with a rounded head, short ears, and short legs with sharp curved claws. Coat of dense, woolly hairs, rather coarse. General coloration buffish grey, tinged with chestnut and marked with numerous indistinct dark brownish black little spots in rows on the upperparts, one on the spine, 4 to 6 on the sides of body. General effect dull and dark at a distance. On the shoulders, two creamy spots. Underparts lighter, grey, tinged with yellowish. Tail very long (at least as long as head and body), fairly thick, somewhat darker than the body, regularly ringed with about 12 narrow blackish rings.

Habitat: Forests and forested savanna. Map, p. 119.

Habits: The Palm Civet is mainly arboreal. Nocturnal, it spends the day hidden among trees or vines. Its diet is diversified and it feeds on vegetable matter, particularly fruit, but also on arboreal rodents, birds, birds' eggs and even Pottos, as well as on insects.

The litter numbers 2–3.

The call recalls the mew of a cat.

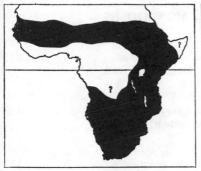

Zorilla, p. 104

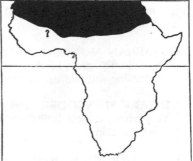

Libyan Striped Weasel, p. 104

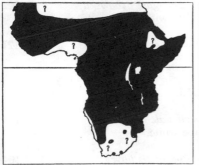

Ratel, p. 105

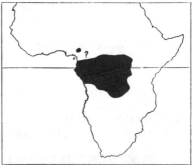

Congo Clawless Otter, p. 106

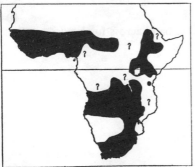

Cape Clawless Otter, p. 108

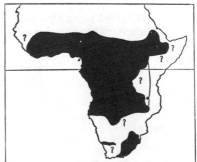

Spotted-necked Otter, p. 108

Plate 19   SMALL MONGOOSES

1. GAMBIAN MONGOOSE   *Mungos gambianus*   *page* 125
   Small; buffish grey; black stripe along side of neck,
   contrasting with buffish white throat.

2. DWARF MONGOOSE   *Helogale parvula*   123
   Very small; stockily built; reddish brown; tail rather
   short and thin.

3. SLENDER MONGOOSE   *Herpestes sanguineus*   122
   Small; slender; reddish brown; tail long, with black tip.

4. POUSARGUES' MONGOOSE   *Dologale dybowskii*   122
   Very small; dark brown; tail longish, without dark tip.

5. CAPE GREY MONGOOSE   *Herpestes pulverulentus*   121
   Small; greyish; tail long.

ZORILLA

6. WHITE-NAPED WEASEL   *Poecilogale albinucha*   105
   Small; very slender; head and nape white.

7. LIBYAN STRIPED WEASEL   *Poecilictis libyca*   104
   Long, soft coat; head black with white band across
   forehead; back mostly white, with indistinct black stripes.

8. ZORILLA   *Ictonyx striatus*   104
   Coat shorter; head black with white band across forehead;
   back white with distinct black stripes.

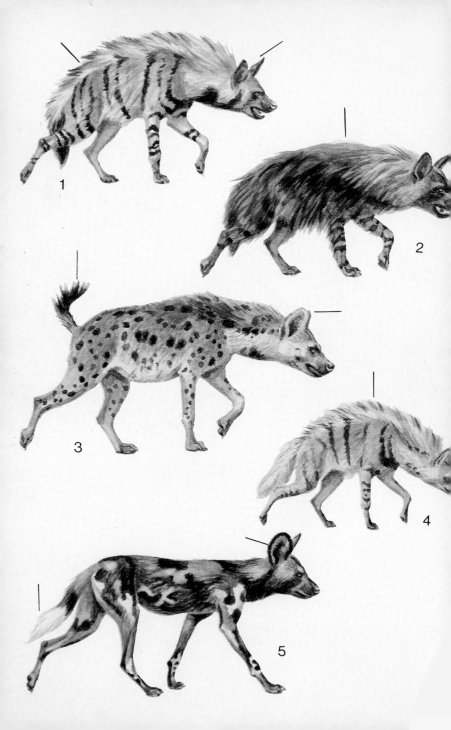

HYAENAS, WILD DOG Plate 20

1. **STRIPED HYAENA** *Hyaena hyaena* *page* 134
Transverse stripes over body; shaggy coat; mane along
spine; long, pointed ears.

2. **BROWN HYAENA** *Hyaena brunnea* 134
Almost uniform dark brown; shaggy coat; long, pointed
ears.

3. **SPOTTED HYAENA** *Crocuta crocuta* 129
Entirely spotted; coat short; short, rounded ears.

4. **AARDWOLF** *Proteles cristatus* 135
Small; narrow muzzle; shaggy coat; mane along spine;
dark stripes; long pointed ears.

5. **WILD DOG** *Lycaon pictus* 101
Long-legged; ears broad and rounded; brown, black,
yellow and white patches, irregularly distributed over
body; tail long with white tip.

COMMON GENET *Genetta genetta* (L.)[1] p. 93
F Genette commune K Kanu[2] G Ginsterkatze
A Kleinkolmuskejaatkat
Identification: Length (without tail) 16–20 in.; weight 5 lb. A genet with proportionately long legs and a short face. Coat of long and coarse hair, with a well developed crest along the spine. Ground colour from greyish to fawn (with a tendency to be greyer than the other species), with a conspicuous dark line along the middle of back. Dark brown or blackish spots on the upperparts and flanks generally small, more or less elongated and arranged in longitudinal rows. Tail well-haired, almost bushy, with 9–10 dark rings, and a whitish tip, occasionally dark.
Habitat: Dry savanna and open country. The only genet found in open dry savanna. Also North Africa, southern and western Europe, Near East and Arabia. Map, p. 119.

LARGE-SPOTTED GENET *Genetta tigrina* (Schreber)[3] p. 93
F Genette tigrine A Grootkolmuskejaatkat G Tiger-Ginsterkatze
Identification: Length (without tail) 16–20 in. A genet with short legs and a proportionately short face. Coat rather soft and short with a distinct dark dorsal line, but without or with only very indistinct spinal crest. Ground colour from brownish grey to pale yellowish or buffy-white, with dark spots showing a tendency to be brown or chestnut more often than blackish, generally large, elongated and more or less arranged in 3–4 longitudinal rows on each side. Tail with 8–9 dark rings and a wide dark tip.
Habitat: Bush, woodland, forest, but not high forest. Map, p. 119.

SMALL-SPOTTED GENET *Genetta servalina* Pucheran[4] p. 93
F Genette servaline G Serval-Ginsterkatze
Identification: Length (without tail) 16–21 in. A genet with long legs and an elongated face. Coat soft, short, with no spinal crest. Ground colour from grey to ochraceous buff, often rich deep buff. Dark, generally black, markings of the upperparts profuse, rather small, narrowly separated by the lighter ground colour; not elongated, but rather quadrangular, never forming longitudinal rows. Underparts dusky instead of light coloured as in other genets. Tail long, with usually 10–12 dark rings, very regularly disposed, wide, clear-cut and well defined.
Habitat: Dense forest. Map, p. 119.

---

[1] Including *felina, dongolana, pulchra, senegalensis*. The taxonomic status of several 'problem forms' from southern Africa is still to be determined.

[2] Apparently a name applied to all genets.

[3] Including the Rusty-spotted Genet, *G. rubiginosa* (probably a colour phase with rusty-red markings, from southern Africa), *mossambica.*

Including *bettoni.*

FOREST GENET *Genetta pardina* I. Geoffroy[1] p. 93
F Genette pardine G Panther-Ginsterkatze
Identification: Length (without tail) 16–20 in. A genet with proportionately long legs. Coat short and rather soft with a short spinal crest. Ground colour from greyish to buff. Black markings very conspicuous, the general effect is predominantly dark. A conspicuous black line on the middle of back. On the upperparts, dark, black or brown spots, elongated, almost confluent and hence forming distinct longitudinal lines. Spots better separated on the flanks (the spots show a tendency to be more numerous and smaller among dense rain forest populations, and less numerous and larger in drier forest populations). Tail almost black, with only 3–4 narrow light rings at its base.
Habitat: Dense forest. Map, p. 119.

GIANT GENET *Genetta victoriae* Thomas p. 93
F Genette géante G Riesenginsterkatze
Identification: Length (without tail) 20–22 in. A large genet (the largest of all), with an elongated face and very long legs. Coat thick and soft. A well developed crest along the spine, particularly visible on the neck. Ground colour yellowish to ochraceous. On the upperparts, black markings very dense; so little of the ground colour is visible that the animal appears almost black at a distance, with a slight ochraceous suffusion. On the flanks numerous small black spots. Limbs black. Tail long, thick and bushy with 6–7 broad dark rings and a black tip; hence mostly black with only narrow light rings.
Habitat: Dense forest. Map, p. 127.

ABYSSINIAN GENET *Genetta abyssinica* (Rüppell) p. 92
F Genette d'Ethiopie G Sennar-Ginsterkatze
Identification: Length (without tail) 15–19 in. A rather small genet with short legs and a shortened face. Coat rather coarse with a poorly developed spinal crest, with a light-coloured central line. General colour pale sandy grey. Along the back, on each side, two distinct black stripes; on the lower flank, two rows of black elongated spots. Thus this genet seems rather striped than spotted. Tail moderately long, with 6–7 dark rings and a dark tip.
Habitat: Highlands. Map, p. 127.

VILLIERS' GENET *Genetta villiersi* (Dekeyser) p. 92
F Genette de Villiers G Villiers-Ginsterkatze
Identification: Length (without tail) 18 in. A genet with short legs and a rather coarse coat. Ground colour greyish fawn, marked with numerous spots varying from chestnut brown to blackish, the general effect often being brownish or rusty fawn. Spots ill-defined, particularly on shoulders

[1] Syn. *maculata*.

and foreparts. On the back, from 3–4 longitudinal lines made by the coalescence of elongated spots; flanks marked with rounded spots. Underparts yellowish grey. Tail very long, well haired, with 7–9 dark rings alternating with light rings; the first bright rufous, the latter darkening to black; thus the tail is tricolor, greyish, rufous and black.
Habitat: Forest. Map, p. 127.

Habits of Genets: All genets are apparently very similar in general habits, though they show various habitat preferences. They can be either terrestrial or arboreal, and all of them are very agile tree-climbers. They are very graceful in their movements, with the long tail carried straight out behind. Entirely nocturnal, they usually spend the day in rock crevices, in burrows excavated by other animals, in hollow trees or on a large branch. They seem to return daily to the same spot. They live singly or in pairs.

Most prey is hunted on the ground, but they climb trees to take nesting or roosting birds. When stalking, they crouch so low as to become completely flat on the ground. Genets can pass through any opening large enough to admit the head as the lithe slender body can also be squeezed through. They are wasteful killers, often eating just the head and breast and killing much more than they need.

They feed on small animals from hares downwards, mostly rodents, birds, snakes, lizards, also insects and some vegetable matter, such as fruits. They are notorious poultry killers.

The litter size is usually 2–3, rarely 4. The kittens are born in burrows.

Genets spit and growl like cats when angered. They also utter clear metallic notes.

AFRICAN LINSANG   *Poiana richardsoni* (Thomson)   p. 92
F Poiane   G Afrikanischer Linsang
Identification: Length (without tail) 13 in. A small genet, with large ears, very long-bodied with short legs and a very soft coat. Ground colour yellowish fawn, sometimes tinged with greyish. Neck with longitudinal dark stripes (the spots run into bands or stripes). Back and sides marked with rounded brownish black spots, in ill-defined rows. Underparts creamy buff. Lower section of limbs almost uniform buff. Tail very long (longer than the head and body), heavily ringed with up to a dozen dark brown rings alternating with light yellowish buff rings.
Habitat: Dense forest, mostly evergreen and montane forest. Map, p. 127.
Habits: Nocturnal, the African Linsang spends the day sleeping among trees or tangled vines, in round nests made of green material; after a few days it moves on and builds a new nest. Omnivorous, it feeds on insects, birds, eggs and vegetable matter. The litter apparently numbers 2.

AQUATIC CIVET   *Osbornictis piscivora* J. A. Allen   p. 92
F Genette aquatique   G Wasserschleichkatze
Identification: Length (without tail) 20 in. A fairly large genet-like animal, with a short face, long and dense pelage, and a striking coloration. Muzzle and forehead fuscous brown; over each eye, a conspicuous elongated white spot; sides of head whitish, almost white under the eye; chin and throat white. Ears blackish, edged with long whitish hairs. Forehead, neck, body, and limbs uniform bright chestnut-red, darker on middle of back, somewhat lighter on middle of underparts, darker again on upper surface of feet. Tail rather long, thick, heavily furred, entirely black.
Habitat: Dense forest. Map, p. 127.
Habits: This rare animal lives near rivers and streams and seems entirely piscivorous. It shows several adaptative characters to this mode of life, such as the small rhinarium, the abbreviated rostrum and the naked palms and soles (convergence with Otters).

WHITE-TAILED MONGOOSE   *Ichneumia albicauda* (G. Cuvier) p. 96
F Mangouste à queue blanche K Nguchiro[1] G Weissschwanzmanguste
A Witstertmuishond
Identification: Length (without tail) 22–24 in.; weight 7–11 lb. A large mongoose, high on the legs, with a rather pointed head and a coarse shaggy coat. Soles of feet furred. General colour grizzled grey or brownish grey with a varying amount of long black hairs, especially on the hind parts. Underparts and limbs dark brown or black. Tail proportionately short, bushy but tapering, dark at its very base, then usually white or buffy white, in sharp contrast with the body; in some individuals, the tail is entirely blackish.
   Young browner, without any speckles.
Habitat: Savanna; dense bush, particularly near water. Also Arabia. Map, p. 127.
Habits: The White-tailed Mongoose is usually solitary and nocturnal, partially diurnal in secluded localities. Terrestrial, and partly arboreal according to some observers, it frequents dense bush, particularly along rivers. It feeds on small animals (frogs, rodents, reptiles, insects, grubs, eggs), also molluscs and crabs (strong teeth enable it to crush hardshelled prey), and vegetable matter (berries, fruits).
   When angry, it utters a loud bark.
   Young (2–3 per litter) are born in a rock crevice. They are browner than adults.

BLACK-LEGGED MONGOOSE   *Bdeogale nigripes* Pucheran   p. 96
F Mangouste à pattes noires G Buschschwanzichneumon
Identification: Length (without tail) 25 in. A large, heavily built mongoose

[1] Apparently a name applied to all mongooses.

showing some otter- or badger-like features, with a thick massive head, a broad and inflated muzzle, and short legs; fur dense, short and soft, except on the tail. Soles well haired, especially the plantar surface. Entire upperparts from head to root of tail, chin and upper neck very light grey, almost whitish, very finely speckled. Belly whitish or greyish. Lower neck, chest and limbs black, in strong contrast with the rest of the body. Tail rather short, covered with long coarse hairs, entirely white, more or less tinged with yellowish.

Similar species: Cannot be confused in the field with any other mongoose, except perhaps the White-tailed Mongoose. But the short coat, the general colour and the entirely white tail are good distinctive characters.

Intraspecific variation: Jackson's Mongoose (*jacksoni*), East Africa, differs from typical *nigripes* (from south-east Nigeria to the Congo) in having the sides of neck and throat deep yellow; smaller and with longer fur.

Habitat: Dense high forest. Map, p. 131.

Habits: Apparently nothing is known on the specific habits of this mongoose, which is reputed to feed on rodents and insects.

BUSHY-TAILED MONGOOSE   *Bdeogale crassicauda* Peters   p. 97
F Mangouste à queue touffue   A Dikstertmuishond   G Iltis-Ichneumon
Identification: Length (without tail) 16–20 in. A rather small mongoose slenderly built, and dark coloured, with a long coarse coat. Upperparts very dark, blackish, the dull buffy underfur being obscured by numerous black and white banded hairs. Underparts lighter. Limbs black. Tail very bushy, entirely black.

Habitat: Woodland. Map, p. 131.

Habits: Very little is known on the habits of this rare mongoose, which feeds on insects (termites), rodents and possibly aquatic animals (crabs). It is reputed to take refuge in hollow trees.

MELLER'S MONGOOSE   *Rhynchogale melleri* (Gray)   p. 96
F Mangouste de Meller A Mellerse Muishond   G Mellers Manguste
Identification: Length (without tail) 20 in.; weight 6 lb. A fairly large mongoose, with a long coarse fur. On the throat and neck, hairs reversed, growing forwards, forming on each side a distinct crest from below the ear to lower shoulder. General colour uniform grizzled fulvous brown, darker on the back, greyer and lighter on head and underparts. Legs darker, feet dark brown. Tail very long, very bushy, coloured like the back at its base, then passing progressively to pure black. The black colour extends sometimes as an indistinct spot to the lower back.

Intraspecific variation: Kershaw's Mongoose (*Rh. caniceps*, Tanzania), originally described as a distinct species, is a mere local representative with a distinctly grey head and more grizzled upperparts.

Habitat: Forested savanna. Map, p. 131.

Habits: Meller's Mongoose is solitary and nocturnal, although also partly

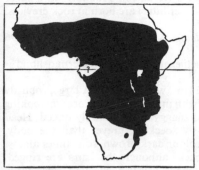

African Civet, p. 109

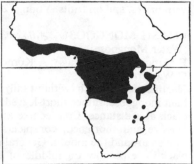

Two-spotted Palm Civet, p. 110

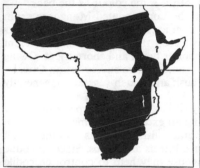

Common Genet, p. 114

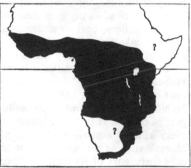

Large-spotted Genet, p. 114

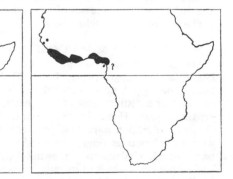

Small-spotted Genet, p. 114

Forest Genet, p. 115

diurnal. Terrestrial, it feeds on insects (termites), probably on smaller vertebrates, and on fruits. Young (2–3 per litter) are born in rock crevices.

MARSH MONGOOSE *Atilax paludinosus* (G. Cuvier) p. 96
(Water Mongoose)
F Mangouste des marais A Kommetjiegatmuishond; Watermuishond
G Wassermanguste
Identification: Length (without tail) 24 in.; weight 5–7 lb. A large, robustly built mongoose, rather short-legged, with uniform dark coloration looking black at a distance. Coat coarse and shaggy. Soles entirely naked. Head massive and shortened, conspicuously speckled, greyer than the body, whitish around the mouth. General colour dark brown, sometimes almost blackish, especially on middle of back, although the hairs are ringed, brownish black and ochraceous, giving a grizzled effect at close view. Underparts somewhat lighter. Limbs darker. Tail rather short, thick and bushy at its base, tapering at its end, of the same colour as the back.
Similar species: Easily confused with the Long-snouted Mongoose, from which it differs, besides anatomical characters (number of teeth), by its entirely naked soles (particularly visible on the hind feet) and different external shape, especially the much shorter head, and shorter legs. Owing to its size, colour and aquatic habits, sometimes mistaken for an Otter.
Habitat: Savanna and forest. Dense bush and marsh vegetation, generally near water. Map, p. 131.
Habits: Nocturnal and often solitary, it is also found in pairs or family parties of 3–4. It is amphibious, being an excellent swimmer. It feeds on every kind of aquatic animal, frogs, crabs, fish as well as on other small animals such as birds, reptiles, rodents, insects and grubs. Since crocodile eggs form part of its diet, this mongoose may help to control crocodile populations. It may inflict damage on poultry.
   Young (apparently 2–3 in a litter) are sheltered in burrows under over-hanging banks or in masses of vegetation.
   The call is a high-pitched bark.

LONG-SNOUTED MONGOOSE *Herpestes naso* (De Winton)[1] p. 97
F Mangouste à long museau G Langnasenichneumon
Identification: Length (without tail) 20–24 in. A large mongoose, stoutly built, long legged, dark coloured and with an elongated face; from nape to shoulder a distinct crest of long hairs. Soles and palms furred on their proximal part. Head distinctly lighter and more greyish than body. General coloration dark blackish brown, although the hairs are ringed with an ochraceous tinge; some individuals are grizzled buff on a dark background. Underparts somewhat lighter, more suffused with rufous. Tail rather short, thick at its base, somewhat lighter than the back.
Similar species: See Marsh Mongoose.

[1] Syn. *Xenogale microdon* J. A. Allen.

Habitat: High rain forest. Map, p. 131.
Habits: Apparently nothing is known on the specific habits of this mongoose.

EGYPTIAN MONGOOSE *Herpestes ichneumon* (L.) p. 96
(Greater Grey Mongoose, Ichneumon)
F Mangouste ichneumon   A Grootgrysmuishond   G Ichneumon
Identification: Length (without tail) 22–26 in.; weight 5–8 lb. A very large mongoose (the largest of African mongooses), with a uniformly grizzled coat of fairly long and coarse hair. Upperparts speckled black and white (the long hairs regularly ringed with white and black) with the woolly underfur buff or yellowish brown, giving a brownish grey appearance. Sides lighter. Underparts buff, partly bare. Head and limbs darker. Tail long and slender, densely haired at its base, then tapering, of the same colour as the back, with a long conspicuous black brush-like tassel at its tip.
Habitat: Savanna, chiefly well wooded and near water. Also in North Africa, southern Spain and Israel. Map, p. 131.
Habits: Mainly nocturnal but also diurnal, the Egyptian Mongoose may be seen singly or in pairs, occasionally in family parties, each animal walking behind the other like a giant snake. Entirely terrestrial, it lives in burrows and crevices between rocks. A holy animal in ancient Egypt.

It feeds on every kind of animal, principally on rodents, game birds and reptiles, even crabs and fish, and may cause damage to domestic animals.

Young—2–4 per litter—are sheltered for a few days in an old Aardvark burrow or in a hollow tree.

CAPE GREY MONGOOSE *Herpestes (Galerella) pulverulentus*
Wagner p. 112
F Mangouste grise du Cap   A Kleingrysmuishond   G Kleinichneumon
Identification: Length (without tail) 14 in. A small, slim mongoose (but heavier and more stoutly built than the Slender Mongoose), with a long and rather loose coat. General colour speckled grey, the hairs ringed black and white. Face darker. Underparts lighter, less speckled than above. Feet uniform dark brown, but not conspicuously contrasting with the body. Tail long and well haired, of same colour as the back, the tip brownish, but not black (only exceptionally, see below).
Similar species: May be confused with the Slender Mongoose, but general colour grey and not reddish, and tip of tail not conspicuously black. Two other forms have been described in southern Africa: *H. nigratus* (Kaoko-veld, South-West Africa), very dark, with a broad black line on middle of back, and tail with a blackish tip; *H. shortridgei* (southern Angola), general coloration chestnut red, tip of tail black. They probably are to be considered respectively as melanistic and erythristic varieties of *pulverulentus*.

Habitat: Savanna. Map, p. 139.

Habits: Mainly diurnal, the Cape Grey Mongoose usually lives singly or in pairs, sometimes in small family groups. It may be seen sunning itself on top of rocks among which it takes refuge. Normally terrestrial, it may climb trees. It feeds on smaller animals of any kind, from hares, ground-squirrels, and springhares to small rodents, lizards, snakes, young birds, birds' eggs and insects.

SLENDER MONGOOSE   *Herpestes* (*Galerella*) *sanguineus* Rüppell
(Lesser Mongoose)   p. 112
F Mangouste rouge, M. naine   A Rooimuishond   G Rotichneumon
Identification: Length (without tail) 12–15 in.; weight 1½ lb. A small and slender, stoat-like mongoose, appearing like a diminutive of the Egyptian Mongoose, with a pointed head, and a rather coarse and wiry coat. General colour yellowish or reddish brown at a distance, in fact grizzled, each hair being ringed with black and buffy brown. Head somewhat greyer. Underparts buff. Tail very long, slender and furry, reddish brown with a conspicuous black tassel at its tip; often held straight up or curled upwards.
Intraspecific variation: There is a large range of intraspecific variation. Some authors distinguish several forms to which they give specific rank, like *cauui, ratlamuchi, ochraceus* and allies. They may be better considered as representing local races or colour phases of a widespread species.
Similar species: May be taken for a Ground Squirrel, as it holds its tail straight up when running.
Habitat: Wide range of habitats, from desert country to dense forest. Particularly rocky places. Map, p. 139.
Habits: The Slender Mongoose lives singly or in pairs and is probably the most frequently seen of all mongooses, being mostly diurnal. Mainly terrestrial, it is able to climb trees. It feeds mainly on rodents (up to ground squirrels) and also on reptiles (snakes), birds' eggs, in addition to insects (orthoptera), larvae and fruits. It may cause damage to poultry.

Young, 2–4 in a litter, are born in hollow trees, rock crevices or holes in the ground. They tame very easily.

POUSARGUES' MONGOOSE   *Dologale dybowskii* (Pousargues)
                                                                                                            p. 112
F Mangouste de Dybowsky   G Listige Manguste
Identification: Length (without tail) 10–14 in. A very small mongoose, with a short snout and a uniform grizzled coloration. Fur short, even and fine. Upperparts dark brown, finely grizzled with yellowish or fulvous to a variable extent. Head darker, distinctly greyer than the back. Underparts lighter, more uniform brownish. Limbs darker, feet almost black. Tail moderately long, well haired at its base, of same colour as the back, with no dark tip.

Similar species: May be confused with the Gambian Mongoose, but has no whitish throat and chest; with the Dark Mongoose, but the fur is much shorter, grizzled and lighter coloured; with the Dwarf Mongoose, but size is larger, and the upperlip entirely haired and not divided by a vertical groove; with the Slender Mongoose, but lacks black tip at tail.
Habitat: Savanna. Map, p. 139.
Habits: Apparently almost nothing is known about the habits of this mongoose which may be at least partly diurnal and hide in hollow trees and termites' mounds. It presumably feeds on insects (termites, grubs, caterpillars).

DWARF MONGOOSE   *Helogale parvula* (Sundeval) and allies   p. 112
(Pygmy Mongoose)
F Mangouste naine   A Dwergmuishond   G Zwerg-Manguste
Identification: Length (without tail) 8–12 in.; weight 1½ lb. A very small mongoose (the smallest of the African species) stockily built, with a short snout. General colour uniform speckled brown or reddish, the hairs being annulated brown and whitish, at a distance appearing dark brown. Underparts somewhat lighter. Feet darker brown. Tail rather short, evenly tapering, not bushy, of the same colour as body, with no black tip.
Allied species: A number of species and local forms of *Helogale* have been described: *hirtula* (Somalia, Ethiopia, north Kenya), *percivali* (Kenya), *undulata* (Somalia, Kenya), others from Uganda, Mozambique and Angola. They are unidentifiable in the field and represent the same type of mongoose all over the savannas of eastern and southern Africa.
Habitat: Dry savanna and woodlands. Map, p. 139.
Habits: Very gregarious, Dwarf Mongoose live in small colonies, up to 15 or even more, taking refuge in the chambers of termitaries or anthills, and also in rock crevices and hollow trees. They are very nomadic and apparently have no fixed place of abode. Diurnal and not especially shy, they may be watched as they peer out from holes or scuttle around. They feed mainly on insects (termites, locusts, beetles), grubs, larvae and spiders, but also on small rodents, reptiles, eggs and young birds. They often attack strategically in mass. Young, 2–4 per litter, are born in holes or hollow trees.

They have a wide vocabulary of bird-like chirrups and whistles, and growl when angered.

DARK MONGOOSE   *Crossarchus obscurus* F. Cuvier   p. 97
(Cusimanse)
F Mangouste brune, Crossarche brune   G Kusimanse
Identification: Length (without tail) 16 in. A small mongoose, with a sharp face and a long projecting and mobile snout, small ears, short legs, a proportionately short tail, and a long, bristly and very coarse coat. General colour uniform dark brown, sometimes almost blackish, lighter

on head and underparts (tips of hairs lighter, giving a very faint grizzled appearance).

Allied species: Two species, closely allied to the Dark Mongoose, have been described:

ALEXANDER'S MONGOOSE (*C. alexandri* Thomas and Wroughton). Larger (length 18 in.); general colour lighter, a coarse mixture of black, brown and pale clay colour. Ubangui and eastern Congo.

ANGOLAN MONGOOSE (*C. ansorgei* Thomas). Smaller (head and body 13 in.); snout not much elongated; general colour sometimes lighter, with a strong tawny suffusion; face cinnamon buff. Only known from the southern Congo and northern Angola.

As yet it is not known whether these two forms represent full species or merely geographical representatives of the Dark Mongoose.

Habitat: Dense high forest. Map, p. 139.

Habits: Gregarious, the Dark Mongoose lives in families or in small parties of up to a dozen or more, which wander in a circular course, returning to the same place from time to time. Very noisy, it has a wide vocabulary of grunting and high-pitched twittering calls. Diurnal, it takes refuge during the night in burrows with several entrances, sometimes dug out in termites' mounds. It is able to climb trees. Both nocturnal and diurnal, it hunts singly, or in parties. It preys on small animals, rodents (up to the cane rat), lizards, birds, eggs, but principally insects and larvae; it eats also berries and other fruits.

NOTE ON *Liberiictis kühni*

Recently the skulls of an undescribed mongoose have been discovered in Liberia and described under the name *Liberiictis kühni*. Skull form and tooth pattern are much like those in *Crossarchus*, but with one premolar more on each side above and below (4 instead of 3); size conspicuously greater. In view of the obvious cranial relationship with *Crossarchus*, we can reasonably expect that this new species might have something of the external appearance of this mongoose. From the dentition, it might be assumed that the diet would be possibly insectivorous. It is hoped that this animal will be met in the flesh in the future. This discovery shows how much is still to be learned in Africa (Hayman, *Ann. Mag. Nat. Hist.* 13, 1, 1958).

BANDED MONGOOSE *Mungos mungo* (Gmelin)   p. 97
F Mangue rayée   A Gebande Muishond
G Gestreifte Mungo, Zebra-Manguste

Identification: Length (without tail) 16 in.; weight 3–5 lb. A small mongoose, well haired, with a coarse and wiry coat, a conspicuous striped pattern and a short tapering tail. Ground colour brownish grey. Behind the shoulder, and becoming more and more definite from the middle of back to the root of tail, a series of conspicuous transverse dark brown bands alternating with light coloured bands of about the same width.

Limbs brownish grey, almost black on feet. Tail bushy at base, then tapering, brownish grey with a blackish tip.

Intraspecific variation: A number of races have been described, varying according to the amount of brown and grey and the intensification of the coloration. As usual, the colour is deeper and more reddish in the more humid habitats.

Habitat: Dry savanna and woodlands, never dense forest, usually not far from water. Map, p. 139.

Habits: Very sociable, Banded Mongoose live in packs of a dozen, sometimes of up to 30–50 individuals. Members of a band often follow one another very closely and move like a huge snake winding here and there among the bush. Very noisy, they have a wide vocabulary of calls to communicate with each other, which includes crooning sounds, high-pitched twittering cries, and when alarmed, a strident chittering. If threatening, they growl or 'spit' like a cat. Sight, hearing and sense of smell are good.

Banded Mongoose are mostly diurnal and look for the sunniest places. They retire at night to warrens, most often recorded in old anthills, or to hollow trees and rock crevices. An entire pack can take refuge in the same shelter. There are several warrens within a pack's territory, between which the pack wanders in an erratic course.

They scratch among dead leaves and under stones for foraging. Insects, grubs and larvae are the most important part of their diet. They feed also on amphibians, reptiles, birds, birds' eggs, rodents, molluscs, as well as on fruits, berries and bulbs.

The exact period of gestation is as yet unknown, but could be about 2 months. The litter is 4–6.

Banded Mongoose are preyed upon mostly by raptorial birds and to a small extent by Lion, Leopard and Wild Dog. Snakes attempt to take some but the pack successfully defend the attacked member and in most cases the snake would be killed. This mongoose is of very mild disposition and is easily tamed.

GAMBIAN MONGOOSE *Mungos gambianus* (Ogilby)   p. 112
F Mangue de Gambie   G Gambiakusimanse

Identification: Length (without tail) 14 in. A small mongoose, with the snout not elongated; body hair coarse, rather short and sparse, lacking underfur. Underparts nearly naked. Upperparts grizzled grey, deep buff and blackish, producing a very coarse grizzled effect. A distinct black stripe on side of neck in strong contrast with the buffy white throat (the only African mongoose with this striking pattern). Underparts golden to deep rusty. Tail moderately long.

Similar species: May be confused with the Dark Mongoose, but lighter and with a much shorter nose; and with the Banded Mongoose, but no dorsal bands. Neck pattern very characteristic.

Habitat: Forested savanna. Map, p. 163.

RED or BUSHY-TAILED MEERKAT[1]   *Cynictis penicillata* (G. Cuvier)
(Yellow Mongoose)   p. 97
F Mangouste fauve   A Geelmeerkat; Rooimeerkat   G Fuchsmanguste
Identification: Length (without tail) 16 in. A small mongoose with a short,
pointed muzzle, and large ears projecting above the head, giving a
triangular shape to the face. Coat fairly long, with thick woolly underfur.
General colour tawny yellowish or orange, brighter on hindquarters,
rarely suffused with greyish. Head greyish fawn, with a white chin. Forelimbs and underparts paler, tawny buff. Tail rather short, thick and bushy,
coloured like the back at its base, becoming conspicuously white towards
the tip.
Habitat: Open country. Map, p. 163.
Habits: This very sociable mongoose lives in colonies or warrens, numbering up to 50 or more individuals, usually in open country; more rarely it
takes refuge in bush or under rocks. It is a great burrower, digging out
underground tunnels and chambers in loose soil. It often associates with
Grey Meerkat and Ground squirrel. Like its relative, it may be seen
sitting up on its haunches or even standing up on the hind legs to have a
better view. Searching for food is done alone or in pairs, during the day,
even during the middle of the day when the weather is cold.
  Hunting alone or in pairs within a radius of a mile or so from its
burrow, it feeds mostly on insects, but also on small vertebrates (up to
hares and game birds). Dung is deposited in certain specific places.
  Young—2–4 in a litter—are born in the burrow.

SELOUS' MONGOOSE   *Paracynictis selousi* (De Winton)   p. 97
F Mangouste de Selous   A Kleinwitstertmuishond   G Trugmanguste
Identification: Length (without tail) 16–18 in.; weight 6 lb. A rather small
but long and slender mongoose (recalling a genet in some ways), with
rather long soft fur. Ears low and wide. Legs fairly long, though the
animal walks in a crouching attitude. Upperparts speckled buffish grey,
the hairs ringed with white, brown and blackish. Top of head browner
than the back, sides of face and forehead whitish. Underparts buffish or
whitish. Hands and feet blackish. Tail fairly long and bushy, tapering
towards its tip, whitish, becoming pure white at the tip.
Habitat: Open country, light woodland. Map, p. 163.
Habits: Selous' Mongoose is assumed to be mainly nocturnal, but may
occasionally be seen in daylight. It lives singly or in pairs. Terrestrial, it is
a burrower and, preferably in sandy soils, excavates underground tunnels
and chambers, with numerous entrances and up to 5 feet deep. It feeds
mostly on insects, particularly locusts, but also on small vertebrates.

[1] This common name derives from some superficial resemblances to monkeys,
due to shape of face, with large eyes and rounded ears.

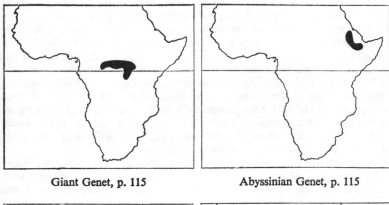

Giant Genet, p. 115

Abyssinian Genet, p. 115

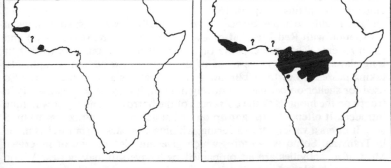

Villiers' Genet, p. 115

African Linsang, p. 116

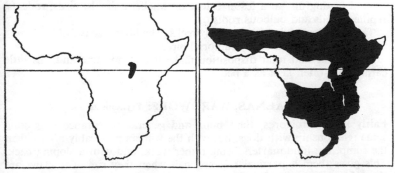

Aquatic Civet, p. 117

White-tailed Mongoose, p. 117

GREY MEERKAT or **SURICATE** *Suricata suricatta* (Erxleben) p. 97
F Suricate A Graatjiemeerkat; Stokstertmeerkat G Surikate
Identification: Length (without tail) 10–14 in. A small mongoose, stockily built, with a narrow and pointed muzzle, and a bulging forehead, very small rounded ears protruding only a little from the fur, very low on the head; a long and soft coat, and a striking pattern. Head and throat dull whitish; ears and conspicuous rings around the eye pure black. General coloration light grizzled fawn with, on the back, from the shoulders to root of tail, a series of dark brown transverse bands, the general effect being of a lozenge-patterned netting. Underparts pale buffy, darker on the lower belly. Limbs buffy yellow. Tail buffish-tawny, proportionately short, not bushy, tapering, with a conspicuous black tip.
Similar species: May be confused with the Banded Mongoose, but shape and pattern of the head very different; the latter with transversal dorsal bands alternating very regularly, instead of the irregular netting of the Grey Meerkat.
Habitat: Dry plains. Map, p. 163.
Habits: Highly sociable, Suricate live colonially in warrens, sometimes in association with Red Meerkat or even Ground Squirrel (*Geosciurus*) and small rodents. They are capable of digging their own burrows with their long claws, but often leave most of the work of excavation to squirrels, taking possession of their burrow system. Crevices among rocks are also used for shelter on occasion. Entirely diurnal, it may be seen gathering in troops on the mounds at the entrances of the burrows, sunning or watching intruders. It often sits straight up on its haunches or even rises on its hind legs. It utters a variety of chattering, whining and barking noises (its name in Transvaal Sotho is *letototo*, which gives an idea of one of its cries). Most of its activities are accompanied by 'conversational' noises. Vision is its most developed sense.

It mostly feeds on insects, grubs, spiders and millipedes captured on the ground or dug up; to a lesser extent on smaller animals, birds, rodents, reptiles, snails and bulbous roots.

The gestation period is about 11 weeks. The litter size is 2–4.

Suricate are preyed on by raptorial birds.

Its sociable and mild disposition make it easy to tame and this little carnivore is often kept as a pet.

HYAENAS, AARDWOLF: Hyaenidae

Fairly large carnivores, their build and general appearance suggesting some relationship with dogs, but with the withers noticeably higher than the rump, the hindquarters being rather weak, and with a sloping back. This gives them a particular loping gait when they run. The claws are short, blunt and non-retractile.

True hyaenas are found through Africa and in Asia. They have a large head with powerful jaws and teeth, which enable them to crush and swallow even the biggest bones with ease. Though they may prey on small mammals and on the young of larger species, occasionally on larger mammals (they are important predators of plains game), their diet consists mostly of carrion, particularly the remains of lion kills. Vultures and jackals compete for carrion, hyaenas taking mainly the bones and other coarse parts with which they are well equipped to deal. Like the other scavengers, hyaenas serve a useful purpose in keeping the country clean.

The Aardwolf is confined to Africa and is often considered as forming a family (Protelidae) by itself. It is small and has very weak, widely spaced teeth, quite unsuitable for chewing meat. It is mainly insectivorous. Some consider it to be a long-degenerate form of hyaena whose diet has changed.

SPOTTED HYAENA *Crocuta crocuta* (Erxleben) p. 113
F Hyène tachetée   K Fisi   G Tüpfel- or Gefleckte Hyäne
A Gevlekte Hiena, Tierwolf

Identification: Height 30–36 in.; weight 100–175 lb. A large hyaena, powerfully built, with very sloping back, a broad and massive head with large eyes, and short rounded ears. Coat short; ground colour very variable, buff to dull grey, irregularly but entirely marked with blackish rounded spots. Face, muzzle and lower parts of limbs dark brown. Throat lighter coloured, unspotted. At a distance seems very dark. A short mane on neck and shoulder. Tail fairly short, with a bushy black tip.

Young blackish, becoming lighter with age; coat shaggy and coarse.

Habitat: All types of savanna, even semi-desert, from sea level up to the snow line in the high mountains. Very rarely in dense forest. Map, p. 167.

Habits: Spotted Hyaena is found all over African savannas south of the tropic of Cancer, in surprisingly high numbers where game is plentiful. Mainly but not entirely nocturnal, it spends the day in thick bush or long grass, in Aardvark holes or in a den among rocky boulders; in plains where there are no natural cavities, it digs out large burrows some 2 to 3 feet below the surface of the soil, 6 feet in width and 5 feet in height. Sometimes more or less sedentary, it follows the game and domestic livestock on their annual wanderings.

It lives singly or in pairs, but also in small packs of up to eight individuals, particularly at a carcass or when mating. Though some gregariousness is observed, it shows little sign of social behaviour, except when several animals together chase a quarry. Hunting packs of over 30 have been recorded.

Very noisy, it has several types of cry, one of which is a most characteristic and gruesome howl which begins as a low hoarse tone and rises sharply to a high-pitched scream, uttered at nightfall when leaving its den. The well known 'laugh', which is peculiar to this species is less often heard; it is made when the animal has found some food, or, with a higher intensity, when mating; it can be very horrible to human ears.

. The sense of smell is very acute and plays the largest part in the life of the hyaena for mutual recognition (in relation to well-developed anal glands) and for finding its way to carrion or other food. But sight is equally important (hyaenas follow vultures to the spot where these birds congregate using them as pointers), as is the sense of hearing.

The Spotted Hyaena is reputed to be a scavenger and actually feeds on carrion, subsisting largely on lion kills. It follows hunting lions and Wild Dogs at a distance and may sometimes force them to leave their kill; but lions, who positively 'hate' hyaenas, keep them away and often kill or mutilate them when they venture too close.

But the Spotted Hyaena is also a proper predator quite capable of pulling down game up to the size of zebra, being the most aggressive of the hyaenas. It forms packs to attack living animals and runs down the victim (attaining a speed of up to about 40 m.p.h.). It kills young, juveniles and even adults of many species, like wildebeest, gazelle and zebra and even lion cubs and young elephant may be attacked. The Spotted Hyaena follows pregnant female antelope and snatches the freshly born young, sometimes killing the female herself when she is in a helpless condition. It kills also domestic stock. It swallows huge pieces of meat and bones, and its powerful jaws and teeth enable it to crack the larger bones and extract the marrow. Owing to the bony nature of its diet, the droppings consist to a large extent of mineral matter; when freshly deposited they are green in colour but become pure white as soon as they dry into hard white balls of crushed bone. Spotted Hyaena defecates in particular open places, conspicuous at a distance, sometimes covering up to a quarter of an acre. According to tribesmen Spotted Hyaena urinates at regular places, showing the dog's 'lamp-post' habit.

Reputed to be cowardly and timid, it can become bold and even dangerous to man, attacking human beings sleeping in the open and causing serious mutilation by biting off the face.

At mating season, the Spotted Hyaena assemble in large meetings, particularly at bright moonlight; the noise is undescribably hideous and a real pandemonium precedes mating. The period of gestation is about 110 days. The litter numbers 1 or 2, sometimes up to 4 (?), young born in burrows. At 6 weeks of age these begin to wander and become independent a few weeks later.

The Spotted Hyaena has few enemies apart from man; lions and Wild Dogs sometimes kill them if they approach too close.

It is widely but quite erroneously believed to be hermaphroditic. This misconception is due to some peculiarities in the external genitalia of the female and to superficial resemblances between the sexes.

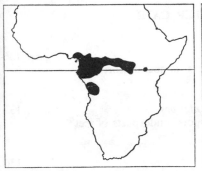

Black-legged Mongoose, p. 117

Bushy-tailed Mongoose, p. 118

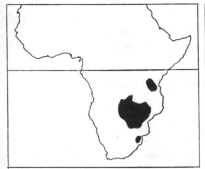

Meller's Mongoose, p. 118

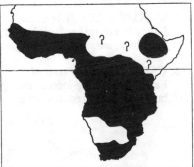

Marsh Mongoose, p. 120

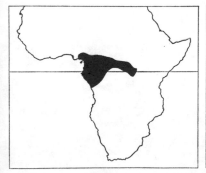

Long-snouted Mongoose, p. 120

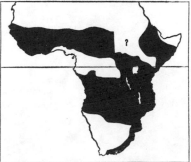

Egyptian Mongoose, p. 121

Plate 21   SMALLER CATS

1. **SAND CAT** *Felis margarita*   *page* 136
   Small; broadened face; broad ears; almost uniformly
   sandy buff.

2. **BLACK-FOOTED CAT** *Felis nigripes*   137
   Small; tawny, with large black spots; underparts of feet
   profusely black.

3. **WILD CAT** *Felis libyca*   136
   Larger; indistinct vertical stripes and spots; tail
   proportionately long.

4. **SWAMP CAT** *Felis chaus*   136
   Fairly large; rather long-legged; no conspicuous
   markings; ears pointed; tail proportionately short.

5. **CARACAL** *Felis caracal*   138
   Fairly large; long-legged; ears pointed, with long black
   tassel; uniform reddish fawn.

1a

1b

1a

2b

2a

2a

MEDIUM-SIZED CATS Plate 22

1. **SERVAL** *Felis serval* *page* 137
   Slender; long-legged; large oval ears; short tail.
   Two colour phases:
   1a. *Serval*. Stripes and large spots. 137
   1b. *Servaline*. Small spots and dots; speckled appearance. 138

2. **GOLDEN CAT** *Felis aurata* 138
   Robustly built; ears rounded; tail long. Highly variable in
   colour; generally reddish brown (2a); sometimes greyish
   or blackish (2b); dark spots more or less conspicuous.

STRIPED HYAENA   *Hyaena hyaena* (L.)   p. 113
F Hyène rayée   K Fisi   G Streifenhyäne
Identification: Height at shoulder 27–30 in.; weight 120 lb. A smaller hyaena with sloping back, massive head and long pointed ears. Coat long, harsh and fairly shaggy; a well developed erectile mane from the nape to the rump. Ground colour from buff to grey, with black transverse stripes all over the body; numerous transverse stripes on legs. Throat mainly black. Tail long and very bushy.
Young the same colour as adult.
Habitat: Also North Africa (still to be found in small numbers in Morocco), south-western Asia and India. Arid savanna. Map, p. 167.
Habits: The Striped Hyaena lives singly or in pairs, more rarely in small packs. It is not as noisy and aggressive as the Spotted Hyaena. Almost entirely nocturnal, it usually remains hidden by day in dense bush or preferably in crevices between rocks or in old Aardvark burrows. Like the Spotted Hyaena, it is a scavenger feeding on carrion, but devouring almost everything and killing small stock in case of necessity. Although living in a dry habitat, Striped Hyaenas drink regularly and wander great distances.

BROWN HYAENA   *Hyaena brunnea* Thunberg   p. 113
F Hyène brune   G Schabrackenhyäne   A Strandwolf, Strandjut
Identification: Height at shoulder 28–32 in.; weight 125 lb. A large hyaena, slightly smaller than the Spotted Hyaena, with some of the features of the Striped Hyaena. Shorter muzzle; long, extremely pointed ears and a distinctly sloping back. Coat coarse and very shaggy, fairly plain coloured, entirely dark blackish brown, except on neck, shoulder and upper back where the long, lighter tawny hairs form a kind of mantle. Some inconspicuous and ill-defined stripes, more clearly visible on legs. Tail bushy, fairly longish, entirely dark.
Habitat: Dry savanna. Map, p. 167.
Habits: Very shy and purely nocturnal, the Brown Hyaena lives singly, hiding by day in Aardvark burrows, crevices between rocks or thick cover, where the young (2–4 in a litter) remain hidden. Like its relatives, it is a scavenger, congregating round carcasses where it feeds on remains. Where its range adjoins the coast, it feeds also on dead marine animals and refuse cast up on the sea shore (hence its name of Strandwolf). It may kill for itself young antelope and damage has been reported among domestic stock. Eggs, insects (locusts), fruits sometimes form part of the diet. Brown Hyaena has a melancholic cry, 'wah-wah-wah', but apparently never the distinctive 'laugh' of the Spotted Hyaena, a much more aggressive animal. Like other hyaenas, it is a great wanderer and covers great distances in search of food.
It has suffered from destruction by farmers who regard it as a danger to domestic livestock; it will probably be exterminated, like other predators, in all inhabited areas.

AARDWOLF   *Proteles cristatus* (Sparrman)   p. 113
F Protèle   K Fisi ndogo   G Erdwolf   A Maanhaarjakkals, Erdwolf
Identification: Height at shoulder 18–20 in.; weight 25–30 lb. Superficially an elegant diminutive of a Striped Hyaena, not bigger than a jackal, with slender legs, narrow, long and pointed ears, and a well developed mane along the dorsal spine from neck to tail; this mane is erected in situation of fright or alarm, when the animal appears much bigger and more formidable than it is. Muzzle narrow and elongated. Coat buffish yellow to reddish brown, throat paler, almost white. A few conspicuous vertical dark brown stripes on shoulders, flanks and thighs. Legs marked with irregular black stripes, darkening towards extremities. Tail fairly long and bushy, terminally black.
Similar species: Sometimes confused with the Striped Hyaena, but very noticeably smaller. When viewed under poor conditions, may be mistaken for a jackal, but the rougher coat, smaller head and conspicuous darker stripes are distinctive characters.
Habitat: Open dry plains and thorn scrub; never forest. Map, p. 163.
Habits: Nocturnal, rarely seen in daylight. The Aardwolf lives singly, in pairs, sometimes in family groups. This very shy and elusive animal takes refuge in Aardvark burrows during the day. It secretes a musky strong smelling substance when attacked.

It feeds on insects, mostly termites and larvae, owing to its small teeth and weak jaws. It has been reported sometimes to eat carrion, but there is no good evidence for this. It may eat rodents and eggs. The litter is 2–4 young, 3 being the usual number, born in a burrow. Several females may raise their young together.

CATS, LION, LEOPARD, CHEETAH: Felidae

Highly specialised carnivores, characterised by their shortened head and the reduced number of teeth. Canines always well developed, cheek-teeth adapted for cutting. Distributed over most of the world, this family is well represented in Africa, where three well characterised groups (subfamilies) can be distinguished. The true cats (Felinae), of small or medium size, and very similar in their general features, are anatomically characterised by a bony hyoid apparatus which allows only feeble cries. Lion and Leopard (Pantherinae) on the other hand are not only larger but can roar; this is possible because the vocal apparatus is suspended on a cartilaginous hyoid and can move freely. The Cheetah (Acinonychinae) show un-cat-like characteristics, chief of which is the inability to retract the claws fully.

Felidae are found in every type of habitat, but many species are adapted to particular environments. There are many differences in the method of hunting and in other behaviour patterns, although all are true flesh-eaters.

SAND CAT *Felis margarita* Loche p. 132
F Chat des sables G Saharakatze
Identification: Height at shoulder 10 in. A smaller cat with an apparently broad face, the ears being low on the head and enlarged; coat rather thick and soft, almost uniform. Face whitish; back of ears with black spots; internal face of ears with long white hairs. General colour sandy buff, darker on the back, lighter on the flanks; belly whitish tinged with buff. Markings inconspicuous all over the body. A few dark brownish stripes across the upper parts of the legs; terminal part of tail with blackish rings. Soles of feet with long grey hairs. Young are more strongly marked than the adults.
Habitat: Sandy deserts. Closely related forms occur in Arabia and Turkestan. Map, p. 167.
Habits: Nocturnal, the Sand Cat lives in burrows in dunes under scrub. It feeds on rodents, sometimes on hares and birds. Litters of 4 kittens have been recorded.

AFRICAN WILD CAT *Felis* (*sylvestris*) *libyca* Forster p. 132
F Chat sauvage d'Afrique; Chat ganté K Paka pori, Kimburu
G Afrikanische Wildkatze A Vaalboskat
Identification: Height at shoulder 14 in.; weight up to 14 lb. A cat of the size and features of the domestic cat, sometimes slightly larger. General colour from greyish to buffish or ochraceous, with rather indistinct dark vertical stripes and spots ('tabby'). Paler on underparts. Back of ears reddish to rufous. Upperparts of limbs and legs marked with broad dark bands. Tail proportionately long, but rather shorter than in the domestic cat, with several dark rings near the dark tip.
Intraspecific variation: There is much colour variation in different parts of the range. As a general rule, Wild Cats are darker in forests and humid habitat than in dry country.
Habitat: All types of savannas. Many authors consider that the African Wild Cat is conspecific with the European species (*F. sylvestris*) distributed through Europe and Asia. Map, p. 167.
Habits: Nocturnal, it remains hidden in thick bush, in tall grass or rock crevices during the day. It feeds on birds (particularly guinea fowl, francolins, rails), rodents, snakes and lizards, as well as on hares, young of small antelopes and even poultry and small stock. Insects and fruits form part of its diet.
The call is a harsh 'meeuw'.
Young are born in rock crevices or among dense bushes. The period of gestation is 56 days; the litter is of 2–5. Wild Cats interbreed with domestic cats, which run wild in great numbers.

SWAMP CAT *Felis chaus* Güldenstaedt p. 132
F Chat des marais G Rohrkatze
Identification: Height at shoulder 16 in. A fairly big cat, considerably

larger than the Wild Cat, robustly built, with long legs and a rather short tail. General colour grizzled sandy fawn with no conspicuous markings. Ears red brown with long black hairs at their tips. Face lighter with a brown lacrymal stripe. Dorsal line more richly coloured reddish. Sides of body very indistinctly spotted; lower parts more rufous. Upperparts of legs marked with inconspicuous dark bands. Underparts lighter, buff. Tail greyer than the back with two very narrow black rings close to the black tip.

Similar species: May be confused with the Wild Cat, but size larger and markings less conspicuous.

Habitat: Low marshy ground, reed beds, sugar cane and other fields. Also Asia from Caucasus and Turkestan to India and Indochinese peninsula. This cat, extra-limital, is confined in Africa to the Nile Delta and valley to a short distance south of Cairo, to the Ahaggar Mountains and probably to the Tassili N'Ajjer.

BLACK-FOOTED CAT *Felis (Microfelis) nigripes* Burchell p. 132
F Chat à pieds noirs A Swartpootwildekat G Schwartzfusskatze
Identification: Height at shoulder 10 in. A small cat, slightly smaller than a domestic cat, with ovate and obtuse ears and rather short legs. General colour tawny, lighter on the underparts. Coat profusely marked with large black spots, rather long and neither annulated nor ocellated, elongated into transverse stripes on shoulder. Three black bands around the legs; underparts of feet black. Tail comparatively short, bushy, spotted with a black tip.

Similar species: May be confused with the common Wild Cat, but the pattern and the large spots should easily distinguish it.

Habitat: Dry country. Map, p. 167.

Habits: Little is known on the habits of this rare little cat which takes refuge in holes in the ground and sometimes occupies old hollow termite heaps and is hence known locally as 'Ant-hill tiger'. It probably feeds on ground squirrels, small rodents, birds and small reptiles, but also larger prey. The litter is of 2–3 kittens.

SERVAL *Felis (Leptailurus) serval* Schreber p. 133
F Serval, 'Chat-tigre' K Mondo G Serval A Tierboskat
Identification: Height at shoulder 22 in.; length (without tail) 28 in.; weight 30–40 lb. A large cat, much larger than the domestic cat, rather slenderly built with a proportionately small head, large oval upstanding ears, elongated legs and a short tail, ringed with black. Coat yellowish buff, heavily marked with black spots, bands and stripes. Underparts whitish or buffy.

Intraspecific variation: Two well defined types are to be distinguished. The typical Serval has stripes on shoulder and back, tending to break up into rows of spots, and large spots on the sides. The number of lines and spots varies according to local races, which are not distinguishable from each other in the field.

The Servaline or Small-spotted Serval, restricted to West Africa (sometimes called *F. servalina* or *brachyura*), shows the same general features, but the coat is greyer and marked with minute spots or dots, giving a speckled appearance to the animal. Formerly considered as a distinct species, the Servaline is a mere colour phase, particularly frequent in Guinean savannas and on the fringe of the forest. Both types may occur in the same litter.

Habitat: Open savannas, from lightly bushed country to forests, particularly near marshy places or rivers. Also on high mountain moorlands. Map, p. 175.

Habits: Nocturnal, sometimes partly diurnal. Serval prey on various small animals, from lizards and rodents (cane rats), hares, and birds (guineafowl) to Duikers and Oribis. They are reputed also to eat fish and vegetable matter. They may be destructive of poultry and small stock. Although terrestrial, as shown by its long legs, it can easily climb trees. The litter is 2–4; young are born in an old antbear or porcupine burrow or in a crevice among rocks.

The call is a high-pitched plaintive cry 'how . . . how . . . how . . .'.

GOLDEN CAT   *Felis (Profelis) aurata* Temminck   p. 133
F Chat doré   G Goldkatze

Identification: Height at shoulder 20 in.; length (without tail) 30 in. A fairly big cat, robustly built, about twice the size of a domestic cat, with rather short legs and a long tail. Ears rounded, blackish outside. Coat short and soft, highly variable in colour; generally deep golden reddish brown, with underparts lighter, sometimes almost whitish; but some individuals are greyish-blue or even blackish. Dark spots generally conspicuous on belly, sometimes obsolete; exceptionally dark spots all over the body.

Similar species: Easily distinguished from the Caracal and the Serval by completely different features, shape of ears and proportion of tail.

Habitat: Closely related to the Asiatic Golden Cat (*F. temmincki*) with which it is probably conspecific. High forest and edge of the Guinea savanna, sometimes high up the mountains. Map, p. 175.

Habits: Almost nothing is known on the habits of this rare and crepuscular cat, very elusive even when present in numbers in some parts of its range. It feeds on rodents, birds and dassies.

CARACAL   *Felis (Lynx) caracal* Schreber   p. 132
(African Lynx)
F Caracal   K Simbamangu   G Karakal   A Rooikat

Identification: Height at shoulder 18 in.; length (without tail) 30 in.; weight 35–40 lb. A fairly big and robustly built cat, with the proportions of a lynx, with a flat head, and long legs, the hind limbs longer than the fore limbs. Coat thick and soft, uniform reddish fawn to brick red-brown

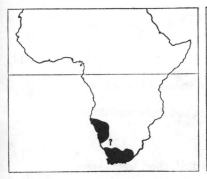

Cape Grey Mongoose, p. 121

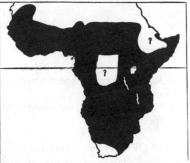

Slender Mongoose, p. 122

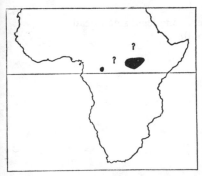

Pousargues's Mongoose, p. 122

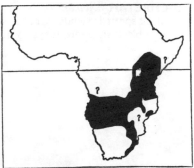

Dwarf Mongoose, p. 123

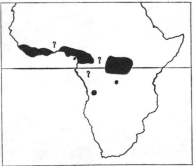

Dark Mongoose, p. 123

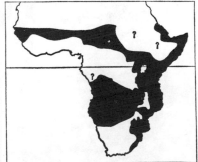

Banded Mongoose, p. 124

Plate 23   BIG CATS

1. **LION**   *Panthera leo*   *page* 142
   Uniform ochraceous; black tuft at tip of tail.
   Male: Larger; mane on neck and shoulder (sometimes absent).
   Female: Smaller; no mane; flanks and limbs sometimes spotted.

2. **LEOPARD**   *Panthera pardus*   144
   Black spotted; long and stout bodied; short legs; long tail.

3. **CHEETAH**   *Acinonyx jubatus*   145
   Black spotted; slenderly built; very long legs; small head, with black stripe from eye to mouth.

1

♂

♀

2

3

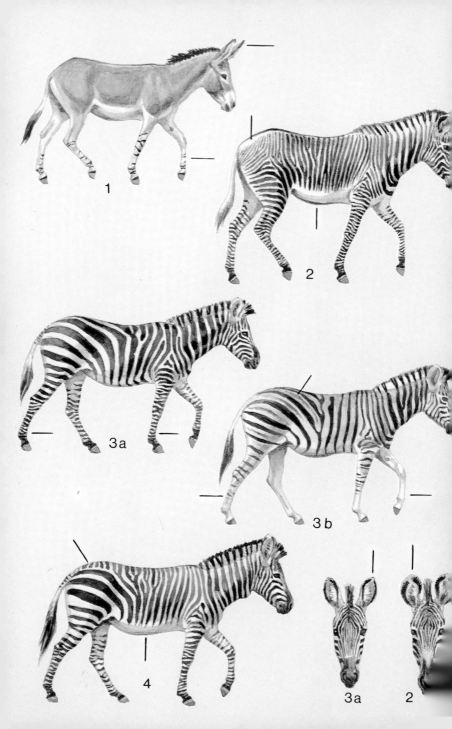

1. **WILD ASS** *Equus asinus* (*somalicus*)   *page* 159
   Long ears; uniform greyish buff with either dark band on
   shoulders or stripes on legs.

2. **GREVY'S ZEBRA** *E. grevyi*   159
   Black stripes numerous, narrow and almost vertical on
   body; white area on rump; white belly; broad, rounded
   ears.

3. **BURCHELL'S ZEBRA** *E. burchelli*   162
   Black stripes less numerous, down to the belly, broad
   and oblique on hindquarters; ears short and rather
   narrow.

   3a. **GRANT'S ZEBRA** *E. b. böhmi*   162
       Ground colour white; legs striped to the hooves.

   3b. **CHAPMAN'S ZEBRA** *E. b. antiquorum*   164
       Ground colour buffy; "shadow stripes"; legs in-
       completely striped.

4. **MOUNTAIN ZEBRA** *E. zebra*   165
   Black stripes numerous and narrow; narrow transversal
   bands across rump ("grid-iron"); white belly; long and
   pointed ears.

with a vinaceous tinge, sometimes darker and even entirely blackish. No stripes or spots. Ears long, sharp and pointed, blackish outside with a long tassel of black hairs. On the face, some white markings, contrasting with a black stripe from eye to nose and a black spot on side of muzzle. Faint indications of spots on the underparts, which are lighter, whitish. Tail short, notably shorter than in any other African cat.

Kittens like the adults, but duller and greyer.

Habitat: All types of savanna; never in dense forest. Also northern Africa, Arabia, the Near East and India. Map, p. 175.

Habits: Little is known on the habits of the Caracal which is mainly nocturnal. It often lives in hilly country where it takes refuge among boulders during the day. It is a good climber. It feeds on various mammals, from small or young antelopes to rodents, hares, dassies and birds, often caught in flight by springing up at them, also on lizards. It may be destructive to small stock and poultry.

The young are hidden in crevices or hollow trees; the litter is 2–4, sometimes 5.

LION *Panthera leo* (L.)   p. 140
F Lion   K Simba   G Löwe   A Leeu

Identification: Height at shoulder 40 in.; length (without tail) up to 100 in.; weight 270–450 lb. Unmistakable. Coat short and uniform, varying from ochraceous silvery-grey to dark ochre brown, somewhat darker on the head. Underparts lighter. Black marks on the back of the ears. Only males have a mane on neck and shoulders, of very variable extent (sometimes with a fringe along the belly) and development, the colour varying from silvery blond through ochraceous and rufous to blackish. Many Lions have no mane or only a very reduced one. Tufts of long hairs on the elbow. Tail rather long, with a black tuft, peculiar to the lion among Felidae.[1]

Lioness notably smaller and more lightly built, maneless; underparts from throat to abdomen almost white.

Cubs with brindled markings, ochraceous rosette-like spots and stripes; coat much more woolly than that of an adult; ears proportionately much larger. The spots disappear progressively with age, but remain visible in sub-adults on the flanks and limbs, particularly in lioness. Young males soon grow whiskers and tufts of hairs on neck and shoulders. The mane takes 4–5 years before reaching full development.

Intraspecific variation: A number of races have been described. They are questionable and there is a wide range of individual variation among the same population, especially in regard to the development of the mane, the size and retention of body spots in adulthood. Generally speaking, at higher altitudes and in colder climates, Lions grow larger and develop darker manes than in warmer regions. The Lions of North Africa and of

[1] A curious horny spur is concealed in the tuft.

the southernmost portion of the continent, both extinct, had a well developed mane, very dark coloured, almost black.

Habitat: Open and lightly wooded grassland, even in montane grassland, up to 10,000 feet. Sometimes subdesert country. Only exceptionally in dense forest. Also formerly widely distributed from North Africa and Asia Minor to India; now limited to the Gir Forest, Kathiawar, India. Map, p. 175.

Habits: Very sociable and rarely seen alone, Lions live together in family groups (prides), with one or several adult males, females and a majority of sub-adults or young; groups numbering up to 30 are sometimes observed. Each group has a wide home range within which it wanders with no regularity. There is no territorial behaviour. They may move on 20 miles a night.

Though hunting mainly during the night, they are more diurnal than any other cat, except where they are disturbed. They spend the heat of the day sleeping under trees and bushes and rarely climb trees, except young lions; they have a strong reputation of being naturally lazy. When fed, they do not trouble the herbivorous species on which they prey, these grazing quietly, sometimes at relatively close quarters.

The sense of smell is good; hearing and sight are excellent. The voice is the well known roar, which can be heard up to 5 miles away; this characteristic call is heard mainly at sunset and before dawn, rarely during the day.

Lions prey on various herbivorous animals from small antelopes and impala to young hippo and elephant, zebra, hartebeest, wildebeest, and also on crocodiles and snakes. Adult giraffe and full grown buffalo may be killed when the Lions attack in a group. Warthogs may be dug out of their burrows. Generally they prey on large species, but old or sick Lions prey on smaller mammals, birds and even rats. Cattle and even man may be taken, and some Lions become 'man-eaters'. The choice of prey is not solely influenced by its relative abundance, for the Lion prefers to hunt certain species rather than others, when the choice offers. The most favoured species as a prey varies from region to region.

Lions hunt by sight and sound, rather than by smell. They approach the quarry, often in the proximity of drinking places, crouching low on the ground and when at close quarters springing on to the back and breaking the neck with their powerful forelegs or killing by strangulation. They never race their quarries like Cheetah, their speed not exceeding 40 m.p.h. They may hunt singly but more often a pride hunts by means of a combined operation, some individuals driving the quarry downwind towards an ambush in which one of them, generally a female, is hidden. Lionesses do the killing more frequently than male Lions. They do not kill every day; the average number of kills per year is sometimes as low as 20 for each Lion. After feeding they usually drink quantities of water.

The Lion is polygamous and the Lioness comes into season every few weeks all the year round. The average period of gestation is 105 days. The cubs—2 to 4 per litter, sometimes up to 6—are born in a hide among dry grass and rocks. Weighing about one pound at birth, they are carefully nursed by the mother. They are very playful. They are weaned at 10 weeks and begin to be independent at one year, but normally remain with their mother until 18 months or so. Mortality rate is very high until 2 years of age, particularly for the males. They are not fully adult before 3 years and may live up to 30 years.

Lions, the most powerful flesh-eaters, are on the top of food chains and have no natural enemy, except man and to a limited extent Wild Dogs.

LEOPARD *Panthera pardus* (L.) p. 140
F Léopard K Chui G Leopard A Luiperd

Identification: Height at shoulder 28 in.; length (without tail) up to 50 in.; weight 110–180 lb. Unmistakable. A big cat, with very elegant shape, powerfully built; body long with comparatively short, stout legs. Coat dense and soft, rather short, marked with numerous black spots, in the form of 'rosettes', on a buff or yellowish-tawny ground colour. Broken bands across the chest. The colour merges into an even grey when seen at a distance. Back of ears black with a conspicuous median white spot. Underparts and inner sides of limbs pure white, less densely spotted. Tail long, spotted, without terminal tuft. Some individuals are black all over.

Female similar to the male, but smaller and more lightly built.

Cubs have dark woolly fur, the spots very close and rather indistinct.

Intraspecific variation: A large number of races have been described from different parts of the range. They are not recognisable in the field and there is a large range of individual variation. The coat is lighter in open country, darker and more heavily spotted in forest where Leopards are often smaller.

Habitat: Very varied habitats from dense forest to open dry country, even on the Saharan border, and up to great altitudes on the East African mountains.[1] Frequently fairly dense bush in rocky surroundings. Also in North Africa, Asia. Map, p. 175.

Habits: Solitary, except during the mating season when male and female live side by side. Small groups of up to 6 may occasionally be observed. Leopards hunt entirely by night and hide during the day among thick bush, rocks, caves or Warthog burrows. They climb trees with the facility of cats, and often spend the day sleeping on a branch up to 15 feet above the soil. They are more silent and cunning than lions. They prey on a wide range of birds and mammals, from francolins and guineafowl to big rodents, tortoises, hares, dassies, Warthogs, River Hogs and smaller antelopes (Impala—their main diet in the Kruger N.P.—Waterbuck, Wildebeest, Duiker, Gazelle, Steenbok, etc.); they are particularly partial to monkeys

---

[1] The body of a Leopard has been found on Mt Kilimanjaro, preserved frozen in the ice.

and baboons. They may also take fish, poultry, cattle (goats and sheep) and especially dogs. The victim is generally seized by the neck and the backbone broken at this level. They carry their prey into a tree, up to 15 ft from the ground, being very agile in trees from which they often spring on their victim. They drink each day, as do most of the carnivores.

The gestation period is 3 months. The litter numbers 2–3 cubs. Although they often kill domestic animals, Leopard are on the whole beneficial to man. They are particularly fond of animals harmful to crops, above all baboons. Thus they play an important role in maintaining the balance of nature and limiting the number of these Primates.

The high price of the skins has resulted in large numbers of Leopards being slaughtered all over Africa.

CHEETAH *Acinonyx jubatus* (Schreber)   p. 140
F Guépard   K Duma   G Gepard   A Jagluiperd
Identification: Height at shoulder 30 in.; length (without tail) 50 in.; weight 100–140 lb. Unmistakable, the 'greyhound of the cats'. A big hollow-backed cat with canine features, looking like a slender leopard with extremely long and thin legs and a small rounded head. Ears short. General colour tawny to pale buff, lighter, almost white on belly. On the head, a characteristic black stripe from the eye to the mouth. Coat rather rough, entirely covered with small solid round black spots, scattered singly and not grouped in 'rosettes' like those of the leopard; less conspicuous on the underparts. On the neck and shoulders, the hair is thicker, forming a slight wiry mane. Tail long, spotted for its greater part, the spots uniting into bands near the rather bushy tip which is white.

Female similar to the male, but smaller and mane less developed.

Cubs at first smoky grey, with long woolly hair and no markings, then becoming yellowish on flanks and limbs and spots more pronounced.
Intraspecific variation: A different 'species', the King or Striped Cheetah (*rex*) has been described from Rhodesia; it is characterised by long, broad stripes, very irregular in shape and length, longitudinal on the back and diagonal on the flanks. In fact it is a mere individual variant or phase of the normal type.
Habitat: Open and semi-arid savannas, occasionally fringes of Guinea savannas, but never forested country. Also in Asia, from Turkmenia and Iran to Arabia; formerly in India where it is now believed extinct. Map, p. 175.
Habits: Cheetah lives singly or in small parties numbering up to 6 individuals. It hunts in daylight, mostly in the morning and evening, sometimes also on moonlit nights (sight is the most important sense). Unlike other cats, instead of hiding near a water hole or along a game track, it quietly approaches its intended prey, then runs it down, being the swiftest animal in the world (speeds up to 75 m.p.h. have been recorded

over short distances, for the Cheetah is essentially a 'sprinter'[1]). The technique is to approach the quarry as closely as possible, then to dart in pursuit, overthrowing the quarry by a side attack and seizing it by the throat. It mainly preys on young or smaller antelopes (Gazelle, Oribi, Impala, Grysbuck), Warthog, hares and also on birds (guineafowl, bustards, ostriches). The capture of larger prey (Waterbuck, Topi, Wildebeest, etc.) is through the fact that Cheetah may hunt in groups. Leopard and Cheetah prey on the same animals but they do not really enter into competition for food, for the Leopard haunts areas with trees or bush or riverine galleries, whereas the Cheetah favours the open plains.

Cheetah are rather silent creatures, uttering a 'chirruping' sort of cry and growling when angered. They purr like cats.

The period of gestation is about 95 days, and the average number in a litter is 2 to 4. Cub mortality is apparently high.

Cheetah are not of a ferocious disposition and have been tamed and used for hunting in Asia for centuries.

Cheetah are timid creatures, unable to withstand changing conditions and increased disturbance. As a result they have been exterminated in much of southern and north Africa,[2] and have become extremely localised throughout the remainder of their range.

[1] The length of the legs and the shape of the claws, which are blunt, only slightly curved and partially retractile, seem adaptations to fast running.

[2] They have not been observed in India since 1948 and are now believed to be extinct throughout their former Asiatic range, except in Iran, Turkmenia and perhaps Afghanistan.

ORDER Sirenia

DUGONG: Dugongidae MANATEE: Trichechidae

Large aquatic mammals, with a long, fusiform body, fore limbs transformed into flippers; no hind limbs. No dorsal fin. Tail transformed into a broad horizontal rudder. Head rounded, massive and heavy, with no external ears, terminated by a broad obtuse snout with a median vertical groove; upper lip forming a labial disk; nostrils separate and with valvules. Mammae located on either side behind the anterior limbs (which has given rise to the legend of mermaids).

May be confused with Pinnipeds'[1] but shape of head quite different; or with Cetaceans, but no dorsal fin. The similarities are superficial ones, due to convergences in adaptation to an aquatic life. The order Sirenia is divided into two families: the Dugong (Dugongidae) and the Manatees (Trichechidae). They occur in fresh and in marine waters along certain tropical coasts.

DUGONG *Dugong dugon* (P. L. S. Müller)
F Dugong G Dugong

Identification: Length 8–10½ ft; weight 400 lb. or more. A large animal with fore limbs developed as flippers with no rudimentary nails. Tail broadly notched into a pair of flukes. In the male, short enlarged tusks. Skin almost naked, sparsely dotted with coarse short bristles; front of the mouth and lower lip covered with thick short bristles. Grey-brown above, underparts whitish grey.

Habitat: Distributed widely through the Pacific and Indian Oceans, from the Red Sea to east coasts of Africa and Madagascar; coasts of Indian Peninsula, to Formosa, the Philippines and north-east Australia. Marine waters along the coasts and a short distance into estuaries. Map, p. 185.

Habits: Dugong live sometimes alone, but more often in family groups of 3–6; they occasionally assemble in very large herds of up to a hundred or more in the shallow waters off the coastal reefs. Very inoffensive, they feed, mostly at night—though this varies, because Dugong prefer to feed on a rising tide—on green seaweed ('dugong grasses') and marine seed-plants (*Zostera*) growing in shallow waters. The vegetable matter is torn off by the strong bristles of the muzzle and ground between the horny palatal plate and the teeth.

Dugong are said normally to remain below water for 5 to 10 minutes before surfacing to breathe, which they can do only through the nostrils.

---

[1] Two Pinnipeds are to be met along the coasts of Africa: the Monk Seal (*Monachus monachus*) (Mauritania) and the Cape Fur Seal (*Arctocephalus pusillus*) (South Africa).

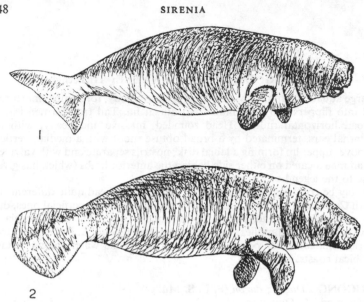

6. Dugong (*Dugong dugon*) (1) and Manatee (*Trichechus senegalensis*) (2)

Senses of hearing, touch and perhaps also of taste are acute, but sight is poor. They have a strong and distinct odour.

Dugong has been heavily hunted for its meat, oil and hide. In spite of being protected by law, its populations have declined very rapidly in most parts of its range.

AFRICAN MANATEE   *Trichechus senegalensis* (Link)
F Lamantin   G Manati
Identification: Length up to 10 ft.; weight up to 1,000 lb. A large animal with fore limbs developed as flippers with rudimentary nails. Upper lip deeply cleft. Body terminated by a horizontal tail, evenly rounded like a paddle. No tusks. Skin almost naked, with the exception of strong bristles on the muzzle. Colour dull grey to blackish.
Habitat: Freshwater lakes and rivers of western Africa; also frequents estuaries and some have been captured along sea coasts. Related species are found in the New World, from south-east United States to north-east South America. Map, p. 185.
Habits: Manatee never come ashore, being incapable of moving on the ground. American Manatee may dive for periods of up to 16 minutes, and

it is probable that the African species does the same. They rest on the surface with the back arched.

Manatee are active throughout the day, but feed mostly at night. Strictly herbivorous, they eat aquatic plants (particularly *Cynodocea*, *Polygonum* and the water hyacinth, *Eichhornia crassipes*) and terrestrial plants hanging over the water (*Rhizophora*). They use their flippers to bring food to the mouth.

One young is born at a time under water and is cared for by the mother for more than a year.

Manatee are seriously threatened throughout most of their range, although protected by law. Unrestricted slaughter for their highly prized meat accounts for the slow but constant decline of their populations.

ORDER Tubulidentata

AARDVARK: Orycteropodidae

The Aardvark constitutes an order (Tubulidentata) by itself with some remote relationship to the hoofed mammals. Its anatomical and biological characters are highly specialised. The teeth are reduced; no incisors or canines; the cheek-teeth are columnar and do not grow simultaneously; those at the front of the jaw develop first, then fall out and are functionally replaced by others farther back. The Aardvark is endemic to Africa.

AARDVARK *Orycteropus afer* (Pallas)
(Antbear)
F Oryctérope   K Muhanga   G Erdferkel   A Erdvark
Identification: Height at shoulder 24 in.; weight 150 lb. An unmistakable animal, the size of a pig, with a massive body and an arched back. Head elongated, terminating in a long tubular snout and a blunt pig-like muzzle. Tongue often protruding. Ears very long, tubular and pointed. A rather short but strong and muscular tail, thick at its base, pointed and conical (somewhat like a kangaroo tail). Limbs short and powerful, with four toes on the forefeet, five on the hindfeet, each with a huge straight claw. Walks on the sole of the foot in a plantigrade manner. Thick skin scantily covered with bristly hairs, dull brownish grey, darker on limbs but often coloured by the earth. Tail sometimes lighter.
Habitat: Open savanna, dry country and light forest; mostly on sandy or clay soil where digging is easy. Map, p. 185.
Habits: Aardvark ('earth-pig') live alone but the young accompanies its mother for a long time. They are very active burrowers, digging into the ground with an amazing speed, and very powerful. During the day, they take refuge in deep burrows. Females are attached to a particular place to which they come back regularly; males seem more vagabond. The burrows may be simple holes with a single entrance, or may form a complicated maze of galleries with up to 20–30 openings, spread over an area of 500 sq. yards. The tunnel ends in a large chamber. Abandoned burrows are used as shelters by a large variety of other animals, from small reptiles, snakes, bats, small carnivores, ground squirrels and owls to Warthogs; they are thus of considerable ecological significance. Nocturnal (rarely active by day), they come out at dusk and are active mainly during the darkest nights. They seem to be almost blinded by daylight.

Aardvark feed exclusively on termites and ants, except for some succulents or fruits (wild cucumbers) which they are said to consume. With their powerful claws, they dig out the termite mounds and catch the insects with their long protractile tongue, wettened with viscous saliva. They go from one termite mound to another, covering as much as 10 miles

7. Aardvark (*Orycteropus afer*)

a night, but rarely visiting the same one on successive nights. They also take termites, as these insects move in long columns by night. They make a hole to deposit their excreta, then cover them up carefully with earth.

Their sight seems poor, but hearing and sense of smell are acute. Generally slow in their movements, they can run fast and are ferocious fighters when cornered. The period of gestation is about 7 months. Only one young is born at a time.

The natural enemies are the Lion and the Leopard.

Although the Aardvark is common in open country where termites abound, its nocturnal habits make it difficult to observe.

ORDER Hyracoidea

HYRAX or DASSIES: Procaviidae

Small and robust animals about the size and with some features of a marmot, a huge guinea-pig or a large rabbit ('rock rabbit' is one of their common names). Head carried on a short neck, with a short and pointed snout and small ears. Legs short and terminated by toes with flattened nails, except for the second digit of the hind foot which has a long curved claw. Soles of the feet are very well adapted for climbing, with firm pads kept continuously moist by a glandular secretion. Tail absent or reduced to a mere stump. Upper incisors well developed, with a wide space between them and the cheek-teeth.

Fur thick, interspersed with long bristles, presumably tactile. On the back is a gland, covered by a patch of hair of a different colour.

Dassies form an order by themselves, and in spite of their rodent-like appearance are more closely related to the elephant than to any other ungulates. Many species have been described, belonging to three genera, two of which are adapted to rocky habitats, the third arboreal. Owing to the scattered, patchy distribution, they have evolved in isolated populations, as local representatives of one of the three genera. Therefore only three species will be listed below, and even these are sometimes difficult to recognise from each other in the field.

Dassies are almost confined to Africa, where they probably originated; only one genus (*Procavia*) is also met in the Near East (the 'coney' of the Bible) and Arabia.

ROCK DASSIE *Procavia capensis* (Pallas) p. 224
F Daman de rocher K Pimbi G Klippschliefer A Klipdas, Dassie
Identification: Height at shoulder 8–12 in.; length 20 in.; weight 5–9 lb. A heavily built Hyrax with short and coarse coat, yellowish or greyish brown, more or less grizzled with black; flanks lighter. In the middle of the back a patch of erectile hairs, varying from black (southern Africa) to yellowish (eastern and western Africa), conceals a naked space (glands). Some forms show two colour phases, a darker and a yellowish. Underparts buff.
Habitat: Also in the Near East and Arabia. Rocky scrub-covered places in savanna, sometimes in very dry country; never in dense forest. Map, p. 185.
Habits: Extremely sociable, Rock Dassies live in colonies of up to 60 individuals, established on rocky hills or among boulders. The colony is made up of family units, with a single adult male, females and young. They climb rocks very easily and jump from one to another, their feet having semi-elastic, rubber-like pads which give the animals purchase on steep slopes. Entirely diurnal but also coming out on moonlit nights, they are

152

very fond of sunning themselves on top of rocks. Some individuals—apparently mostly old males—watch and warn the others at the approach of a potential enemy. When alarmed, they dash into the depth of a rocky cleft or under boulders. Their sense of sight and hearing is very keen. For intercommunication they have an extensive range of sounds, largely comprising warning and alarm cries. The commonest call is a high pitched mewing note, audible at great distances.

Exclusively vegetarian, they feed mostly on grass but also on berries, small fruits, bark, lichens and leaves (even latex-bearing fig leaves). They feed in close proximity to their haunts, but when vegetation becomes scarce they may venture farther, though never far from rocks to hide in case of danger. They drink very little, but may travel distances of up to 700 yards in search of fluid.

Dassies usually defecate and urinate in specific spots, where the droppings accumulate.[1]

The period of gestation is 7 months (abnormally long for an animal of this size). Two or three young, sometimes even up to six, are born at a time, in a shelter under rocks; they are active shortly after birth, and are cared for by the whole colony.

Rock Dassies are preyed upon by Leopard, Wild Dog, eagles and other large birds of prey, and also mongooses. Owing to the destruction of their natural enemies, they have increased enormously in some districts and have become a nuisance.

YELLOW-SPOTTED DASSIE *Heterohyrax brucei* (Gray) p. 224
F Daman de steppe, Daman gris A Geelkoldas K Pimbi
Identification: Height at shoulder 12 in.; length 18 in.; weight 9 lb. A Hyrax with short and coarse coat, usually brown mixed with whitish and black; flanks lighter. Generally a conspicuous white patch above the eye. On the middle of the back, a wide patch varying from white and yellowish to chestnut, concealing a naked spot (glandular area). Underparts whitish.
Habitat: Rocky places, savanna and mountains, up to 11,000 feet. Map, p. 185.
Habits: Yellow-spotted Dassies live in colonies, sheltering in rock crevices, and abandoned termites' mounds. They are mostly diurnal and enjoy sunning themselves on boulders or chasing each other in play. Very alert and agile, they seek refuge among rocks when alarmed, uttering shrill screams. They are also to some extent arboreal. Their senses of hearing and sight are very keen.

They feed, mostly in the early morning and in the evening, on grass, bulbs and roots, also on certain insects (locusts).

The period of gestation is about 7 months and the young are active a few hours after birth.

---

[1] In former times these were used as medicine (*hyraceum*) in epilepsy, convulsions and women's diseases.

Their natural enemies are pythons, leopards, mongooses and birds of prey.

TREE DASSIE   *Dendrohyrax arboreus* (A. Smith)   p. 224
F Daman d'arbre   K Perere   G Baumschliefer   A Bosdas
Identification: Height at shoulder 12 in.; length 16–24 in.; weight 9 lb. A Hyrax with long, thick and often soft coat, dark brown, sometimes almost blackish. In the middle of the back is a wide patch of white hairs concealing a naked area (glands).
Similar species: In life the three Dassies are so much alike that it is almost impossible to differentiate between them in the field (the three genera are distinguished by cranial and skeletal characters). Moreover they show a wide range of variation according to localities, particularly in intensity of coloration and in colour of dorsal spot.

In western Africa, where the Yellow-spotted Dassie does not occur, the Tree Dassie is distinguished from the Rock Dassie by its much darker coat. In southern Africa, the Rock Dassie has the dorsal patch blackish, while in the Yellow-spotted and the Tree Dassies it is yellowish. In eastern Africa, where the three species coexist, it is almost impossible to distinguish between the living animals. The Yellow-spotted Dassie generally has conspicuous spots above the eye.

Habitat: Forests up to 14,500 ft. Races restricted to high mountains (*ruwenzorii, adolfi-friederici*) live among rocky boulders. Map, p. 185.
Habits: With some remarkable exceptions (see below), Tree Dassies are arboreal and nocturnal and are less gregarious than the other species. They live in hollow trees or dense foliage, sometimes very high up, remaining hidden during the day and descending at dusk to feed. They walk with some difficulty, but climb with great ease, which is surprising in an animal lacking particular anatomical adaptations to arboreal life.

After dusk and in the early morning, they utter very loud cries (louder and harsher than those of the Yellow-spotted Dassie), rising to a piercing scream (an ascending scale terminating on a false note). These sounds appear to be emitted when the animal ascends or descends the trees.

They feed only on vegetable matter, mostly leaves of Leguminosae, but also certain fruits.

Like Rock Dassies, they always seem to defecate and urinate on the same spot.

The period of gestation is about 7 months. One or two young are born at the same time, rarely three. The young are precocious.

Tree Dassies frequent the cliffs, caves and boulders on the Ruwenzori and on volcanoes of eastern Congo where they live on the upper treeless zones. Thus they fill the niche occupied in other mountains by Rock Dassies. Their habits are there most similar to that of Rock Dassies. They are partly diurnal, and can be seen in the daytime, sitting on rocks.

ORDER Proboscidea

ELEPHANTS: Elephantidae

Elephants are classified in an order by themselves and their characteristics are too well known to need description. Their enormous size, height (almost equal to length) and elongated nose (trunk or proboscis) used to carry air and olfactory stimuli, and as a tool for foraging and handling materials, make them easily recognizable. They are represented by two types, one in south-eastern Asia, the other in Africa. The African Elephant is a much larger animal than the Asian, with wider ears, a flatter, straighter head; larger tusks and a trunk showing two finger-like organs at its tip.

AFRICAN ELEPHANT *Loxodonta africana* (Blumenbach)
F Eléphant d'Afrique   K Tembo, Ndovu   G Afrikanischer Elefant
A Olifant

Identification: Height at shoulder up to 13 feet (females always smaller). Unmistakable. Their most conspicuous external feature is the flexible trunk, a great elongation of the nose. Huge head, with enormous fan-shaped ears (much larger than in the Asiatic Elephant). The upper edge of the ear tends to flop over with increasing age. Elephants, the largest living land mammals, are highly adapted to their mode of living. In spite of their very massive features and a weight from $3\frac{1}{2}$ to over $6\frac{1}{2}$ tons (bulls), locomotion is very easy owing to the shape of the animal, the weight of which rests on pads of elastic tissue. However, having the legs straight with the bones placed vertically one above another, they are quite incapable of leaping. They have highly adapted teeth, with the tusks (upper incisors) which are very variable in length (always smaller in cows). The longest tusk ever measured was 11 ft. $1\frac{1}{4}$ in. long; the heaviest was 226 lb. Most of these giants, the big tuskers being particularly frequent in East Africa, have disappeared through ivory hunting and in many countries one observes a gradual decrease of length and weight of tusks due to selective shooting for sport or ivory. Tusks above 100 lb. are exceptional in most countries of Africa. Tusks show a strong tendency to be asymmetrical and one of them is often more worn than the other, being used as a tool. The tail is long and terminates in a long tuft of coarse hairs.

Intraspecific variation: Two distinct types of African Elephants formerly considered as full species can be recognised. The Bush Elephant (*africana*) is larger ($9\frac{1}{2}$ to 13 ft. high at the shoulder) and has large broad ears with a sharply pointed lower lobe. The ears cross on the back of the neck when held against the body. The tusks are longer and are usually curved forwards. The Forest Elephant (*cyclotis*) is smaller ($7\frac{1}{2}$ to 9 ft. at the shoulder) and has smaller rounded ears with less pronounced lappets, and straighter, thinner and shorter tusks, usually projecting downwards. There is undoubtedly intergradation between the two forms.

The status of a third type, the Pygmy Elephant, considered by some as a full species (*pumilio*) is very controversial. Confined to the swampy forests of Gabon and the Congo, it is said to be recognised by its much smaller size, not exceeding 6½ ft. at the shoulder, and very small tusks. They are reputed to live in small herds and to be very aggressive. Their recognition as a different species does not seem justified. According to some authors, they are young animals forming distinct groups. But it is probably better to consider them merely as an ecological subspecies, adapted to an unfavourable habitat and therefore of much smaller size.

Habitat: Formerly northwards to northern Africa, where elephants, still common in Roman times, have disappeared through hunting and conversion of the country to desert. Very small elephants still occur in parts of Mauritania.

From rain and montane forests (bamboo, *Hagenia*, up to 9,000 feet) to subdesert country, but mostly in forested savanna. Usually not far from water owing to the need to drink daily. Map, p. 197.

Habits: Gregarious, elephant live in herds averaging from 10 to 20 head, sometimes up to 50, led by an old female. The composition of herds varies considerably. There is usually a master bull, one or two immatures, and a number of cows and calves of various ages. Bulls lose the herd instinct as they get older and are often solitary. Sometimes, particularly in severe drought, the herds are much larger and number up to several hundreds. However, these gatherings never form a single herd and are merely the congregation of many smaller groups.

Highly sociable, elephant can be very noisy and produce a variety of sounds to communicate. These calls indicate alarm, identification, distress or keeping in touch. Most signals take the form of a rumble issued either through the trunk or mouth. The most alarming noise is a loud, high-pitched trumpeting scream, uttered when the animal is in despair or frightened. When charging, the elephant will often give a shrill trumpeting sound, followed by short, sharp blasts.

They are also capable of rumblings, and it has been suggested that these are produced by the stomach and the digestive processes. Since these noises are controlled at will when elephant are alerted, this explanation seems unlikely, for it would appear impossible for them to control the involuntary muscles of the stomach. It is probable that these noises are made by the vocal organs and that elephant keep in touch with each other by this growl. In addition to sounds, elephant use trunk posture and spreading of ears as expressive behaviour.

The sense of sight is not very developed, but scent and hearing are excellent.

Under normal conditions elephant are tolerant animals, but they can be temperamental and unpredictable. They have very elaborate behaviour-

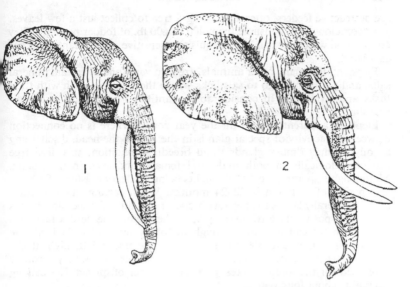

8. Head of Elephants (*Loxodonta africana*): Forest Elephant (*cyclotis*) (1); Bush Elephant (*africana*) (2)

patterns and a high sense of sociability: there are numerous cases of elephant helping a wounded member of the herd to make its escape. Herds are constantly on the move, mostly at night, according to their food requirements. The average walking pace is about 4 m.p.h., but a charging elephant can reach a speed of 25 m.p.h. for a short distance. The causes of these movements analogous to migrations have an alimentary origin, with water playing an important role. Elephant have large water requirements and drink vast quantities daily. They draw up water in the trunk and pour it into the mouth. They also enjoy bathing just as much as dust baths, and will cross rivers deep enough to immerse them completely. Elephant migrations involving hundreds of animals occur sometimes as a result of severe drought.

Much of their time is spent feeding. Very adaptable in diet, they are both grazers and browsers and feed on various vegetable matter, mostly leaves, twigs, terminal shoots, bark, roots and fruits (like those of *Borassus* palms, *Irvingia*, *Pachylobus*, *Sclerocarya* or Mugongo, one of their favourites). They break and fell trees up to 50 inches in diameter and can cause deforestation when the carrying capacity of the habitat is surpassed (overcrowding of elephant has caused damage in the Tsavo N.P., Kenya, and in Parc National Albert, Congo). Sometimes grass (particularly *Pennisetum*) can constitute 80 per cent of their diet. They also may destroy crops, especially banana trees, cassava root, maize and sugar-cane. They are destructive feeders, often uprooting a tree to collect just a few leaves. Very voracious, they consume from 400 to 600 lb. of fodder per day. They collect food with their trunk, an exquisitely sensitive organ adapted for use as a hand.

Elephant, like many other animals, are also very fond of certain mineral salts, and periodically go to salt-licks where they dig out earth with their tusks and swallow it in considerable quantities (? purgative and anti-parasite).

Elephant apparently breed all the year round. There is no connection between the activity of special glands in the side of the head, discharging an oily product ('musk glands') and breeding condition; this discharge occurs periodically in both male and female, and even in the young. Mating fights are rare, most of the fights being made for mastery of a herd. The period of gestation is 22–24 months. When calving, the expectant mother generally leaves the herd with one or two other females and retires to a quiet spot where birth takes place. They rejoin the herd a few days later, when the calf is strong enough to follow the adults. At birth the calves weigh about 270–300 lb. and are a little under 3 ft. high at the shoulder. They are very playful. The maternal instinct is very strongly developed for the mother takes great care of her offspring. The calving interval is about four years.

Elephant are weaned at two years old, and grow until 25 years, sometimes longer; tusks continue to grow later and the cheek-teeth are replaced in a peculiar manner. Elephants reach puberty at about 10–12 years, and full maturity at 18 or more. The normal life span is 60–70 years, some individuals may live longer, possibly up to 120 years. The 'elephant cemeteries' are a myth and remains of dead may be found everywhere through the bush, especially near water where sick animals gather.

Adult elephant have no natural enemies, but young may be attacked by Lions.

ORDER Perissodactyla
(Odd-toed Ungulates)

ASS, ZEBRA: Equidae

Horse-like hoofed mammals, characterised by the reduction of the number of toes to one (adaptation to fast motion on hard soil). Zebra, the only striped Equidae, are confined to Africa, as are the Wild Ass. Wild horses and forms intermediate between horses and asses are found in Asia. All of them are animals of open habitat, sometimes even desertic.

WILD ASS   *Equus (Asinus) asinus* L.   p. 141
F Ane sauvage   K Punda   G Afrikanischer Wildesel
Identification: Height at shoulder 43 in. An ass, with a big head, long ears, white inside. General colour uniform, buff or greyish, with a dark spinal line and a dark band crossing the shoulders. Underparts white. Legs with or without dark stripes.
Intraspecific variation: Two races may be distinguished in Africa. The Nubian Wild Ass (*africanus*) is greyish buff or grey and has no dark markings on the legs. The Somali Wild Ass (*somalicus*) is reddish-fawn; the shoulder-band is ill defined or absent, but the legs are conspicuously marked with dark transverse bands.
Similar species: Wild Ass may be easily confused with feral asses, which are numerous in most of their range as well as in the Sahara. Their plain coloration, similar to the dominant colours of their habitat, their greater size, their extreme wariness and their ability to walk among rocky mountains may help to distinguish them, often a very difficult task.
Habitat: Mountains, broken country and open grass plains. A closely related Wild Ass inhabited North Africa up to the fourth century B.C. This stock has contributed to domestication, probably in Egypt. Map, p. 197.
Habits: Wild Asses are remarkable climbers and move with ease among rocks and cliffs. They retire to the mountains during the day and come down to the valleys to graze at night.

They live singly or in small herds of up to 10 individuals, sometimes up to 30.

The populations have declined very substantially during the last half century, due to overshooting, destruction by herdsmen and competition with domestic livestock in a country where the available pasture is limited. Many have been captured for crossing with domestic stock. A gradual deterioration of the wild strain through inter-breeding with domestic or feral donkeys also occurs.

GREVY'S ZEBRA   *Equus (Dolichohippus) grevyi* Oustalet   p. 141
F Zèbre de Grévy   G Grevy-Zebra
Identification: Height at shoulder 60 in.; weight 780–950 lb. A large zebra,

Plate 25 RHINO, HIPPO

1. **BLACK RHINOCEROS** *Diceros bicornis* *page* 166
Smaller; head short; upper lip triangular.

2. **WHITE RHINOCEROS** *Ceratotherium simum* 169
Larger; head very long; broad square muzzle; massive
hump on neck.

3. **PYGMY HIPPOPOTAMUS** *Choeropsis liberiensis* 172
Small; head relatively small; black.

4. **HIPPOPOTAMUS** *Hippopotamus amphibius* **171**
Huge; head enormous; dark brownish grey, pinkish on
head.

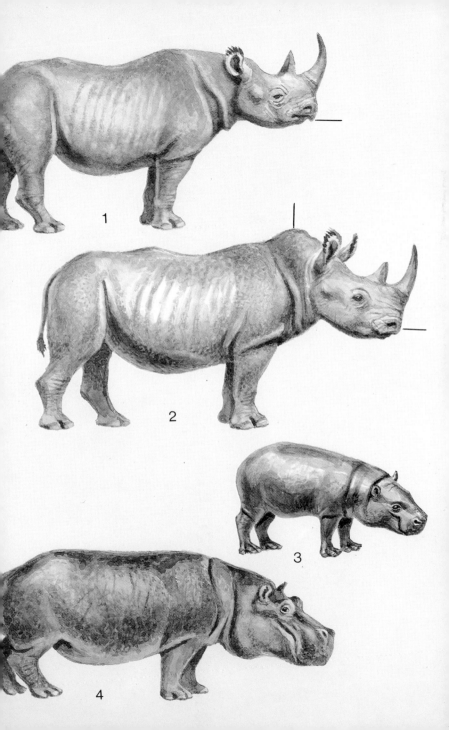

1

2

3a

3b

4

WILD PIG Plate 26

1. **WILD BOAR** *Sus scrofa* *page* 173
Long, pointed head; tusks small.

2. **WARTHOG** *Phacochoerus aethiopicus* 174
Enormous flattened head with warts; coat scarce, except
whiskers and mane; tusks long; tail carried erect when
alarmed.

3. **BUSH-PIG** *Potamochoerus porcus* 178
Elongated face; coat long; ears with tassels; face whitish.

   3a. **WESTERN BUSH-PIG** *P. p. porcus* 178
     Bright rufous.

   3b. **SOUTHERN BUSH-PIG** *P. p. koiropotamus* 178
     Dark brown.

4. **GIANT FOREST HOG** *Hylochoerus meinertzhageni* 179
Large; massive snout; coat long, entirely black.

somewhat resembling a mule, with prominent broad rounded ears, thickly haired on the inner side and with a black margin, except for a white tip. Head long and narrow, especially the muzzle. A brown patch on muzzle, separated from the striped blaze by a white area. A mane of stiff hairs along the neck. General colour white; numerous narrow black stripes, vertical across neck and body to the rump. On the rump and base of tail, narrow black stripes upwardly concave, and never disposed like a 'grid-iron'; a broad blackish brown spinal stripe, extending from the middle of back to the tail, set away from the striping of the sides of rump by a white area. Underparts pure white with no stripes. Legs with numerous narrow transverse stripes down to the hooves.

Similar species: Differs from any zebra of the Burchell's Zebra group, by the larger size, different shape, the size of the ears, and much narrower and more numerous stripes.

Habitat: Subdesert steppe and arid bushland. Map, p. 197.

Habits: Grévy's Zebra are sociable and usually live in small herds of from 4 to 14 individuals; stallions may be solitary; where their range overlaps with that of Grant's Zebra (northern Kenya), mixed herds are formed.

They are grazers, but may take some foliage in addition to grass. They seem less dependent on water than Burchell's Zebra.

Their call is a bray like that of an ass.

BURCHELL'S ZEBRA *Equus (Hippotigris) burchelli* Gray   p. 141
(and related forms)

F Zèbre de Burchell   K Punda milia   G Steppenzebra
A Bontkwagga, Zebra

Identification: Height at shoulder 50–55 in.; weight 500–700 lb. A zebra with horse-like features, without dewlap and with short ears. An upright mane of stiff hairs along the neck. General colour white or buff, with dark stripes, very broad and oblique over the hind parts. Stripes extending very low on the flanks to the belly. No 'grid-iron' pattern at the base of the tail, where the stripes are longitudinal.

Foal with coarser coat, especially on the back; dark stripes brownish.

Intraspecific variation: Burchell's Zebra show considerable geographical variation which has led to description of a number of local races, some distinguishable in the field. The wide range of individual variation (some freaks are even spotted) makes it difficult to delimit populations; it is impossible to find two zebras exactly alike, even in the same herd. There is, however, a general tendency for the stripes on the hindquarters to become less well defined from the north to the south of the range. The following races may be recognised in the field.

GRANT'S ZEBRA (*böhmi*=*granti*) (from southern Sudan, Ethiopia and Somalia to the upper Zambesi and southern Tanzania). Black stripes and white interspaces broad and less numerous, strongly contrasting. Legs striped to the hooves.

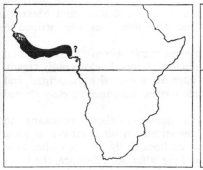

Gambian Mongoose, p. 125

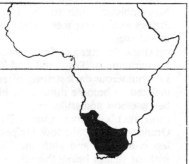

Red Meerkat, p. 126

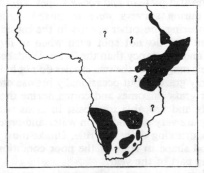

Selous' Mongoose, p. 126

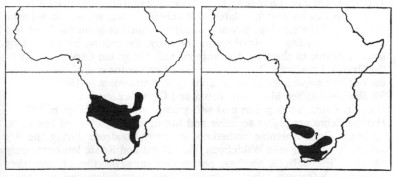

Grey Meerkat, p. 128

Aardwolf, p. 135

SELOUS' ZEBRA (*selousi*) (from the lower Zambesi and northern Mozambique south to the Limpopo; eastern Zambia and Malawi). Stripes and interspaces narrower and more numerous. Legs striped to the hooves.

CHAPMAN'S ZEBRA (*antiquorum=chapmani*) (from Benguela and Damaraland to Transvaal and Zululand). Ground colour buffy cream. Less numerous dark stripes, often alternating with 'shadow stripes', and inclined to become diffuse on hindquarters. Legs incompletely striped below elbow and stifle.

BURCHELL'S ZEBRA (*burchelli*) (originally southern Botswana to Orange River). 'Shadow stripes' numerous on hindquarters, striping less contrasted and with indistinct outlines. Belly almost white. Legs without stripes below the elbow and the stifle. At a distance, the hindquarters seem almost uniformly brownish, the striping being apparent on the foreparts only. True Burchell's Zebra are probably extinct.

The true Quagga (*quagga*), now extinct, generally considered as a distinct species but closely related to Burchell's Zebra, showed an extreme reduction of the striping; it was distinctly banded only on the head and neck, with only faint indications on the body, the ground colour varying from isabelline to chestnut. Its range extended from the Cape Province to the Orange Free State. It was exterminated before the end of last century; the last living specimen died in captivity in Amsterdam in 1883.

Similar species: See Mountain Zebra and Grévy's Zebra.

Habitat: Open grassy plains and well grassed woodland. Map, p. 197.

Habits: Zebra are highly sociable and live in family parties of from 5 to 20 head. These assemble sometimes in many hundreds during the dry season. They often join Wildebeest, Hartebeest and Roan, less commonly Eland or Giraffe. In the northern part of their range (northern Kenya) they overlap with Grévy's Zebra, in spite of their basic differences in habitat: they prefer the grasslands and the undulating country while Grévy's Zebra alone occur on the arid plateau and rocky slopes. Up to two-thirds of the zebras counted during surveys were in mixed herds, Grévy's Zebra generally outnumbering the other species in the mixed herds, which are relatively constant and do not split even when in flight. They show a greater cohesion and constancy than the Zebra-Wildebeest associations in other parts of their range. But the two species do not hybridise in the wild.

Zebra are mainly grazers, but occasionally browse on leaves and scrub. They also dig for grass rhizomes and corms during the dry season. They graze very closely and are able to subsist in areas with poor or coarse grass cover. They are very dependent on water and never wander very far from water holes, drinking daily as a rule. Unlike most antelope, they are invariably in good shape in spite of the poor conditions prevailing over their range during part of the year.

Sometimes sedentary, they may also wander great distances during the dry season in search of the most favourable places.

They are noisy and their voice is a very characteristic bark; a whistling intake of breath is followed by a succession of calls: "kwa-ha ha . . . kwa-ha ha . . .", hence the name 'Quagga'.

Rival stallions fight very fiercely by kicking and biting. They gather a group of mares together. The period of gestation is about 12 months. One foal is born at a time.

Zebras are very inquisitive where they have not been molested. They are fond of rolling in sand or dust. They run very fast and with endurance. They are much preyed upon by Lions, rarely by Wild Dogs and by hyaenas.

MOUNTAIN ZEBRA   *Equus* (*Hippotigris*) *zebra* L.   p. 141
F Zèbre de montagne   A Bergzebra   G Bergzebra

Identification: Height at shoulder 47–51 in.; weight 600 lb. A zebra with asinine features, a rather short plump head, proportionately long, pointed and short-haired ears, and a distinct dewlap. Extremity of the muzzle black, with a bare reddish patch above. General colour white or buff with conspicuous black stripes. On neck and body, stripes numerous and narrow (as in Grévy's Zebra). Thighs marked with three broad oblique bands (as in Böhm's Zebra); a number of short narrow transverse bands across the middle of rump and base of tail, forming a 'grid-iron' pattern. Underparts not striped, white. Legs transversely striped to the hooves.

Similar species: Resembles the Burchell's Zebra group, differing in the asinine proportions of head and body, and the striping, especially the 'grid-iron' on the rump.

Intraspecific variation: Two subspecies are recognised: the true Mountain Zebra (*zebra*) (southern mountains of the Cape Province), ground colour whitish and black stripes broader and in strong contrast, mane short; and Hartmann's Zebra (*hartmannae*) (mountains of South-West Africa and Angola to Mossamedes), ground colour creamy or buff and the black stripes narrower and more numerous, mane well developed. Individual variations are to be observed.

Habitat: Dry stony mountains and hills. In South-West Africa, Hartmann's Zebra ranges deep into the desert when rains have brought about a growth of grass. Map, p. 197.

Habits: Though gregarious, Mountain Zebra very seldom live in large herds but rather in smaller groups of 7 to 12 scattered over the hills; sometimes they assemble into herds numbering up to 50. Old stallions may be solitary. They are very agile climbers and favour arid situations in precipitous country.

They graze on tufted grass, mostly in the morning and late afternoon, resting during the heat of the day under thorn bushes. They do not drink regularly and may go for three days or so without water. However, they cannot dispense with it for longer periods, and will travel far to get it. They may dig for water in river beds down to three feet or so.

The voice is a low snuffling neigh or whinny, resembling that of a horse, quite different from the bark of the Burchell's Zebra.

Their range overlaps in the central and eastern Kaokoveld with that of this species and they can be seen on the same plain. But their herds never mix and they do not hybridise in the wild.

Mountain Zebra of the nominate race have been exterminated throughout most of their former range as a result of settlement. Saved from extinction by the efforts of some landowners, they are now strictly protected in the Mountain Zebra National Park, near Cradock, and on some private farms. No more than 75 were supposed to be living in 1965. Hartmann's Zebra is still relatively numerous in some parts of its rather restricted range.

RHINOCEROSES: Rhinocerotidae

Odd-toed ungulates (three toes), very massively built, standing low on the legs. Neck short, eyes small; head bearing two solid horns (the front horn being the larger) of dermal origin, growing from the skin and with no skeletal support. Skin practically naked, grey in colour and very thick, making folds on shoulder and hindquarters. Two species in tropical Africa; other representatives in south-eastern Asia, some with only one horn.

BLACK RHINOCEROS *Diceros bicornis* (L.) p. 160
(Hook-lipped Rhinoceros)
F Rhinocéros noir K Faru G Schwarzes Nashorn, Spitzmaulnashorn
A Swartrenoster

Identification: Height at shoulder 60 in.; weight 2,000 to 3,000 lb. A Rhino with proportionately short head, and a narrow muzzle. No hump on the neck; line of back concave. Upper lip triangular in shape, prehensile and very mobile. Ears relatively small, almost hairless. Two horns, very variable individually in proportions and shape, measuring up to 53 in. Front horn sometimes projecting forwards; rear horn as a rule much smaller, invariably flattened from side to side.

Female similar to the male, with generally longer and more slender horns.

Similar species: Distinguished from the White Rhino by its smaller size, lighter features, lack of nuchal hump, and by the smaller head which is carried high, giving a different silhouette; also by the pointed upper lip, which is distinct from the square muzzle of the White Rhino.

Habitat: Dry bush country and particularly thorn scrub. Also mountains up to 11,500 ft. (Mount Kenya) in the cloud-soaked moorlands. Map, p. 197.

Habits: Sedentary, Black Rhino are usually solitary, especially the males. Pairs are formed by a cow and her calf, which lives with the mother for a

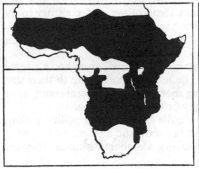

Spotted Hyaena, p. 129

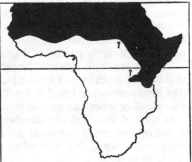

Striped Hyaena, p. 134

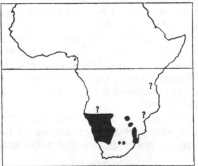

Brown Hyaena, p. 134

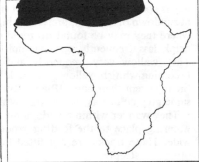

Sand Cat, p. 136

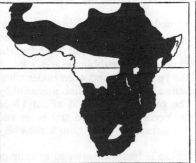

Wild Cat, p. 136

Black-footed Cat, p. 137

long time: sometimes the female is accompanied by two calves, one well grown and one small. The female walks ahead of her calf, contrary to the White Rhino mother who follows her young, guiding it with her front horn. Male and female are found together only during the brief mating season. Very rarely parties of 4 or more are seen.

They have a fairly extended vocabulary. They growl, grunt and also emit slight short squeaks, not unlike pigs, quite disproportionate to their size. The most commonly heard is a puffing snort, repeated several times, as an alarm call or when the animal is angry or begins to charge.

In spite of their bulk, Rhino show a quite extraordinary agility, making a turn on the spot. Their usual gait is a fast walk and a bouncing trot when frightened; they gallop only when charging. On short distances, they can reach 30 m.p.h.

They have very poor sight, but a good sense of smell and excellent hearing.

Rhino feed during the early morning and at dusk; the remainder of the day is spent resting in the shade of trees. Normally they drink once a day, at sundown or at night, preferably in stagnant water. In subdesert country, where they may be found up to 30 miles from any water hole, they may drink less frequently, getting moisture from succulents or euphorbias. They wallow very frequently and roll in the dust, their colour then becoming whitish, yellowish or reddish according to the colour of the soil (in any event their name 'Black' Rhino is misleading for their skin has the same grey colour as that of the 'White' Rhino).

They wander within a wide home range, moving 5 to 15 miles from the watering place to the feeding grounds, along regular paths some $1\frac{1}{2}$ ft. wide. These tracks are not fitted to the contours as elephant paths and often rise steeply.

Black Rhino browse on twigs, leaves and bark of trees (acacias, euphorbias) and bushes, using the prehensile upper lip; they rarely graze. They defecate in particular places, where they scatter the dung with their hind legs.

They are rather ill-tempered and sometimes charge without apparent reason. They are vicious in areas where they have been much disturbed and should never be taken on trust. Males defend a kind of territory, the limits marked by dung heaps, urination spots and rubbing places.

Mating takes place at any time of the year. Fights between males when a cow is coming into season are frequent and mating is often preceded by attacks on the bull by the female. The gestation period is about 17–18 months, and one calf is born at a time. Young are weaned at 2 years and maturity is not reached before 5 or even 7 years of age. Rhino breed every 3 years or so.

Like the other Rhinos, the Black Rhino is badly threatened in spite of the protective legislation adopted in all the territorities in which it still survives. The survival of such a big animal with a wide range and specific

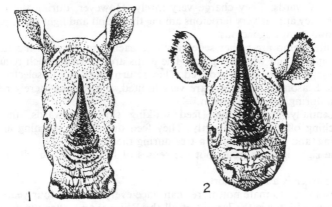

9. Head of White Rhinoceros (*Ceratotherium simum*) (1) and of Black Rhinoceros (*Diceros bicornis*) (2)

ecological requirements is almost incompatible with the transformation of the habitat and the development of the country. Poaching is prevalent in many countries. The total population is estimated between 11,000 and 13,500 head. They will only be preserved, like most big game, in wide, protected areas.

WHITE RHINOCEROS   *Ceratotherium simum* (Burchell)   p. 160
(Square-lipped Rhinoceros)
F Rhinocéros blanc, Rh. de Burchell   A Witrenoster
G Weisses Nashorn, Breitmaulnashorn
Identification: Height at shoulder up to 70 in.; weight 3½ tons, up to 5 tons. Much larger and heavier than the Black Rhino, especially in regard to the height at shoulder. A distinct massive hump on the neck; middle of back slightly but distinctly arched. Head very long, carried low, terminating in a broad square muzzle with no trace of protruding lip. Ears large, pointed, fringed by thick hair. Horns generally longer (front horn up to 62 in.), thinner and straighter than in the Black Rhino.

Female similar to the male, with generally longer and more slender horns.
Similar species: See Black Rhino.
Habitat: Grassland and open savannas with scrub. Map, p. 203.
Habits: White Rhino are much more sociable than their Black relatives. They are seen in family groups of 2 to 5 head, or even in parties up to 10. Herds of 24 head have been observed. They are very placid and even-tempered animals and it is a relatively simple matter to approach them

within 30 yards. They charge very rarely. However, during the mating season they appear very ferocious among their kind and fight fiercely; even the cows seem pugnacious.

White Rhino are rather sedentary and each family group has its own grazing area and watering place. The paths are used with such regularity that they become deeply grooved. They return every day to selected dung heaps. Seasonal movements are very limited, the Rhinos merely retiring uphill during the rainy season.

Essentially grazers, they feed walking slowly forwards, the jaws munching off the grass shortly. They feed during the morning and the evening, and they rest under a tree during the day.

The sight is quite poor, but the senses of hearing and smell are very good.

The voice is a harsh snort.

Cows seem to mate not more than once every three to four years.

White Rhino are the largest of all the Rhinos, and after the elephants the largest living land mammals.

Status: Formerly distributed over much of the perennial grassland of tropical Africa, their range is now limited to a few areas in south-eastern and north-central Africa where they are well protected. Extinct outside these sanctuaries because of overshooting for sport and horn. Except in some parts of their present range (West Nile), White Rhinos are increasing at a very satisfactory rate and in Natal have even become too numerous. Translocation to other areas within their former range seems a good solution to the surplus of population. Several hundreds have already been moved from the Natal reserves to the Kruger N.P. and other sanctuaries. Nevertheless the total number does not exceed 4,000 head.

ORDER Artiodactyla
(Even-toed Ungulates)

HIPPOPOTAMUS: Hippopotamidae

Huge to medium-sized mammals, very massively built, with a big head, a broad muzzle, short legs terminated by 4 toes, the lateral digits being nearly as well developed as the median ones. Incisors and canines growing continuously. A 3-chambered, but non-ruminating stomach. Aquatic or semi-aquatic. Restricted to Africa.

HIPPOPOTAMUS *Hippopotamus amphibius* L. p. 160

F Hippopotame K Kiboko G Flusspferd, Nilpferd A Seekoei

Identification: Height at shoulder 55–63 in.; weight averaging 2,500–3,000 lb., sometimes up to 5,800 lb. Unmistakable. A huge, fat animal, with short legs, an enormous head with an extremely broad muzzle, short neck and a barrel-shaped body, the belly carried only a short distance above the ground. Ears, eyes and nostrils prominent so as to emerge when most of the animal is submerged. Long tushes (canines) strongly curved, and elongated incisors, the lower ones growing straight forward, and the upper ones downward. Skin, except for a few bristles on the muzzle and tail, nearly naked and forming folds on neck and shoulders. Colour uniform brownish grey, lightening to pinkish around the muzzle, eyes and throat; sometimes the body is coloured red by a secretion of glands ('blood sweat').

Female similar to the male, smaller.

Habitat: Streams, lakes and ponds with permanent water bordered by grassland; up to an altitude of 8,000 ft. Map, p. 203.

Habits: Very gregarious, sedentary and attached to a particular place, Hippo live in schools of 5–15 head, sometimes up to 30, which during certain seasons may join together in larger herds. Density of population may be very high in some districts (up to one Hippo every 6 yards, along the Upper Semliki, Congo). Females seem to form schools with their young, and around the bulls are settled according to the hierarchy, the dominant adult bulls being the nearest. However, this social organisation is controversial and according to some observers a master bull is responsible for the whole group.

Hippo are semi-aquatic, truly amphibious, and well adapted to living in water, their natural refuge when disturbed. They swim very well and dive for periods averaging 2 minutes, but they can stay under water much longer, up to 6 minutes. Their specific gravity being higher than that of water, they can walk on the bottom.

They spend the entire day sleeping and resting on sand banks or in water; often birds of various species (from Cormorants and Egrets to

Wagtails) perch on their back. At dusk, they leave the water (the adult males being the last) and walking within the limits of their pearshaped home range (their territory seems only around their water refuge, the only spot actually defended), along well defined pathways, about 2 ft. wide, beginning as grooves in the banks of rivers. They go to forage on pastures, sometimes several miles away from their aquatic haunts. Entirely herbivorous, they feed on grasses (*Themeda*, *Panicum*, *Heteropogon*, etc.) and on aquatic plants (*Pistia stratiotes*). They have been found eating fruits of the sausage tree (*Kigelia pinnata*). Very voracious, they eat up to 130 lb. of vegetable matter during a night. They urinate and defecate in water or on land in well-defined places, dispersing the excreta with the tail; this behaviour has no territorial significance, but probably is in relation with nocturnal orientation on land. Excreta sometimes form deposits 2 ft. high along the shores of rivers or lakes.

After a period of gestation of 233 days, females give birth to a single calf on land or in water; the young weighs about 100 lb. and is suckled at first on land, then in the water. Its mother takes great care of it, and teaches it to swim and to wallow. It begins to graze regularly at 4–6 months of age. Sexual maturity is reached at 4 years or more. The life span is about 30 years; in captivity, a Hippo reached the advanced age of 46 years. The voice is a kind of low whinnying; they also grunt and bellow.

In spite of their placid appearance, Hippos, especially bulls, fight very frequently and more fiercely than most other animals. They inflict frightful wounds on each other with their teeth, the scars being visible on the thick skin. They also threaten each other by a display with their jaws wide open, showing the interior of the mouth and the teeth. They may even be dangerous to man, if any one is surprised between the Hippo and its water refuge. They can attack canoes, usually as a result of wounding.

Hippo sometimes destroy fishermen's nets, but they are of benefit to fishing as their movements stir up the bottom mud, thus liberating nutrients into the water, and their excreta constitute a very valuable fertiliser. In fact the protection of the Hippo seems essential to a continued heavy yield of fish.

Hippo relaxing in water are often surrounded by a particular fish, belonging to the genus *Labeo*, which feeds on vegetable matter and excreta.

The young are preyed on by Lions and by crocodiles.

PYGMY HIPPOPOTAMUS *Choeropsis liberiensis* (Morton)   p. 160
F Hippopotame pygmée   G Zwergflusspferd
Identification: Height at shoulder 31 in.; weight 600 lb. A hippo-like creature, but not at all a mere reduction of its huge relative, being more pig-like. Size of a large Wild Boar. Body massive, but lightly built. Back much arched and rump sloping away behind. Head relatively small, not enormously inflated, rounded, with the eyes not markedly prominent but

rather set to the side. Limbs proportionately longer, with feet approximating to those of pigs, widely spread out, with sharp nails. Skin naked, uniformly blackish, somewhat lighter below.

Habitat: Swampy forests and along streams and creeks in dense forests. Map, p. 203.

Habits: Not gregarious, Pygmy Hippo never live in herds, but singly or in pairs. Nocturnal, they wander at night along fixed paths through the undergrowth which with time come to resemble tunnels, to feed on various vegetables, succulents, tender shoots, roots, grasses and fallen fruits.

They are good swimmers, but are far less aquatic than their huge relative and if pursued take refuge in dense thickets.

Never numerous, this little known species has declined alarmingly in spite of total protection.

WILD PIGS: Suidae

Medium-sized animals, with four toes on each foot, the middle toes being the longer, the lateral ones located higher and not reaching to the ground. Head terminating in an elongated mobile snout, the tip forming an expanded, truncated and naked disc. No head appendages, but canines often very long (tusks). Two-chambered, non-ruminating stomach. Widely distributed throughout the world, except Arctic regions and Australasia. Three types, well defined and easily recognisable, are met with in tropical Africa, on the northern limit of which occurs the Wild Boar, a Palaearctic species.

WILD BOAR *Sus scrofa* L. p. 161
F Sanglier G Wildschwein

Identification: Height at shoulder 31 in.; weight 200 lb. A pig with a relatively long and pointed head, without any warts. Tusks relatively small; the upper turning outwards and upwards, the lower biting against the upper and forming a sharp edge. Coat coarse and bristly, rather long. General colour grizzled brownish, becoming greyer with age.

Female similar to the male, smaller, with tusks much smaller.

Young with longitudinal stripes, yellowish buff on a dark brown ground colour. Becoming plain brownish with age, then blackish.

Intraspecific variation: The Egyptian Wild Boar (*sennaarensis*) is the African representative of the Wild Boar of Europe and Asia, from which it differs only slightly: smaller size, snout somewhat longer, coat shorter and thinner. The Wild Boar may be confused with feral pigs, which live in several districts of the Sudan. According to some observers, the populations from the Sudan are entirely feral and thus the distribution of the Wild Boar would be limited to northern (palaearctic) Africa. This seems questionable.

Habitat: Forest and thick undergrowth. In the hills during the summer

Almost extralimital; also in Morocco, Algeria and Tunisia. Extinct in northern Egypt. Map, p. 203.

Habits: Gregarious, Wild Boar live in small family parties (sounders); old boars are solitary. Nocturnal, they spend the day under dense cover or in the shade of rocks. They feed on all kinds of vegetable matter, grass, shoots, leaves and fruits, and also small animals and carrion. The litter numbers 8–10.

WARTHOG *Phacochoerus aethiopicus* (Pallas)   p. 161
F Phacochère   K Ngiri   G Warzenschwein   A Vlakvark
Identification: Height at shoulder 30 in.; weight 140–300 lb. (♂) 120–150 lb. (♀). An ugly pig-like animal, with an elongated body and an enormous head; face much flattened, with an expanded muzzle, and two pairs of large warts, the upper immediately below the eye, the lower between the eyes and the tusks. Tusks very unusual; the upper turning outwards, then upwards and inwards, forming a semi-circle; the lower wearing against the base of the upper tusk, forming a sharp cutting weapon. Coat very sparse and bristly, adults almost naked with the exception of light coloured brush-like whiskers on the edge of jaw, and a mane of long stiff hairs on neck and shoulders. Skin greyish or blackish, but often coloured red or yellow through the animal's habit of wallowing in mud. Tail thin and long, with a terminal tuft; carried vertically upright in a very characteristic way when the animal is running.

Sow similar to the boar, but without prominent warts; tusks smaller.

Young uniformly coloured, rosy grey during the first week, then plain grey.

Habitat: Open savannas, particularly where water is available to drink and wallow. Also found in the very dry habitats of the Sahelian zone where water is not available 6 months of the year. Map, p. 203.

Habits: The Warthog is gregarious, though old males live alone; it is mostly found in family parties (sounders), with male, female and the youngsters of one or two successive litters; groups may join temporarily into larger bands, in which each party more or less retains its individuality.

Mainly diurnal, it sometimes feeds on moonlit nights and may lie up during the warmest hours of the day. It often sleeps and usually breeds in Aardvark burrows, which have been enlarged and adapted; otherwise it sleeps in sheltered hollows, etc. Burrows and hollows are lined with grass. It enters the burrow backwards, the better to defend itself with its tushes.

Its sight is poor, but the senses of smell and hearing are very acute.

Usually silent, the Warthog utters grunts when alarmed.

Essentially a grazer, it feeds largely on short grasses and herbs which are plucked selectively with the incisors, the animal often going down on its horny, densely-haired 'knees' to graze. It may also take leaves and fruits and in some areas roots for bulbs and tubers, behaving then very much

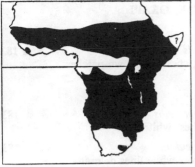

Serval, p. 137

Golden Cat, p. 138

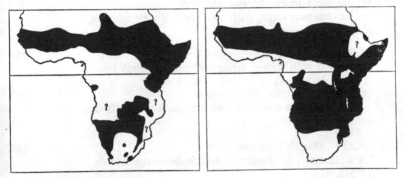

Caracal, p. 138

Lion, p. 142

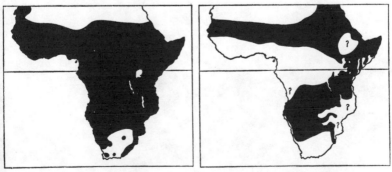

Leopard, p. 144

Cheetah, p. 145

Plate 27   GIRAFFE, OKAPI

1. **GIRAFFE**   *Giraffa camelopardalis*   *page* 182
   Huge; very long neck; long legs; chestnut brown patches
   on buff ground colour.

   NORTHERN GIRAFFE

   1a. **Nubian Giraffe**   *G. c. camelopardalis*   183
   Broad geometrical dark patches; white legs.

   1b. **Reticulated Giraffe**   *G. c. reticulata*   183
   Well defined network of narrow white lines delimin-
   ating broad dark patches; white legs.

   1c. **Baringo Giraffe**   *G. c. rothschildi*   183
   Patches very dark, with star-like features; white legs.

   SOUTHERN GIRAFFE

   1d. **Kenyan Giraffe**   *G. c. tippelskirchi*   183
   Dark spots with jagged, irregular outlines; buffy legs
   with dark spots.

   1e. **Southern Giraffe**   *G. c. giraffa*   183
   Dark patches with well definited outlines; buffy legs
   with dark spots.

2. **OKAPI**   *Okapia johnstoni*   184
   Dark chestnut; hindquarters and limbs conspicuously
   striped.

1a

1b

1c

1d

1e

2

ELAND, BONGO

Plate 28

1. **GIANT ELAND** *Taurotragus derbianus* 186
Ears broad and rounded; prominent dewlap from point
of chin; numerous white stripes on body; horns long,
diverging.

2. **CAPE ELAND** *Taurotragus oryx (oryx)* 187
Ears narrow and pointed; prominent dewlap only along
throat, with tuft of black hairs; stripes inconspicuous;
horns shorter, slightly diverging.

3. **BONGO** *Boocercus euryceros* 190
Heavy; bright chestnut red with conspicuous white
stripes; horns massive; well developed spinal crest.

as Bushpigs usually do, particularly in areas where water is scarce. Therefore Warthogs are generally not detrimental to cultivation.

The average litter is 3–4, but according to some observers, the same sow
frequently takes care of up to 8 piglets.

Warthogs are preyed on by Lions and Leopards.

BUSH-PIG   *Potamochoerus porcus* (L.)   p. 161
(Red River Hog)

F Potamochère   K Nguruwe   G Flussschwein, Pinselschwein A Bosvark

Identification: Height at shoulder 25–30 in.; weight 120–180 lb. A domestic
pig-like animal, with an elongated face and a short, laterally flattened
body. Coat long and bristly; a long dorsal whitish crest, often extending to
the ears, erected when the animal is excited. Ears with terminal tassels of
long hairs. General colour variable; either from reddish brown to bright
rufous, head with a conspicuously contrasted pattern of blackish and
white markings; or dark grey to brownish black, with the same pattern of
white and black markings on the head or a generalised bleaching, the
entire head being whitish. In old males, two well developed warts on snout.
Tusks very sharp, but short. Tail long and thin, reaching to the hocks,
hanging down when the animal is running.

Young with longitudinal stripes, pale yellowish buff, on a dark brown
ground colour; in a short time the markings disappear and are replaced
by a rufous brown colour, with a black and white dorsal crest.

Intraspecific variation: A large range of variation in the colour of the coat,
according to age (becoming darker with increasing age) and partly to
geographic origin. The southern and eastern races (*koiropotamus*, Southern
Cape Province to Natal; *nyassae*, Nyasaland, and allies) are very dark,
sometimes nearly black; on the contrary, the western races are bright red
or rufous, the coat being often shorter and denser, so that no portion of
the skin is visible.

Habitat: High forests, their fringes and thick bush country; also montane
forest. A related race (*larvatus*) represents this genus in Madagascar, the
only Suidae found in that island (? introduced). Map, p. 203.

Habits: Gregarious, Bush-pig live in sounders usually of from 6 to 20
individuals with a large master boar; herds of up to 40 have been observed.

They are essentially nocturnal, or at least hide in very dense thickets but
never in Aardvark burrows during the warmest hours of the day. They are
swift on foot and swim very well. They move to some extent according to
food supply and their home range is very wide.

They utter snorts and harsh grunts, like pigs, when alarmed or as they
feed.

Essentially omnivorous, they take animal as well as vegetable food,
eating even insects and larvae, birds' eggs, reptiles and carrion. But roots
and bulbs form the most important part of their diet, as well as grass, seeds
and fruits. They 'root' about for their food, digging with their snout. Their

excavations may have an appearance of devastation, the ground torn up, overturned shrubs and debris scattered on a wide area. They may be very destructive to crops (cassava roots, ground nuts, etc.).

The average litter is 3 to 6. The populations are increasing, despite attempts to control them. The persecution of Leopards, their principal predator, is partly responsible.

GIANT FOREST HOG *Hylochoerus meinertzhageni* Thomas   p. 161
F Hylochère   G Riesenwaldschwein
Identification: Height at shoulder 40 in.; weight up to 500 lb. A huge pig, the largest of the African Suidae, heavily built, with an elongated body, relatively long limbs, the rump being higher than the shoulder. Head long and massive, with an elongated and flattened snout, and large swollen excrescences below the eyes. Ears pointed, proportionately small. Tushes protruding from the mouth, smaller than those of the Warthog. Coat long, coarse, becoming sparse in old individuals, consisting of bristles standing nearly erect on the back of the head and neck, entirely jet black; skin blackish grey. Tail long and tufted, never carried upright.

Young plain-coloured, blackish brown, lighter than the adults.
Habitat: Dense forest; in eastern Congo, even at edge of the forest, feeding in the plains. Often high in the mountains. Map, p. 213.
Habits: Giant Forest Hog live in small family parties of 4–12 individuals, and sometimes in herds numbering up to 30 head; males form small troops and old boars live by themselves. Essentially nocturnal but also diurnal in protected areas, they roam the dense bush along regular pathways, which become clearly visible tunnels. They root about very little for their food and in some areas no trace is to be found of any rooting. On the forest edge, they feed on grass and herbaceous plants, but in the depths of the forest they eat mainly leaves, fallen fruits, berries and certain roots. They may be destructive to crops.

The average litter is 2 to 6.

CHEVROTAIN: Tragulidae

Very small hoofed mammals related to deer (Cervidae); showing some affinities with Suidae. Head small and pointed, without horns or antlers, but with canines well developed in males, protruding below the lips. Legs long and thin, with 4 well-developed digits. Ruminants (stomach with 3 compartments). Only one species in Africa, the others in south-eastern Asia.

WATER CHEVROTAIN *Hyemoschus aquaticus* (Ogilby)   p. 257
F Chevrotain aquatique   G Zwergmoschutier, Wassermoschutier
Identification: Height at shoulder 14 in.; weight 30 lb. Unmistakable. A very small antelope-like animal, with a little pointed head, small rounded ears, a hunched back, the hindquarters being higher than the shoulder and

Plate 29   KUDU, NYALA

1. **GREATER KUDU** *Tragelaphus strepsiceros*   *page* 191
   Larger; abundant fringe of hairs from chin to neck;
   striped; horns very long, largely divergent, spreading in
   open spirals (male).

2. **LESSER KUDU** *Tragelaphus imberbis*   194
   Smaller; no fringe of hairs under throat; conspicuously
   striped; two white patches under neck; horns long,
   moderately diverging, spreading in close spirals (male).

3. **MOUNTAIN NYALA** *Tragelaphus buxtoni*   195
   Stripes ill-defined; a few spots on thighs; horns long,
   widely divergent, spreading in no more than 2 open
   spirals.

4. **NYALA** *Tragelaphus angasi*   195
   Male dark slaty-brown; lower legs orange; conspicuous
   black mane along underparts. Female bright chestnut;
   with no mane.

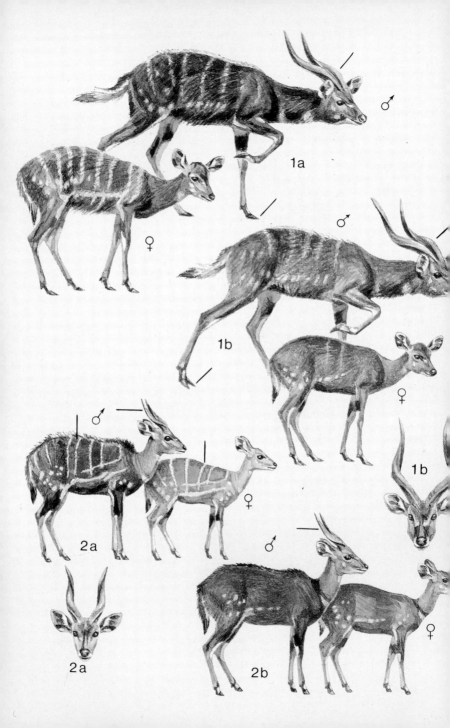

SITATUNGA, BUSHBUCK Plate 30

1. **SITATUNGA** *Tragelaphus spekei* *page* 196
   Larger; coat long and shaggy; long pointed hoofs; horns
   long (male.)

   1a. **WESTERN SITATUNGA** *Tragelaphus s. gratus* 198
   Conspicuously striped. Male deep chocolate brown;
   female reddish brown.

   1b. **SELOUS' SITATUNGA** *Tragelaphus s. selousi* 198
   Nearly without stripes. Male drab grey brown; female
   often of same colour.

2. **BUSHBUCK** *Tragelaphus scriptus* 198
   Smaller; coat not shaggy; hoofs normally shaped,
   horns smaller (male).

   2a. **WESTERN BUSHBUCK** *T. s. scriptus* 199
   Bright chestnut red, with conspicuous stripes and
   spots ("harnessed" bushbuck). Female smaller and
   lighter coloured.

   2b. **SOUTHERN BUSHBUCK** *T. s. sylvaticus* 199
   Dark brown, almost uniform.

short, slender legs. No horns, but (in adult males) upper canines exceedingly long, extruding from the lips, used as weapons when fighting. General colour rich dark rufous brown. On the face a blackish chevron, more or less distinct, from the muzzle to below the eyes; a white stripe along the upper jaw and across the cheek to below the ear. On the back and along the upper flanks, 6–7 ill-defined vertical rows of whitish or yellowish spots; a conspicuous lateral stripe of same colour from shoulder to rump; below some ill-defined lines on lower flank and across the thigh, hence lighter than the back. Throat and lower part of neck white, crossed diagonally by two dark bands. Underparts white. Tail very short.

Female similar to the male, without protruding canines.

Similar species: Cannot be confused with any Duiker or Pygmy Antelope, due to its characteristic light spots and stripes.

Habitat: Dense high forest, along rivers and streams. Map, p. 213.

Habits: Very elusive and difficult to observe, Chevrotain are nevertheless quite common. They live alone, in pairs during the mating season, and have a small home range. They are nocturnal.

They lead a semi-aquatic life, swimming very easily and taking refuge in the water. They feed on fruits, leaves, seeds and water weeds, not unlike Duikers. But surprisingly an important part of their diet consists of animal matter, fish, insects and flesh of dead animals.

Males utter series of short calls during the mating season.

Water Chevrotain show some similarities to pigs in their behaviour.

GIRAFFE, OKAPI: Giraffidae

A very peculiar group of hoofed mammals, restricted to Africa, with highly specialised morphological and anatomical features. Feet with two hoofed digits; no false hooves. Horns ill-defined, without horny sheaths and covered with skin and hair. Neck moderately to very much elongated (7 neck vertebrae as in other mammals, but each greatly elongated). The two well defined animals, Giraffe and Okapi, are unmistakable.

GIRAFFE   *Giraffa camelopardalis* (L.)   p. 176
F Girafe   K Twiga   G Giraffe   A Giraf, Kameelperd

Identification: Height at shoulder 10–12 ft., at top of head 14½–18 ft.; weight up to 2,600 lb. Unmistakable. The silhouette of this very large animal, the tallest in the world, its very long neck with a short stiff mane, its sloping back, and its long limbs make it very easy to identify. A long tufted tail. Colour pattern consisting of chestnut brown cut into patches by a network of light buff lines, very variable in shape and size. Underparts light and faintly spotted. One pair of short frontal horns, covered with skin and hair, on top of head; a median horn, sometimes only a knob, on the forehead; sometimes a pair of very small 'horn-like' protuberances on the occiput.

Female smaller, lighter coloured, with smaller horns.

Intraspecific variation: Giraffe show a very wide range of variation over their extensive range. Many subspecies have been described. The following trends may be observed.

NORTHERN GIRAFFES. White legs, especially the shanks, more or less spotted but not under 'knees'. Median horn well developed. There is a gradual decrease in the reticulation from east to west, the spots becoming less and less defined. The Reticulated Giraffe (*reticulata*) (north-east Africa, Somalia and northern Kenya) has a deep chestnut general colour, marked with a well defined network of narrow white lines delimiting large geometrical patches. (This Giraffe has sometimes been considered a distinct species.) The Nubian Giraffe (*camelopardalis*) shows a pattern of coloration approximating to that of the Reticulated Giraffe, but the dark patches are separated by broader, buffy white lines, as also in the Baringo Giraffe (*rothschildi*). In the Western Giraffe (*peralta* and allies), the patches show a tendency to split up and to be more numerous. The light interspaces are from deep yellowish fawn to white.

SOUTHERN GIRAFFES. Roughly from south of the Equator in eastern Africa, the giraffes have darker coloured (fawn or tawny) legs and shanks. Median horn reduced or absent. The populations from Kenya and Tanzania (*tippelskirchi*) have dark spots, very irregular in shape, with a jagged outline. The populations from South Africa (*angolensis*, *wardi*) show a clear tendency towards the netted or 'blotched' type, the patches being large, sub-quadrangular and with well defined outlines.

Giraffe show intermediate stages between all these different types of coloration.

Habitat: Formerly a wider distribution through Africa. Their presence in the Central Sahara is attested by rock paintings in caves; increasing aridity expelled them from these now desert regions. They have been exterminated over most of west Africa through overshooting.

Dry open country, covered with bush and acacia; they penetrate into light forest, but never into dense forests. Map, p. 213.

Habits: Gregarious, Giraffe live in herds of from 2 or 3 to 40 head, sometimes up to 70. Old bulls are often solitary. Bulls also form herds by themselves, sometimes consisting only of full adults, sometimes a large male followed by younger. Mixed herds consist of one, sometimes up to 8, big males with cows, subadults and calves of various ages. They are loose associations, dominated by the big bull and generally led by a female.

Giraffe gallop at a good speed, up to 35 m.p.h., in a curious manner. The hind feet are swung forward of and to the outside of the fore feet, with the neck and head swinging freely and the tail curled high over the back. Both forelimbs and both hindlimbs move together, instead of diagonally as, for example, in a horse. When moving slowly, they amble along.

Contrary to general belief, Giraffe are not voiceless, but are in fact able to utter low moans and snorts. But noises apparently are not much used to communicate with each other.

Hearing is acute, sight excellent, but the acuteness of the sense of smell is questionable.

Giraffe browse on leaves and twigs of a large variety of tall trees, especially Leguminosae, their principal diet. Their long neck allows them to browse up to 20 feet above ground, collecting twigs and leaves with their long prehensile upper lip and extensible tongue. Thorns do not harm them. They spend most of the day and a part of the night feeding, especially the early morning and late afternoon. They drink very irregularly when water is scarce; but they drink freely if possible. To bring their head down to the water level, they have to spread their forelegs wide apart in a series of peculiar movements.

Males fight a great deal by sparring in a particular manner often called 'necking'. They stand side by side facing the same or opposite directions. Suddenly one lowers its head and swings it at his opponent's head or body. The blows can be very heavy and often are perceptible some distance away. The fighters move around a great deal. Fighting among the males takes place all the year round. Mock fights are also frequently observed. Courting behaviour is relatively rare; the most common sexual behaviour is urine testing, the male collecting some of the urine of the female in his mouth or tongue. Apparently there is no breeding season, the young being born all the year round after a period of gestation of 450 days. Twins are occasionally recorded. Young begin browsing very early, at about 2 weeks.

To defend themselves, Giraffes kick with their forelegs. They are preyed on by Lions, particularly when drinking or feeding on the ground.

OKAPI   *Okapia johnstoni* (Sclater)   p. 176
F Okapi   G Okapi

Identification: Height at shoulder 63 in.; weight 500 lb. Unmistakable. A large animal, very peculiar in shape; body short and compact, with sloping back like the giraffe, but neck much shorter, not longer than in an antelope. Legs rather long in proportion to the length of the body. Ears very broad. Short horns projecting backwards, covered with hair. An ill-defined mane on the neck in young. General colour velvety dark chestnut, almost purplish black. Sides of head light grey. Upper parts of forelegs, lower rump, thighs and buttocks with conspicuous transverse black and white striped markings, sharply contrasted. Lower parts of limbs creamy white, except for a longitudinal stripe in front of the forelegs under the 'knee' and for a broad black band well above the hooves on each leg. Tail rather short, not reaching to the hocks, with a small terminal tuft.

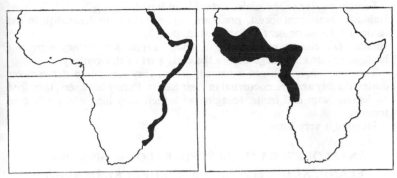

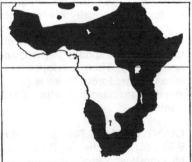

Dugong, p. 147

African Manatee, p. 148

Aardvark, p. 150

Rock Dassie, p. 152

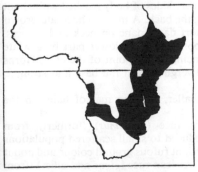

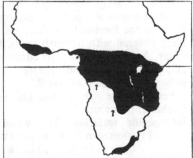

Yellow-spotted Dassie, p. 153

Tree Dassie, p. 154

Female similar to the male, but without horns.

Habitat: Dense rain forest, preferably in very dense undergrowth in the secondary forest or near streams. Map, p. 213.

Habits: The elusive way of life of Okapi explains why they were not brought to our knowledge before the early part of this century.

They live singly and are extremely wary; they retire into dense cover during the day and are nocturnal in their habits. Purely browsers, they feed on leaves, twigs and fruits, foraging with their very long and protractile tongue.

Hearing is very acute.

ANTELOPES, GAZELLES, BUFFALO and allies: Bovidae
ELAND, KUDU, NYALA and BUSHBUCK: Tragelaphinae

In spite of considerable differences, especially in size, the Tragelaphinae share several very distinct characteristics. Most have stripes and spots on the body, and usually a white chevron on the forehead. A crest of long hairs runs along the spine, at least on the shoulders. Sometimes a mane under the neck. The horns (present in males only, except in the Eland and the Bongo) are spirally twisted, and keeled in front and behind; they are never ringed. These antelopes live mostly in a closed habitat, sometimes even in dense forest. Voice is normally a bark or a deep grunt. They have an elaborate courtship, which distinguishes them from most other horned ruminants.

GIANT ELAND *Taurotragus derbianus* (Gray)[1] p. 177
F Elan(d) de Derby G Riesenelenantilope

Identification: Height at shoulder up to 69 in.; weight 1,000–2,000 lb. A very large antelope, with ox-like massiveness and 'bovine' appearance like the next species. Ears broad and expanded. General colour ruddy fawn, or chestnut, turning to bluish grey with age. Sides of body marked with about 14 white stripes. A black stripe along the back. A mat of chocolate brown hairs on the forehead (adults); a short dark mane on neck and withers. Neck covered with blackish hairs, bordered at its lower part by a white collar. A prominent dewlap commencing at the point of the chin. Horns (35; 48¾) very large and massive, diverging from the base and straight, with a close screw-like spiral.

Female more lightly built and smaller, with no mat of hairs on the forehead; horns smaller.

Intraspecific variation: The western race (*derbianus*) (formerly from Senegal to northern Nigeria; now reduced to small scattered populations in grave danger of extinction) has a bright rufous ground colour and about 15 vertical white stripes. The central African race (*gigas* and allies) (from the Cameroons through southern Chad to the Bahr el Ghazal, Sudan, and

[1] Sometimes considered as conspecific with the Cape Eland.

the Garamba N.P., Congo), is somewhat larger, has a sandy ground colour and 12 vertical stripes.

Similar species: See Cape Eland.

Habitat: Woodland and forested savannas, interspersed with stones; never far from water. Map, p. 213.

Habits: Gregarious, Giant Eland occur in herds of up to 60 head, but usually 15–25. They feed mostly on leaves, shoots, sometimes on grasses. Their movements are largely determined, at least during the dry season, by the presence of trees of the genus *Isoberlinia*, the young leaves of which form one of their favourite foods. They feed mainly at night, but unlike most tropical game, do not rest during the heat of the day.

They are exceedingly shy and show the same lack of aggressiveness as the Cape Eland. The sense of smell and hearing are excellent.

Giant Eland have paid a heavy toll to rinderpest to which they are more susceptible than any other antelope. Uncontrolled hunting (notably with fire) also contributed to reduce their numbers, particularly in western Africa where they have been exterminated throughout much of their former range.

CAPE/LIVINGSTONE'S ELAND *Taurotragus oryx* (Pallas) p. 177

F Elan(d) du Cap K Pofu, Mbunju G Elenantilope A Eland

Identification: Height at shoulder 70 in.; weight 1,300–1,500, sometimes up to 2,000 lb. A very large antelope, with ox-like massiveness and 'bovine' appearance. Ears narrow and pointed. General colour fawn or tawny, turning to greyish or bluish grey with age, except lower part of legs. Sides of body uniform or lightly striped. A mat of chocolate brown or black hairs on the forehead (adults), a short brown mane on the back of neck. A black stripe along the back. A prominent dewlap commencing on the throat (not on the chin), with a tuft of black hairs on the lower part. Tail long, reaching to the hocks, with a terminal black tuft. Horns (29; 43½) large, massive, slightly diverging and lying backwards in line with the profile of the face, with a close screw-like spiral in the basal half.

Female like the male but smaller and more slightly built; general colour rufous fawn; no mat of hairs on the forehead, horns lighter but often longer.

Intraspecific variation: Several subspecies may be recognised according to coloration and pattern. The Cape Eland (*oryx*) (from Natal (Giants Castle Game Reserve) and the northern Cape Province to Zambezi River and northern South-West Africa) is characterised by absence of stripes in adults. Livingstone's Eland (*livingstonii*) (from Zambezi River to central Tanzania; Angola) has a deeper colour, and 6 to 10 distinct vertical white stripes on the flanks. The East African Eland (*pattersonianus*) (from central Tanzania through Kenya to the Tana River, westwards to Rwanda (Kagera) and Uganda) is slightly more rufous, with white stripes; an incomplete white chevron across the forehead usually present.

188

Plate 31   ADDAX, ORYX

1. **ADDAX**   *Addax nasomaculatus*   *page* 200
   White or greyish; thick dark mat on forehead; horns
   long and spirally twisted.

2. **SCIMITAR-HORNED ORYX**   *Oryx dammah*   201
   Neck and chest ruddy brown, contrasting with white
   body; horns long, with bold backward curvature.

3. **BEISA ORYX**   *Oryx beisa*   201
   Head with definite black and white pattern; black stripe
   along flank; horns nearly straight, almost parallel.

4. **GEMSBOK**   *Oryx gazella*   202
   Head with definite black and white pattern; black stripe
   along flank; dark patches on rump and hind legs; horns
   nearly straight, diverging rather widely.

5. **ROAN ANTELOPE**   *Hippotragus equinus*   204
   Reddish fawn; ears long and sickle-shaped; horns
   relatively short, curved backwards. A mane along neck.

6. **SABLE ANTELOPE**   *Hippotragus niger*   205
   Glossy black, horns very long, curved backwards. A mane
   along neck.

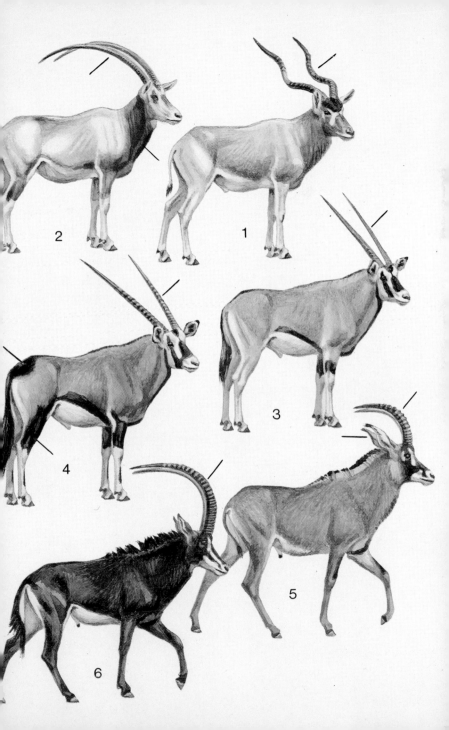

1a ♂

♀

1b

2

3

4 ♂

♀

KOB

Plate 32

1. **KOB** *Kobus kob* *page* 210
Bright rufous to dark brown; whitish area around eyes;
black markings on legs; horns long.

   1a. **THOMAS' KOB** *K. k. thomasi* 211
   Rich rufous.

   1b. **WHITE-EARED KOB** *K. k. leucotis* 211
   Dark brown (ad. male); conspicuous white ears.

2. **PUKU** *Kobus vardoni* 212
Bright golden yellow; no head markings; no black
markings on legs; horns rather short.

3. **COMMON WATERBUCK** *Kobus ellipsiprymnus* 210
Large; dark brown, shaggy coat; white ring across rump;
horns with single crescentic curvature.

4. **DEFASSA WATERBUCK** *Kobus defassa* 206
Large; greyish brown, shaggy coat; broad white patch
on rump; horns with single crescentic curvature.

Similar species: See Giant Eland.

Habitat: Open plains and savannas; also dry mopane, light forests and montane grasslands; sometimes giant heath and highland forest up to 14,000 ft. Map, p. 213.

Habits: Gregarious, Cape Eland occur in herds from a few individuals up to 200, occasionally considerably larger (during migration or periods of severe drought), but usually of from 25 to 70 head, with one or two mature bulls. They may assemble with Roan, Gemsbok or Zebra. Old bulls are often solitary. Their power of leaping—up to 8 feet—is an unexpected feature of such a heavy antelope (they can jump one over another from almost a standing start). Browsers rather than grazers, they feed on leaves (even the oily mopane leaves) and bushes; they also eat certain fruits, even wild melon, and use their hooves to dig for large bulbs and tuberous roots. They use their horns to collect twigs, grasping and breaking them by a movement of the neck. They sometimes feed on grass during the early rains, particularly in montane habitats. They are largely independent of water, although drinking regularly when it is available. They move about a great deal at all seasons, but this tendency is particularly marked in the dry season.

The hearing and the sense of smell are acute, but sight seems poor.

The voice is a deep grunt or a snort. They are rather silent.

Cape Eland are lacking in aggressiveness and are readily tamed. As they are more easily fattened, more than any other African antelope, and as their flesh and milk are excellent, they have been kept in semi-captivity and even semi-domesticated (South Africa, Rhodesia and Ascania Nova, U.S.S.R.).

BONGO *Boocercus euryceros* (Ogilby)   p. 177
F Bongo   G Bongo

Identification: Height at shoulder 50 in.; weight up to 500 lb. The largest and heaviest forest antelope, one of the most brightly coloured of all, with the line of the back not straight but hunched. Ears very large and broad. General colour bright chestnut red, becoming darker with age. A black and white spinal crest and 12–14 transverse narrow, but well defined, white stripes on the shoulders, flanks and hindquarters. Muzzle blackish; a conspicuous white chevron between the eyes, and 2 large white spots on the cheek. Lower neck with a distinct light yellowish crescentic white band. Underparts blackish. Legs with a striking pattern of black and white. Tail long with a terminal tuft of black hairs. Horns (30; 39½) large and very massive, smooth, forming an open spiral, black with light yellowish tips.

Female similar to the male, paler, horns more slender, shorter, rather parallel, sometimes deformed (at least in the eastern race). Young lighter than the adult.

Intraspecific variation: The western race (*euryceros*) (from Sierra Leone to Katanga) is characterised by more numerous white stripes on the sides of the body, while in the eastern race (*isaaci*) (Kenya) the number of stripes is reputed to be fewer.

Similar species: The Sitatunga is easily distinguished by its slender features, its darker, brown colour, the less conspicuous stripes and (if visible) the greatly elongated hooves.

Habitat: Typically dense forest, very seldom light forest. It may sometimes be found in forest remnants, isolated there by the surrounding open country. In East Africa only recorded from rain forest and bamboos, in montane regions. Map, p. 219.

Habits: Mostly nocturnal, but also diurnal, and very elusive, Bongo live in pairs or small groups, occasionally consisting of as many as 35 individuals. Old bulls live alone. They walk easily through dense undergrowth and may run at considerable speed in a crouching position with the head up and the horns extended along the back. They do not jump willingly. Entirely browsers, they feed on leaves and shoots of shrubs and creepers; they are fond of rotten wood and bark, raising themselves on their hind legs to reach trees. Bamboos apparently do not form part of their diet. Very shy, and with excellent hearing, they move to dense cover during the heat of the day.

The voice is somewhat similar to that of the Eland and of a domestic calf (a bleat). They are rather silent.

GREATER KUDU   *Tragelaphus strepsiceros* (Pallas)   p. 180
F Grand Koudou   K Tandala mkubwa   G Grosser Kudu   A Koedoe

Identification: Height at shoulder 63 in.; weight 600–700 lb. (♂), 400–470 lb. (♀). A large antelope, slender and very elegant. Ears large. General colour from bluish grey to greyish brown and rufous. Sides of body conspicuously marked with 6 to 10 vertical white stripes. Head darker, with a white chevron between the eyes and three white spots on the cheek below the eye. No white markings on the throat. An abundant fringe of hairs from the chin to the neck, with 1–2 dark brown bands. A crest from the occiput to the root of tail, brown and long on the neck and withers, less developed and white on the back. Tail not reaching to the hocks, bushy with white underside and black tip. Horns long (45–50; 71½) and impressive, rising slightly above the plane of the face at the base, largely diverging, spreading in 2–3 open spirals.

Female smaller and more slender, ground colour fawn, with no horns. Young more reddish.

Intraspecific variation: The Southern Greater Kudu (*strepsiceros*) (from South Africa to Angola and Zambia) is larger; body colour darker, grey in old males, 9–10 transverse stripes. The East African Greater Kudu (*bea*) (from Tanzania to Eritrea) is brighter-coloured, with 6–8 stripes. The Western Greater Kudu (*cottoni*) (from Chad to Ethiopia) is paler, with fewer stripes.

Similar species: Lesser Kudu is smaller and more graceful; the throat has

192

Plate 33   **LECHWE**

1. **NILE LECHWE**   *Kobus megaceros*   *page* 214
   Male: Dark; white stripe along nape, and large white
   patch on shoulder; horns very long, S-shaped.
   Young male: Fawn, darkening progressively; pattern ill--
   defined.
   Female: Uniform fawn.

2. **LECHWE**   *Kobus leche*   214
   Neck and shoulder of same colour as body.

   2a. **BLACK LECHWE**   *K. l. smithemani*   212
       Blackish brown (ad. male).

   2b. **KAFUE LECHWE**   *K. l. kafuensis*   212
       Dark shoulder patches (ad. male).

   2c. **RED LECHWE**   *K. l. leche*   212
       Bright chestnut fulvous.

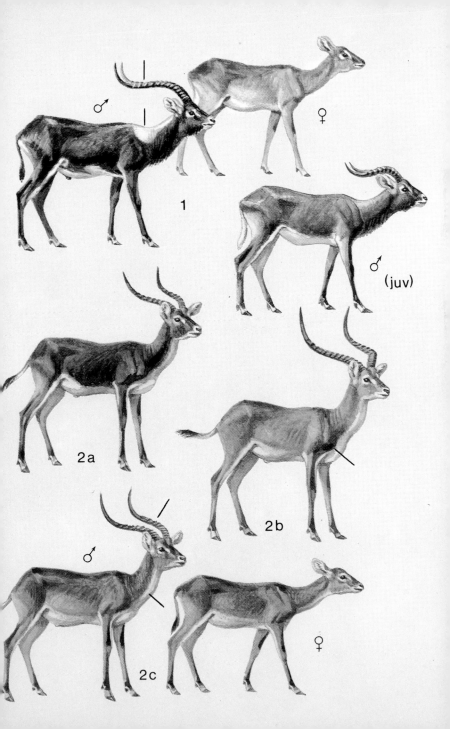

♂

♀

1

♂ (juv)

2a

2b

♂

2c

♀

REEDBUCK

Plate 34

(Notice round patch of grey naked skin below ear)

1. **BOHOR REEDBUCK** *Redunca redunca* *page* 215
   Smaller; horns short, but thick, forming hooks.

2. **MOUNTAIN REEDBUCK** *Redunca fulvorufula* 216
   Smaller; horns short and slender.

3. **SOUTHERN REEDBUCK** *Redunca arundinum* 216
   Larger; horns longer, divergent.

4. **VAAL RHEBUCK** *Pelea capreolus* 217
   Smaller; ears long and narrow; horns short, vertical.

two well defined white patches and has no fringe of hairs. Stripes are more numerous and contrasting. Horns smaller, forming a closer spiral and less diverging.

Habitat: Light forests or fairly thick bush, often in rocky, mountainous or hilly country, seldom far from water, as in most regions they drink regularly. However, they sometimes occur in waterless regions. They may come down to the plains during the rainy season, but generally avoid open country. Map, p. 219.

Habits: Greater Kudu usually live in small herds or family groups of 4–5 head, often without adult males; but aggregations of 30 or more have been recorded. The herds may split during the rains. Bulls are inclined to be solitary, but sometimes form bachelors' herds. Largely nocturnal, Kudus rest in the shade of trees during the heat of the day, preferably in high country, visiting the feeding grounds from late afternoon to early morning. Essentially browsers, they feed mainly on shoots and leaves of a very wide variety of plants (even plants which are considered to be poisonous are eaten without any harm), on seeds, and very seldom on grass, which may be taken during the early rains or after a fire. In the driest part of South-West Africa they obtain the greater part of their liquid nutriment from wild water melons.

Kudu are accomplished jumpers and a fence over 7 ft. high is needed to keep them out of fields. They run heavily and clumsily, throwing the tail up and showing the white underside. They are very sensitive to sound.

Their call is a loud hoarse bark, the loudest of any antelopes. Bulls roar during the mating season.

LESSER KUDU *Tragelaphus imberbis* Blyth   p. 180
F Petit Koudou   K Tandala ndogo   G Kleiner Kudu
Identification: Height at shoulder 40 in.; weight 120–230 lb. A medium-sized, slender, attractive antelope. General colour brownish grey becoming blue grey with advancing age. Sides of the body marked with 11–15 narrow but well defined vertical white stripes. Head of deeper colour, with an incomplete white chevron between the eyes. Two conspicuous white patches, one on the upper, the other on the lower part of neck. A short crest from the occiput to the root of tail, brown and longer on the neck and withers, less developed and white on the back. No fringe of hairs under throat. Tail not reaching to the hocks, bushy, with white underside and black tip. Horns long (30; 36), moderately diverging, forming usually two and occasionally three close spirals. Female with no horns, smaller, lighter coloured, reddish fawn, only tinged with grey, white markings on throat less contrasted.

Similar species: See Greater Kudu.

Habitat: Acacia thickets, dense scrub and semi-arid bush country. Never met in open grass plains. Map, p. 219.

Habits: Lesser Kudu usually live in pairs, often accompanied by their young. Females may constitute small herds. Very shy, they spend the heat of the day in dense bush and move mostly at dusk and in the early morning. Essentially browsers, they feed on leaves, young shoots and twigs. They drink regularly when water is available, but may dispense with liquid for long periods during the dry season, often inhabiting much drier country than the Greater Kudu.

Their call is a loud bark, not unlike the call of the Bushbuck.

Like the Greater Kudu, they are good jumpers.

MOUNTAIN NYALA *Tragelaphus buxtoni* (Lydekker) p. 180
F Nyala de montagne   G Bergnyala
Identification: Height at shoulder 50 in.; weight 450–500 lb. A large antelope with some features like the Greater Kudu. Coat rather shaggy. Ears large. General colour greyish chestnut. Head marked with a white chevron between the eyes and 2 white spots on the cheek. Two white patches on the underside of the neck, the upper very large, the lower crescent-like. Back and upper flanks with about four white ill-defined stripes; a few white spots on the thighs. A short dark brown mane on the neck continued on the spine as a brown and white crest. Tail not reaching to the hocks, bushy, with white underside and black tip. Horns long (34; 46¾) and heavy, widely divergent, spreading in two open spirals.

Females without horns, general colour like the male. Young lighter coloured.
Habitat: Forest (*Hagenia*) and heathland in mountains above 9,500 ft., up to 12,500 ft. Avoids very open terrain. Map, p. 219.
Habits: Mountain Nyala, discovered only in 1908, occurs singly or in small herds, up to 15, but usually 5–10. Females outnumber males. Old males are usually solitary. The herds are constantly moving. Very shy and wary, it will sometimes squat in heath till the observer is at close range. Mostly active by night, it feeds normally in evening and early morning, but where common it may be found in early afternoon. Mainly a browser, it feeds on heath and leaves, but takes some grass, leguminous herbs and *Alchemilla*.

The voice is a deep grunt.

The Mountain Nyala is much reduced in number in parts of range (Arussi) and the calving rate is apparently low. But it is still common in Bale Mountains, and the total population may exceed 4,500 head.

NYALA *Tragelaphus angasi* Gray p. 180
F Nyala   G Nyala   A Nyalabosbok, Inyala
Identification: Height at shoulder 42 in.; weight 220–280 lb. A large, but slenderly built and very narrow bodied antelope, not unlike a large Bushbuck, with a rather shaggy coat, enormously developed on the underside, differing in this respect from all other antelopes. Ears large. General colour dark slaty brown, with a purplish tinge and some reddish on forehead and around the eyes. A white chevron between the eyes and 2–3 spots

on cheek. Sides of body marked with 8–14 white stripes, and a few white spots on thighs. A conspicuous crest of long hairs from the occiput to the root of tail, brown on the neck and white along the back. Underside of neck with a very long mane of black hairs, continued along the underparts, with a white crescent-like patch on lower neck. Buttocks and upper part of hind legs fringed with very long black hairs. Lower legs orange chestnut, contrasting strongly with the dark coat. Tail very bushy, dark brown, with white underside. Horns well developed (28; 32⅜), usually with a single open curve, dark brown or black with ivory coloured tips.

Female very different, much smaller, without horns; general colour much lighter, bright chestnut, with the white lateral stripes numerous and very conspicuous. No white chevron between the eyes. No mane on the underside; a short dark crest from shoulder to rump. Young like the female. Young males early develop the white chevron between the eyes, and gradually assume the adult coloration. Fully horned males with female coloration have been recorded (young males may be confused with Bushbucks, but the orange 'stockings' are characteristic).

Habitat: Low country, dense bush and savanna veld, never far from water. Map, p. 219.

Habits: Nyala are usually found in small parties, sometimes consisting only of females and young, sometimes with one or more bulls. They may congregate in herds of up to 30 head. Solitary animals are not uncommon. They feed from late afternoon to early morning, but they are not decidedly nocturnal and move freely by day. They are exclusively browsers, except when grass is young and tender. They feed on leaves, twigs, pods and fruits ('kaffir oranges' (*Strychnos*), wild figs). Voice a deep roaring bark and a hoarse grunt. The gait is similar to that of the Greater Kudu and the tail is also thrown up, displaying the white underside. Their habits in general resemble those of the Lesser Kudu and bear little resemblance to those of the Mountain Nyala.

SITATUNGA *Tragelaphus spekei* Sclater   p. 181
F Sitatunga, Guib d'eau   K Nzohe   A Waterkoedoe
G Sitatunga, Wasserkudu, Sumpfbock

Identification: Height at shoulder 45 in.; weight 100–240 lb. A large antelope with truly amphibious habits; hindquarters higher than the forequarters, giving the animal a peculiar hunched appearance. Coat very shaggy and fairly long. General colour from chocolate to drab grey brown, with white markings, sometimes with faint stripes. Head with an incomplete white chevron between the eyes, and some white spots on the cheek. Neck with two white patches, one under the throat, the other on lower parts. Long, pointed hooves, widely separated at tips. Tail not very bushy, merely tufted at the tip. Horns long (25; 36⅜).

Female smaller, without horns, brown or bright chestnut, more conspicuously striped.

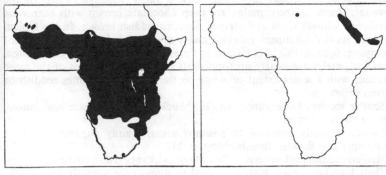

African Elephant, p. 155

Wild Ass, p. 159

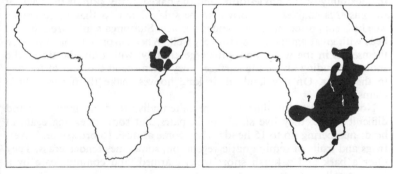

Grévy's Zebra, p. 159

Burchell's Zebra, p. 162

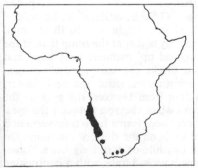

Mountain Zebra, p. 165

Black Rhinoceros, p. 166

Intraspecific variation: Sitatunga show a fairly wide variation. In the western form (*gratus*), males are deep chocolate brown with numerous white or whitish spots and stripes; females reddish brown. In the typical form, Spekes' Sitatunga (*spekei*) males are greyish brown, with a faint striping; females bright chestnut. In the southern form (Selous' Sitatunga, *selousi*), males are nearly uniform drab grey brown, females of the same colour with a lesser extent of white on the throat, sometimes reddish or even yellowish.

Similar species: Differs from the Bushbuck by its larger size and longer, more twisted horns.

Habitat: Strictly confined to swampy areas, mainly papyrus and reed swamps; also flooded forests. Map, p. 219.

Habits: Sitatunga (formerly called Marshbuck) are true aquatic antelopes. Their long hooves are highly adapted to support the animals on the soft, boggy soil and marsh vegetation without sinking deeply into the ground; the flexibility of the ankle-joints and the naked horny skin at the back of the pasterns enables the hooves to be splayed out so that the animal's weight is supported on an expanded surface. Sitatunga slink through reed beds with great agility and swim very well. When surprised, they immerse themselves in the water and submerge entirely, with only the tip of the snout protruding above the surface. They often spend the heat of the day in the water. On dry land, their long hooves make them run a little clumsily.

Nocturnal but also diurnal where quite undisturbed, normally shy and difficult to see, they live singly or in pairs, but sometimes aggregate in herds numbering up to 15 heads. They come at dusk to browse on leaves, twigs and fruits of semi-aquatic vegetation, sometimes tender grass. They utter a bark and a harsh snort when alarmed, and communicate by a bleating call.

BUSHBUCK *Tragelaphus scriptus* (Pallas) p. 181
F Guib harnaché K Mbawala, Pongo G Schirrantilope A Bosbok

Identification: Height at shoulder 27–37 in.; weight 70–170 lb. A small antelope, elegant, but robustly built, slightly higher at the rump than at the shoulder, therefore running in a 'hunched up' manner. Ears large and broad. General colour varying from bright chestnut to dark brown, passing into black on underparts in adult males. Head and neck lighter, fawn colour; a blackish band extending from between the eyes to the muzzle. A white spot on the cheek; no white chevron between the eyes. Two white patches on throat. The 'harnessed' forms have transverse and vertical stripes, white or whitish, and spots on the sides of the rump. On the middle of the back, a spinal crest of white or dark long hairs. Sometimes a blackish collar around the lower neck. Limbs with a contrasting pattern of dark and white. Tail bushy and long, but not reaching to the hocks, white below with a black tip. Horns short (13; 22½), almost straight

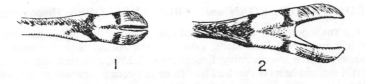

10. Hooves of Bushbuck (*Tragelaphus scriptus*) (1) and of Sitatunga (*Tr. spekei*) (2)

and only diverging a little, strongly keeled, forming the first loop of a spiral.

Female smaller and without horns, lighter than the male and more conspicuously striped (western forms), or duller and redder (eastern and southern forms).

Intraspecific variation: Bushbuck vary considerably in coloration and in size over their wide range and more than 40 races have been described, distinguished mainly by the degree of striping and intensity of coloration. Western and northern forms (*scriptus, pictus, bor*) are bright chestnut red with conspicuous white stripes and spots so arranged as to have given rise to the name 'Harnessed Bushbucks'. Eastern Bushbucks (*massaicus* and allies) are larger and browner; the stripes are broken up into rows of white spots, which become obscure in some races. Southern forms (*sylvaticus* and allies) are dark brown or even blackish, sometimes practically uniform, with no white markings except a few indistinct spots behind the shoulders and on the rump. Others, like *ornatus* (Angola, Botswana), are conspicuously marked with white spots and stripes. Bushbuck from Ethiopia (*meneliki, powelli*) are much darker, sometimes almost black, and less spotted.

Habitat: Forest thickets and dense bush, usually never far from water; but they also occur in some entirely waterless country, being able to do without water when necessary. They live in a very wide range of habitats, from the fringe of dense forest and in clearings to the Sahelian zone into which they penetrate along galleries. Map, p. 223.

Habits: Bushbuck live singly or in pairs, sometimes in small family parties (females and young). Nocturnal, they usually spend the heat of the day in dense bush, and are attached to one particular spot, not moving more than a short distance. Almost entirely browsers, they feed on leaves, tender shoots and acacia pods; they dig up various tubers and roots, and feed on grass only when it is young. Still numerous over a great part of their range, they are elusive and very shy; nevertheless they are among the most pugnacious of antelopes and if attacked may be dangerous. They are a favourite prey of the Leopard and pythons.

The voice is a loud clear bark, sometimes repeated (not unlike that of a baboon), and also series of grunts.

ADDAX, ORYX, ROAN and SABLE ANTELOPES: Hippotraginae

Large antelopes, with well developed horns, borne by both sexes, almost straight or curved backwards, except in the Addax in which they are spirally twisted. Muzzle hairy. Except in the Addax, a mane along the neck of stiff straight hairs (Roan and Sable), or projecting forwards towards the head (Oryx). Tail long and tufted. They are found in open country and light woodland, some even in the desert.

ADDAX   *Addax nasomaculatus* (Blainville)   p. 188
F Addax   G Mendes-Antilope
Identification: Height at shoulder 41 in.; weight 180–270 lb. Unmistakable. A large antelope, rather heavy and clumsy in form. Head light smoky grey with a conspicuous broad white patch from the middle of the cheek to the upper portion of the nose in front of the eye. Chin, lips and inside of the ears pure white. On the forehead, a thick mat of dark brown hairs, resembling a wig. A faint mane of longish hairs under the neck. Neck, back and flanks greyish white in spring and summer, darker in autumn and winter. Rump, underparts and limbs pure white. Tail rather long but not reaching to the hocks, 'bovine', with a black tuft at tip. (Intensity of coloration shows a wide range of individual variation, with no relation to sex, age or geographical origin; some individuals may be entirely white.) Horns long (35; 43) rather thin, diverging and spirally twisted, conspicuously ringed on the basal half. Hooves considerably enlarged (adaptation to walking on soft, sandy soil).
Female similar to the male, but with thinner horns.
Habitat: Formerly throughout the entire Sahara, north to southern Algeria and Tunisia. Addax are typical desert-dwellers, living in the most arid parts of the Sahara, far away from any water-hole, in sandy country as well as in stony desert (reg). Map, p. 223.
Habits: Addax live in herds, averaging about 20 head, but sometimes up to 200. Their movements (or 'migrations') are determined by rains which are rare and irregular in both timing and distribution. Patches of desert vegetation (including species of *Aristida, Boerhavia, Cornulaca*) grow with incredible rapidity after rainfall; these pastures are sought by the Addax, which are supposed to possess a special sense of perception to find them. Apparently they do not require free water to drink and their water need is provided by their diet, in which some succulent plants are found. Addax probably have a physiological device enabling them to exercise great water economy.
The Addax, one of the most threatened antelopes, is decreasing very rapidly throughout its present range, except in some absolutely uninhabited districts. They are actively hunted by nomads, oil surveyors and soldiers, often with motor cars.

SCIMITAR-HORNED ORYX *Oryx dammah* (Cretzschmar)[1]
(=*algazel; tao*) (White Oryx)   p. 188
F Oryx algazelle   G Sabelantilope

Identification: Height at shoulder 47 in.; weight 450 lb. A large antelope, rather heavy, very pale coloured, with no striking pattern on the body. Head white, with a brownish patch on the blaze, another on the forehead; a lateral stripe of the same colour across the eye. Neck and chest ruddy brown. Body white, more or less washed with russet, particularly on flanks and upper limbs. A faint longitudinal stripe on the lower flank. Tail long, with a large hairy dark brown tuft, reaching to well below the hocks. Horns scimitar-like, very long (40; 50½) and parallel, with a bold backward curvature. Hooves enlarged (but less than in the Addax).

Female similar to the male, but horns more slender.

Habitat: Sahel and semi-desert, never penetrating into true desert or the Sudan zone. Formerly over most northern Africa, north to southern Tunisia. Map, p. 223.

Habits: Scimitar-horned Oryx usually live in herds of about a dozen, sometimes up to 60 individuals and even more, seldom singly. Old males may join herds of Dama Gazelle. At certain seasons, when rain falls in particular districts, they concentrate in enormous herds numbering thousands. Extremely nomadic, they wander great distances through their range during migration-like movements in search of grazing. They usually feed on grasses, Leguminosae, acacia pods, succulents and some fruits.

The voice is a grunt and a kind of bellow.

Scimitar-horned Oryx were kept in captivity by the ancient Egyptians as a domestic animal. Today, like the Addax, they are hunted so severely by desert tribesmen, oil surveyors and soldiers, as to be close to extermination in parts of their range. They are one of the most endangered of all the antelopes, particularly in the northern part of their range.

BEISA ORYX *Oryx beisa* (Rüppell)   p. 188
F Oryx beisa   K Choroa   G Eritrea-Spiessbock

Identification: Height at shoulder 47 in.; weight 290–450 lb. A large antelope, with a well defined pattern on head and body. Head white with a black patch on forehead, from the base of the horns, joined by a narrow black stripe to a broad patch of the same colour on the blaze. Another broad black stripe across the eye extends from the base of horns to lower cheek; a third from ear to ear across the throat. Ears rather large, with a black tip. Body sandy fawn with a black spinal stripe. From the interramal area to the chest, a narrow black stripe. A black stripe separating the lower flank from the white underparts. No dark patch on the rump and thighs; buttocks white. Forelegs white, with a narrow black ring above the 'knee'; hind legs whitish with no black markings. Tail long, reaching to the hocks,

---
[1] According to some authors, all oryx are conspecific.

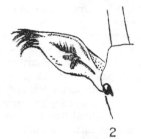
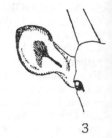

1   2   3

11. Shape of ears of some Oryx
    1 Beisa Oryx (*Oryx b. beisa*)   2 Fringe-eared Oryx (*Oryx b. callotis*)
    3 Gemsbok (*Oryx gazella*)

with a black tuft. Horns nearly straight with a slight backward curve, very long (30; $41\frac{7}{16}$) and heavily ridged, almost parallel.

Female similar to the male, but horns more slender although often longer.

Intraspecific variation: Two races may be recognised. The Beisa Oryx (*beisa*) (from Eritrea to the Tana River) is greyer and duller, and has no fringe or tassel on the ears. The Fringe-eared or Tufted Oryx (*callotis*) (from the Tana River to Tanzania) is a richer brown, and its ears bear a very distinctive tuft of long black hairs; horns heavier than in *beisa*.

Similar species: May possibly be confused with the Roan Antelope with which it shares some similarities in head markings; but horns are quite different.

Habitat: Dry open bush and short grass savanna, often very far from water. Map, p. 223.

Habits: Beisa live in herds ranging from 6 to 40 head or more, often in association with Grant's Gazelle and Zebra. Bulls are often solitary. They mostly feed on coarse grasses, but also browse on thorny shrubs. Where water is available, they drink each day, but may survive long periods without drinking. They are very pugnacious and their long, sharp horns are very effective weapons; in fighting, they lower their head between the forelegs in order to impale their enemy. Even Lions have been killed in this manner.

The voice is a snort or a grunt. Sight is very keen.

GEMSBOK *Oryx gazella* (L.)   p. 188
F Gemsbok   G Südafrikanischer Spiessbock   A Gemsbok, Gensbok
Identification: Height at shoulder 48 in.; weight 450 lb. A large antelope with a striking pattern on head and body. Head white with a conspicuous black 'harness'. A black patch on the forehead, at the base of the horns, joined by a narrow black stripe to a broad patch of the same colour on the blaze. A black stripe extending from the base of the horns across the eye

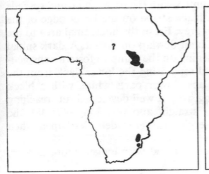

White Rhinoceros, p. 169

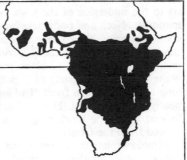

Hippopotamus, p. 171

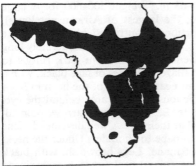

Pygmy Hippopotamus, p. 172

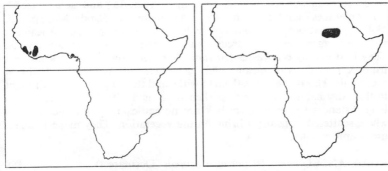

Wild Boar, p. 173

Warthog, p. 174

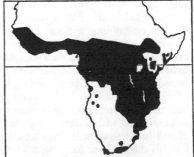

Bush-pig, p. 178

to the corner of the mouth, where it unites with the nasal patch and spreads on to the underside of the jaws. A black stripe on the lower edge of the mandible. Neck and body pale fawn grey. From the interramal area to the chest, a narrow black stripe with a faint dewlap on throat. A dark spinal stripe from the nape to the tail, widening on the rump to form a conspicuous dark patch. A broad black band separating the lower flank from the white belly. Upper parts of legs black, lower parts white, with a black longitudinal patch in front. Tail long, with a well developed tuft reaching nearly to the ground. Horns nearly straight and very long (42; 48), the longest of all the Oryx, ringed, diverging rather widely, V-shaped when viewed from the front.

Female similar to the male, but smaller and with longer, more slender, horns, sometimes slightly curved.

Habitat: Formerly distributed throughout South Africa, from the Karoo districts northwards in the dry west. Typically dry plains and even sub-desert (they favour red dunes with sparser vegetation and isolated trees), but sometimes found in savannas and in mopane woodlands. Map, p. 223.

Habits: Gregarious, Gemsbok usually live in herds of up to 30–40 head but sometimes aggregate in hundreds. Old bulls sometimes lead a solitary life. They feed mainly on grasses (*Aristida, Panicum, Schmidtia*), but also eat fruits, especially wild melons and cucumbers, as well as the bulbs of succulents. This diet enables them to withstand the long periods of drought in their dry habitat. They drink when water is available, and may travel long distances to get it. Gemsbok are nomadic and aggregate in areas where scattered rainstorms bring on the vegetation. They make frequent use of mineral licks.

ROAN ANTELOPE *Hippotragus equinus* (Desmarest) p. 188
F Hippotrague, Antilope chevaline, Antilope rouanne   K Korongo
G Pferdeantilope   A Bastergemsbok
Identification: Height at shoulder 50–63 in.; weight 500–600 lb. A large antelope (after the Eland and Kudu, the largest of African antelopes), slightly resembling a horse in proportions. Contrasted black and white face markings, very long, pointed ears, tufted at their tip, moderately long horns strongly curved backwards. General colour from dark rufous to light reddish fawn. Underparts white. Blaze and sides of face black, with a broad pure white stripe extending from near the base of the horn in front of the eye to the cheek. A less conspicuous, whitish area behind the eye. Muzzle and interramal area pure white. Ears long and narrow, pointed, sickle-shaped with a dark brown tassel at their tip. A well developed mane of stiff hairs, fawn with dark tips, from nape to shoulder. Under the neck, longish dark hairs, forming a kind of mane. Legs brownish, with black patches. Horns strong, evenly divergent, curved backwards, heavily ringed at the base, relatively short (30; 39) for the size of the animal.

Female similar to male, but horns smaller and less heavily ridged.

Intraspecific variation: The western race (*koba*) (from Gambia to the Cameroons and Central Africa) has a pale brown general coloration. The East African race (*langheldi*) (from Uganda to Zambia) is pale rufous-roan, while the southern race (*equinus*) (from southern Congo and Uganda to South Africa) is greyer. The Angolan race (*cottoni*) is characterised by a rich rufous ground colour.

Similar species: See Sable.

Habitat: Open or lightly wooded country, often in rough broken ground and grassy valleys, never far from water. Absent from densely forested country. Map, p. 223.

Habits: Roan live in small herds, up to 20 individuals, sometimes 50 when water or food become short. Each herd is led by a master bull. Bulls in mating condition are solitary and in season take the females out of the herds. The pair lives then for a while together. After having given birth, the females form a herd by themselves, then come back to their males in their territories. During the dry season, many herds may join and constitute large concentrations. Very pugnacious and aggressive, Roan fight from a very early age.

The voice is a blowing snort.

Roan are mainly grazers (90 per cent of their food is made of grass) and rarely feed on leaves and fruit. Like many grazers, they are particularly susceptible to drought and they move to a variable extent according to seasons; if the conditions are favourable all the year round, they can be very sedentary.

SABLE ANTELOPE   *Hippotragus niger* (Harris)   p. 188
F Hippotrague noir   K Palahala, Mbarapi   G Rappenantilope
A Swartwitpens

Identification: Height at shoulder 43–54 in.; weight 400–550 lb. A large antelope, very dark coloured, with conspicuous head markings. General colour glossy black. Pure white underparts in strong contrast to the sides. Face largely white, with a broad black blaze from the forehead to the nose and a black stripe from below the eye to the muzzle. A well developed mane of long stiff hairs from the top of the neck to the shoulder. Ears long and narrow, light chestnut outside, white inside, not tufted at their tips. Horns very long (40; 64⅞), almost parallel to each other, strongly ridged, rising vertically and sweeping backwards in a pronounced curve.

Female similar to the male, but paler, more or less tinged with dark chestnut; sometimes bright golden chestnut; horns less massive, shorter, and less curved. Calf fawn-coloured, with indistinct facial markings.

Similar species: May be confused with the Roan, but distinguished by its black colour, the strong contrast between dark sides and snowy belly, the different pattern of the head, the absence of tufts at the tip of the ears, and the longer, more robust horns. Sable prefer wooded areas and Roan open grassland, but their ranges may overlap.

Intraspecific variation: The Giant Sable (*variani*), from Angola (between the Upper Cuanza River and its tributary the Luando), sometimes considered as a full species, has a darker, almost black face; the horns are much more massive and much longer than in the typical race.

Habitat: Dry light woodland, or mixed bush and grassland, never far from water. Avoids extensive open grassy plains. Map, p. 229.

Habits: Sable live in herds, usually of from 10 to 20 head, occasionally up to 80. Herds are generally led by a master bull accompanied by females, young and subadults. Bulls often become solitary or associate together in small parties. Very pugnacious, Sable are prone to fighting between themselves and ably defend themselves against carnivores, even Lions, which seldom attack them. Bulls take the female in mating condition out from the herd like the Roan.

They are grazers (90 per cent of their food is made of grass) but feed also on leaves to some extent. They move, following a cyclic route, according to seasons.[1]

WATERBUCK, KOB, LECHWE and REEDBUCK: Reduncinae

Smaller, medium or large antelope, most of them heavily built, with well developed horns (males only), curved backwards then upwards and forwards at their tips, never twisted, but strongly ringed. Muzzle naked. Most species live in marshes or near water from which they never go far. All are mainly grazers.

Three groups may be distinguished, easily recognised from each other by their general features, the shape of the horns and their habits: the true Kob, the Reedbuck (characterised by a bare patch below the ear) and the Rhebuck.

DEFASSA WATERBUCK   *Kobus defassa* (Rüppell)[2]   p. 189
F Cobe defassa, Cobe onctueux   K Kuru
G Defassa-Wasserbock, Hirschantilope   A Tropiese Waterbok
Identification: Height at shoulder 47–53 in.; weight 350–600 lb. A large antelope, heavily built, but elegant and with imposing features; coat coarse and shaggy. General colour from rufous to greyish brown. Sides of face lighter, muzzle darker. A long superciliary stripe and the tip of muzzle white. Ears rounded, broad and large, very hairy, white inside, tipped with

---

[1] In former times, a third species of *Hippotragus*, apparently related to the Roan Antelope, the Bluebuck or Blaauwbok (*Hippotragus leucophaeus*) lived in South Africa (Swellendam district). Its general colour was bluish grey, with no conspicuous head markings and with an ill-developed mane; it was smaller than the Roan or Sable. The Blaauwbok was the first African mammal to have become extinct as a result of human activity. It disappeared as early as 1800, owing to over-shooting of a species with very limited distribution and small numbers.

[2] According to some authors, conspecific with the Common Waterbuck.

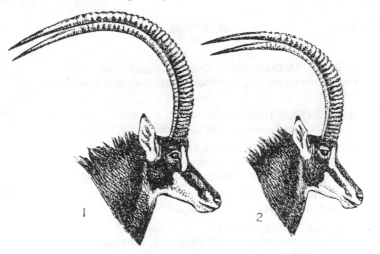

12. Head of Sable Antelope (*Hippotragus niger*): Giant Sable (*variani*) (1); Common Sable (*niger*) (2)

black. Sometimes a white patch under the throat. Buttocks pure white. Limbs darker (except in younger individuals) with a white ring above the hooves. Tail moderately long with a darker tip. Horns long (30; 39½) and heavy, strongly ringed, diverging widely at the base, rising backwards and upwards in a single crescentic curve.

Female similar to the male, generally somewhat lighter, without horns.
Similar species: May be confused with the Common Waterbuck, but the Defassa has a wide white patch instead of a crescent-like marking on the rump. The two species interbreed on the border of their range (along the eastern escarpment of the Rift Valley), at least in the Nairobi National Park and near the Ngorongoro crater; a great variety of rump patterns results.
Intraspecific variation: The typical Defassa (*defassa* and allies) (from Ethiopia through Kenya to central Tanzania) is bright rufous, with much white on face and throat. The populations from the southern Sudan to western Tanzania and Zambia (*harnieri*, *crawshayi*, and allies) are grey, even dark iron-grey, without any rufous tinge. Those from southern Gabon to Angola (*penricei*) are dark blackish brown with a bluish tinge. The western populations (Sing-sing Waterbuck, *unctuosus*), from Senegal to Central African Republic and the Congo, are light rufous, with the white area on face much reduced. Horns are on the average smaller in the west than in the east of the range.
Habitat: Woodlands, clearings, flood plains, even stony hills. Map, p. 229.

Plate 35   HARTEBEEST

1. **BUBAL HARTEBEEST** *Alcelaphus buselaphus*   218
   Frontal region forming a pedicle; blaze generally concolor to
   body.

   1a. **WESTERN HARTEBEEST** *A. b. major*   220
       Dull sandy brown; horns U-shaped.

   1b. **SWAYNE'S HARTEBEEST** *A. b. swaynei*   220
       Deep chocolate brown; horns slender and expanded,
       forming a bracket; blackish patches on upper legs.

   1c. **JACKSON'S HARTEBEEST** *A. b. jacksoni*   220
       Reddish brown; horns V-shaped.

   1d. **COKE'S HARTEBEEST** *A. b. cokii*   220
       Sandy fawn; horns short, expanded, forming a
       bracket.

2. **LICHTENSTEIN'S HARTEBEEST** *Alcelaphus
   lichstensteini*   222
   Frontal region very wide, not forming a pedicle; horns
   thick, with basal part forming a circle when viewed
   from in front.

3. **RED HARTEBEEST** *Alcelaphus caama*   221
   Frontal pedicle greatly expanded; dark blaze; blackish
   patches on upper legs; conspicuous whitish patch on
   rump; horns V-shaped.

TOPI, SASSABY, BONTEBOK Plate 36

1. **TOPI** *Damaliscus korrigum* *page* 226
   Glossy purplish red; dark patches on face and upper limbs.

2. **HUNTER'S HARTEBEEST** *Damaliscus hunteri* 228
   Uniform rufous tawny; white chevron between eyes; long
   whitish tail; horns long, thin, almost parallel.

3. **SASSABY** *Damaliscus lunatus* 227
   Glossy purplish red; dark patches on face and upper
   limbs; horns crescentic.

4. **BLESBOK** *Damaliscus d. phillipsi* 227
   White blaze interrupted by dark band between eyes;
   pale patch on rump inconspicuous; legs dark.

4a. **BONTEBOK** *Damaliscus d. dorcas* 227
   White blaze not interrupted by a dark band between
   eyes; conspicuous white patch on rump; lower legs
   white.

Habits: Although they usually live near water and take refuge in it or among reed beds, Waterbuck are by no means truly aquatic like the Sitatunga or the Lechwe. They may wander considerable distances from water to feed but they are not nomadic since their habitat has plenty of cover and grass at all times of the year. The coat is impregnated with an oily secretion exuding from glands in the skin (French: *Cobe onctueux*). Waterbuck have a peculiar musky odour, which can even be detected where the animals have been standing. The meat may have the same smell in old males, and is therefore considered unpalatable by many, unless care has been taken in butchering to assure that the meat does not come in contact with the hide or the oily secretion.

Gregarious, Waterbuck live in small herds of 5–25 head, sometimes more, usually composed of females, young and subadults, with a master bull. Adult males are polygamous; they have a territorial behaviour and defend areas in which females may wander and graze at random. Young bulls form small herds by themselves.

They are almost entirely grazers and feed on tender shoots; they drink very freely.

Rather silent. The sense of smell seems poorly developed, as in Lechwe and Puku.

They are chiefly preyed on by Lions.

COMMON WATERBUCK *Kobus ellipsiprymnus* (Ogilby) p. 189
F Cobe à croissant   K Kuru   G Ellipsenwasserbock
A Waterbok, Kringgat
Identification: Height at shoulder 47–53 in.; weight 450 lb. A large antelope, with the general features of the Defassa Waterbuck. General colour grizzled-grey or brown, sometimes almost blackish on back, paler on flanks. A long superciliary stripe and the tip of the muzzle white. Ears rounded, broad and large, white inside, tipped with black. A white collar under the throat. A very conspicuous white crescent-like ring across the rump (the only antelope with such a pattern) in strong contrast with the dark rump and buttocks. Limbs darker, with a white ring above the hooves. Tail moderately long with a black tip. Horns long (30; 39¼) and heavy, strongly ringed, diverging widely at their base, rising backwards and upwards in a single crescentic curve.

Female similar to the male, generally somewhat lighter, but without horns.
Similar species: See Defassa Waterbuck.
Habitat: Woodlands and clearings, usually never far from water. Map, p. 229.
Habits: Same as Defassa Waterbuck.

KOB *Kobus* (*Adenota*) *kob* (Erxleben) p. 189
F Cobe de Buffon, C. de Thomas   G Schwarzfuss-Moorantilope
Identification: Height at shoulder 39–43 in.; weight 150–200 lb. A medium-

sized antelope, strongly but gracefully built; coat short and glossy, never coarse. General colour from bright gold fulvous to dark brown. Head marked by a whitish area around the eye, sometimes extending to the base of the ear. A white patch on throat and upper neck. Underparts white, sharply defined on the flanks. Black markings on the front of legs; a white ring above and a bare patch behind the hooves. Tail moderately long, falling short of the hocks, with a black tuft. Horns (20; 27½) thick, strongly ringed, with a double curvature, rising at a marked angle from the head, bending backwards then forwards (when viewed from the side, they have the shape of the letter S).

Female similar to the male, but smaller and without horns.

Intraspecific variation: Kob are very variable in colour. The Western Kob or Buffon's Kob (*kob*) (from Gambia to Chad and the Central African Republic) is slightly smaller, with shorter horns; general colour bright fulvous, with white areas above the eye, back of ear reddish brown. In the White-eared Kob (*leucotis*) (from Sudan to Ethiopia), young males are chestnut-red, like the females, but with age most of them develop a darker colour which spreads from the forehead to the whole upper surface; adult males are generally dark seal-brown, almost black; conspicuous white rings round the eyes; ears of the males entirely white, buff with darker tips in the females and young; size larger, horns longer. Uganda or Thomas's Kob (*thomasi*) (from the southern Bahr-el-Ghazal to Mount Elgon, Kenya and the Rwindi-Rutshuru plains) is also larger; general colour rich dark rufous, with the white areas of the face less extensive; ears buff.

Habitat: Savanna country, flood plains, never far away from water. Map, p. 229.

Habits: Kob live in herds of 20–40 head, sometimes up to 100 and in former times to thousands, as it still occurs in some areas during the dry season (southern Sudan). Still one of the commonest African antelopes, they are bold and often do not retire into cover during the heat of the day, sunning for long hours and less nocturnal than the Waterbuck. However, they often go into the water during the middle of the day. They will then feed on aquatic vegetation; the males in particular appear to be partial to this.

In densely populated districts, adult males defend each a territory more or less circular, from 30 to 150 ft. in diameter, the central area of which is heavily trampled. These territories form a territorial ground located on a ridge or a slightly raised area; the average ground is occupied by about 15 males in a central area of concentrated activity and twice as many on peripheral territories. These areas are primarily copulatory grounds, the males having to leave them to graze and drink. Females enter the territories for mating and move freely on a given ground. Males not on territorial ground join herds of females and young moving in the proximity.

Kobs are purely grazers.

PUKU *Kobus* (*Adenota*) *vardoni* (Livingstone) p. 189
F Puku G Gelbfuss-Moorantelope A Poekoe
Identification: Height at shoulder 31–40 in.; weight up to 200 lb. A medium-sized antelope, much like the Kob with a rather long coat. General colour bright golden yellow. No clearly defined head markings; whitish hue around eyes, on the sides of muzzle and throat. Underparts whitish. No black markings on the legs, which are uniformly rufous. Horns rather short (18; 21), thick, strongly ringed, curving outwards and backwards and then forwards.

Female similar to the male, but with a brownish crown and without horns.

Similar species: Differs from the Kob by the absence of black markings on legs, and shorter horns. Cannot be confused with the Lechwe owing to its shorter and less divergent horns, and absence of black on the legs.

Habitat: Open flats bordering marshes or river banks, never far from water. Map, p. 229.

Habits: Puku usually live in small parties of 3–10 head, sometimes up to 15 or even more. Males are often solitary or form small troops by themselves. During the mating season, they occupy and defend territories widely spaced on a territorial ground, like the Uganda Kob. At the end of the breeding season females with their young make up herds numbering up to 50 head.

The voice is a low whistle uttered when alarmed.

They are grazers, but occasionally browse on acacias.

LECHWE *Kobus* (*Adenota*) *leche* Gray p. 192
F Cobe lechwe G Litschi-Moorantilope A Basterwaterbok
Identification: Height at shoulder 39 in.; weight averages 170 lb. (♀) and 220 lb. (♂), up to 280 lb. A medium-sized antelope, with rather short and conical muzzle, the hindquarters noticeably higher than the shoulders, and a rather long and rough coat. General coloration either bright chestnut fulvous or blackish. No pronounced head markings, only a faint whitish stripe over the eye. Underparts from chin to belly white, sharply set off from the colour of the upperparts. Conspicuous black markings running down the legs, with a white patch above the hooves. Back of pasterns naked; hooves long and pointed. Horns long (28; 36½) and relatively thin, lyre-shaped, bowed, rising upwards, then curving outwards and backwards, almost vertical in their final section, forming a double curve.

Female similar to the male, more lightly built, without horns.

Intraspecific variation: The Red Lechwe (*leche*) (from Botswana to western Zambia) is bright chestnut fulvous, only the legs being marked with black. The Black Lechwe (*smithemani*) (north-eastern Zambia and south-eastern Congo) may be blackish brown on back and sides. This coloration appears very progressively with age in males, while young and females are chestnut fulvous. A third race (*kafuensis*), distinguished by its particularly fine horns

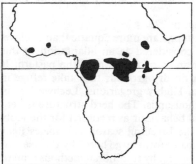

Giant Forest Hog, p. 179

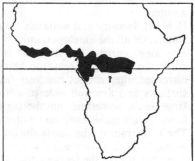

Water Chevrotain, p. 179

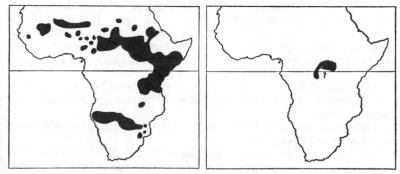

Giraffe, p. 182

Okapi, p. 184

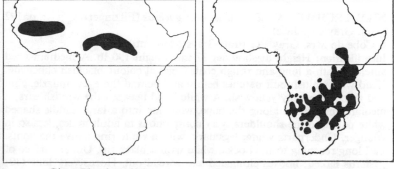

Giant Eland, p. 186

Cape and Livingstone Eland, p. 187

and dark shoulder patches in adult males, occurs in the Kafue Flats, Zambia.

Habitat: Swamps and wetlands. Map, p. 229.

Habits: Of all the antelopes, only Sitatunga are more aquatic than Lechwe. The long, narrow hooves may be considered as an adaptation to this particular habitat as may the hairlessness of the skin of the pastern. If disturbed, they cannot run very fast on dry ground; they take refuge in shallows and are well able to swim. Highly gregarious, Lechwe live in large herds, sometimes numbering thousands. The herd structure is very loose. Adult males have no territorial behaviour as recorded for the Kob. The sexes mix in the herds during the breeding season and males fight viciously. Out of the mating season, males form large herds by themselves. They outnumber the females due to hunting by traditional methods (chila), the females being more easily killed than males.

Lechwe feed on grass (*Echinochloa, Oryza, Panicum, Acroceras, Paspalum, Pennisetum, Digitaria*) and on water plants. The water-meadow pastures offer them greenery throughout most of the year. The herds follow the falling flood and retreat before the rising flood in a fairly regular migration, being then confined to rather narrow belts. They graze in water up to 2 ft. deep, favouring areas where there are about 2 to 8 inches of water.

The sense of smell is poor. The voice is a whistle and a polysyllabic 'whinny-grunt'. Males often emit series of staccato grunts during the breeding season.

Lechwe are preyed on by Hyaena, Cheetah, Leopard, Lion, Wild Dog, and larger predatory birds.

There has been an alarming decrease of Lechwe in recent years. This antelope has disappeared from many parts of its range and even in its main strongholds—the Kafue flats and the Bangweulu swamps—its populations are reduced to a tenth of the numbers of 30 years ago.

NILE LECHWE   *Kobus (Adenota) megaceros* (Fitzinger)   p. 192
(Mrs. Gray's Lechwe)
F Cobe de Mrs. Gray   G Frau Grays Moorantilope
Identification: Height at shoulder 37 in.; weight 190 lb. A medium-sized antelope with a long and rough coat. General colour blackish chocolate. Head with whitish buff patches before and behind the eyes; muzzle, chin and throat generally yellowish. A white band between the whitish ears; a median white stripe along the nape, widening into a large saddle-shaped white patch on the shoulders, very conspicuous in adult males, less so in younger. Underparts white, legs dark, with a white ring above the hoofs. Tail long reaching to the hocks, white with a black tip. Under surface of pasterns naked; hooves elongated and spread out. Horns very long (30; 34½) and thin, strongly ringed, sub-lyrate, curving backwards, diverging widely before curving upwards and a little inwards.

Female uniform chestnut fawn, lighter on underparts and buttocks, without horns.

Habitat: Swamps and wetlands traversed by the White Nile, the Bahr-el-Ghazal and their tributaries. Map, p. 235.

Habits: Nile Lechwe live in large herds, up to 50 or more. Males often form separate groups which are close to but not within the main herd. They have the same aquatic habits as their nearest ally, the Lechwe, which lives 2,000 miles to the south. They feed on grass and aquatic plants.

The alarm call is a croaking grunt.

BOHOR REEDBUCK   *Redunca redunca* (Pallas)   p. 193
F Redunca, Nagor, Cobe des roseaux   K Tohe
G Riedbock; Isabellantilope

Identification: Height at shoulder 27–35 in.; weight 80 lb., up to 110 lb. A small antelope, light and graceful, with a rather long and thick coat. General colour uniform bright yellowish or reddish fawn. Face with light rings around the eyes, but without conspicuous markings. A round light greyish patch of bare skin below the ear. Underparts white. Tail short, very bushy, fawn above and white below, the white underside forming a conspicuous recognition mark when the tail is held erect. Horns thick at their base, short (10; 16⅝), ringed, evenly and widely divergent, curved backwards, then very sharply upwards and forwards forming hooks at their ends; often with a rounded fleshy swelling at their base.

Female similar to the male, but without horns.

Intraspecific variation: Several races have been recognised according to colour and shape of the horns. The Nagor Reedbuck (*redunca*) (from Senegal to Ghana) is somewhat smaller, with no dark stripe along the forelegs, and short but very stout horns. The Nigerian form (*nigeriensis*) (from Nigeria to the Congo) is larger, with usually a dark stripe along the forelegs and rather long horns. The Abyssinian form (*bohor*) (Ethiopia) is duller in colour, and has short, stout horns. The Sudan form (*cottoni*) is distinguished by its long and thin horns with a wide spread, which is usually greater than the horn length itself. The eastern form (*wardi*) (from the Tana River and Uganda to south-western Tanzania) is the most deeply coloured of all, tawny rufous, with the dark stripe on the forelegs well marked. Horns large and stout, forming a very well-marked lunate curve, and sharply hooked forwards and inwards at the tips.

Similar species: See Southern Reedbuck.

Habitat: Grassland, never far from water. Map, p. 235.

Habits: Bohor Reedbuck live in pairs or in small family parties, sometimes singly; young males form small herds of 3 or 4. But they are not truly gregarious and are more often seen in closer proximity to other antelopes than those of their kind. They lie up among reed beds or bush during the heat of the day, making formlike shelters in tall grasses, and graze in the early morning and at dusk. They will sometimes squat very close bolting only at the last moment from cover and run with a 'rocking horse' motion.

They feed principally on grass. The voice is a characteristic shrill whistle uttered when alarmed, particularly as they bound away (some think that this sound is produced by the inguinal pouches).

SOUTHERN or COMMON REEDBUCK
Redunca arundinum (Boddaert) p. 193
F Cobe des roseaux   K Tohe   G Grossriedbock   A Rietbok

Identification: Height at shoulder 33–37 in.; weight 120–170 lb. A medium-sized antelope (the largest of the Reedbucks), light and graceful. General colour uniform greyish fawn, tinged with brown; head and neck lighter fawn. No facial markings except sometimes a blackish patch on the nose or crown. Ears broad and rounded, very hairy, white inside. A round whitish patch of bare skin below the ear (covered with velvety-white hairs in younger animals). Belly white. Legs with a dark stripe in front. Tail short, thick and bushy, pure white below. Horns rather short (15; 18) for an antelope of this size (but longer than in any other Reedbuck), ringed for their basal half, evenly and widely divergent, curved backwards then upwards and forwards, not strongly hooked at their tips: often a rounded fleshy swelling at their base.

Female similar to the male, a little smaller, without horns.

Similar species: Distinguished from the Bohor Reedbuck by its considerably larger size and the shape of horns, which are less sharply curved forwards, not forming hooks at their tips. The Mountain Reedbuck is much smaller and is generally not found in the same habitat.

Habitat: Treeless or sparsely wooded country, with water holes and rivers. Map, p. 235.

Habits: Seldom gregarious, Southern Reedbuck usually live singly or in pairs, sometimes in small family groups, rarely in groups of up to 15. They spend the heat of the day in reed beds or among tall grass, usually near water. They are very reluctant to enter or cross water. Entirely grazers, and very partial to burnt bush, they sometimes make depredation on standing crops.

They utter a shrill whistle when disturbed and make a clicking sound when galloping. They run off with a rocking gait, the tail thrown up showing the white underside.

MOUNTAIN REEDBUCK   *Redunca fulvorufula* (Afzelius)   p. 193
F Redunca de montagne   K Tohe   G Bergriedbock   A Rooiribbok

Identification: Height at shoulder 24–30 in.; weight 50–60 lb. A small antelope, delicate and graceful, with a long, soft and woolly coat. Ears very long and narrow. A bare patch under the ear. General colour greyish fawn, brighter and largely tinged with rufous on the neck and head. Chin and upper throat buff; a dark nose-stripe. Belly largely white. Legs with no defined blackish markings. Tail short and bushy, white below. Horns

WATERBUCK, KOB, LECHWE AND REEDBUCK 217

slender, short (7; 10 1/16) ringed at the base, evenly curved upwards and forwards, with no hooks at the tip.

Female similar to the male, but much greyer, slightly larger and without horns.

Intraspecific variation: The Southern Mountain Reedbuck (*fulvorufula*) (south-east Africa, south of the Limpopo River) is rather larger and more intensively rufous. Chanler's Mountain Reedbuck (*chanleri*) (from southern Ethiopia and the Sudan to Kenya) is smaller and greyer with less rufous tinge. An apparently related form (*adamauae*), of smaller size, has been found in the Adamawa Mountains, Northern Cameroons.

Similar species: See Southern Reedbuck. When, as occasionally occurs, Mountain Reedbuck consort with Southern Reedbuck, the two species may be confused. The Mountain Reedbuck is distinguishable by its smaller size, shorter and less hooked horns, dark nose-stripe, and red neck. May be also confused with Vaal Rhebuck at a distance, but has much more white on the underparts.

Habitat: Distribution largely broken, owing to restriction to a mountainous habitat. Broken hilly country and mountains either stony, with bushes and trees or grassy; seldom on summits. Map, p. 235.

Habits: The Mountain Reedbuck lives on the slopes of hills, even the roughest and steepest. It tends to seek cover amongst rocks and boulders or in patches of scrub. More gregarious than the Bohor Reedbuck, it lives in small parties up to 10 head. Very shy and alert, it takes refuge at higher elevation when disturbed. It proceeds with a kind of 'rocking-horse' action, like other Reedbucks. The call is a sharp whistle.

It feeds on grass, but also browses on leaves and twigs. It feeds and drinks in the morning and evening on lower slopes and in valleys and retires to higher elevations during the heat of the day, when it rests in shady places amongst rock or scrub. The greyish colour merges well into the background of its environment.

VAAL RHEBUCK   *Pelea capreolus* (Forster)   p. 193
F Rhebuck, Pelea   G Rehbok   A Vaalribbok

Identification: Height at shoulder 30 in.; weight 50 lb. A small antelope, gracefully built with a long slender neck, and a soft, thick and woolly coat. Ears long, narrow and pointed. No bare patch under the ear. General colour brownish grey, tinged with fulvous on head and limbs; underparts scarcely paler than the back. Tail short, bushy with white underside and tip. Horns short (8; 11½), nearly straight and vertical, parallel to each other, ringed only at the base.

Female similar to the male, but slightly smaller, without horns.

Similar species: May be confused with Mountain Reedbuck where the two species coexist. Distinguished by absence of well marked white underparts which characterise Mountain Reedbuck, and by straight horns.

Habitat: Grassy hills and mountains, up to the flat tops. Map, p. 235.

Habits: Vaal Rhebuck live in family parties, with a master ram, females and immatures. Parties numbering up to 30 head may be found, but they are usually composed of less than a dozen animals. Old males live singly.

Vaal Rhebuck live in a variety of hilly or mountainous regions. Usually higher grassy slopes or plateaux are selected, more exposed and with less cover than the environment preferred by the Mountain Rhebuck. Where they occupy isolated hills, Vaal Rhebuck may leave them to feed on lower ground in the morning and evening. They are very wary and, when alarmed, take flight with a kind of 'rocking-horse' action, the hindquarters being jerked up in the air. Males are aggressive and are reputed to attack the Mountain Reedbuck which occurs in the same habitat.

They are entirely grazers.

They are sometimes considered inedible, due to the presence of parasitic larvae of the bot-fly under the skin. They are reputed to kill occasionally sheep and goats, also Mountain Reedbucks.

The voice is a sharp coughing snort, and for the males a deep guttural note during the mating season.

TOPI and allies, HARTEBEEST and WILDEBEEST: Alcelaphinae

Large antelopes with some very peculiar features. All of them have the withers higher than the rump, and the face, often long and narrow, with a clumsy, rather 'stupid' appearance. Three well defined types may be distinguished, all unmistakable. The Topi and allies are the most 'normal'. The Hartebeest are well characterised by their sloping back and their very long head, surmounted by a frontal appendage on which are inserted the horns. Both have the tail bordered with a fringe of stiff black hairs on the upper edge (except Hunter's Hartebeest). The Wildebeest,[1] due to their head and general appearance, with peculiar hair ornaments (beard, mane, and horse-like tail), have a 'prehistoric' appearance. All of them live in open habitats, especially on the great plains.

Very gregarious in habits, they generally live in large herds.

BUBAL HARTEBEEST *Alcelaphus buselaphus* (Pallas) p. 208
F Bubale K Kongoni G Kuhantilope
Identification: Height at shoulder 47–57 in.; weight 280–450 lb. A large antelope with unmistakable features. Shoulder considerably higher than the rump, the back sloping at quite a considerable angle. Head extremely long and narrow, the frontal region more or less expanded upwards into a bony pedicle growing from the summit of the skull, imparting a 'stupid' aspect to the animal. General colour almost uniform, varying from sandy fawn to bright reddish, more intense on middle of back, lighter on hind-

[1] Wildebeest are regarded by some as aberrant members of the Bovinae (Leakey).

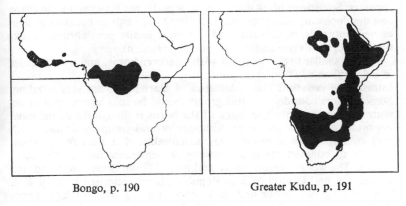

Bongo, p. 190

Greater Kudu, p. 191

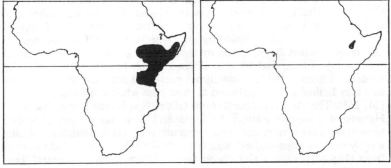

Lesser Kudu, p. 194

Mountain Nyala, p. 195

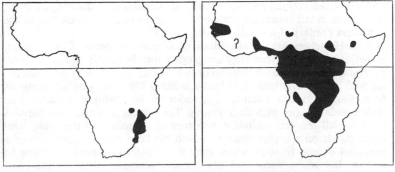

Nyala, p. 195

Sitatunga, p. 196

quarters. Sometimes black markings on legs. Horns very variable in shape and development, doubly curved, first rising outwards or backwards, then curved outwards, or forwards and upwards, finally bent abruptly backwards or upwards (see under intraspecific variation).

Female similar to the male, but with slenderer horns, and usually paler in colour than adult males.

Intraspecific variation: The systematics of Hartebeests are very puzzling. Some authors consider that this group should be split into several forms with full specific rank. The shape of the horns is thought to be the most important diagnostic character. Although several groups of forms, which may overlap to some extent, are recognisable, it is wise for practical reasons to consider them as geographic representatives of the same species. The western group (*major* and allies[1]) (from Senegal to Chad, the Cameroons and Central African Republic) is characterised by large size, dull sandy brown colour and dark shading along front of legs; horns thick and massive, U-shaped at their base when viewed from in front (24; 27½). The central group (Lelwel Hartebeest, *lelwel*; *tschadensis*, *roosevelti*, *jacksoni*) (Chad, Central African Republic, Northern Cameroons, Kordofan, Bahr-el-Ghazal, Uganda, Kenya (Lake Baringo), is also large, but it is distinguished by the extreme length of the head and of the frontal pedicle, and by a uniform reddish brown colour; blackish shading in front of the legs sometimes present; horns diverging outwards to a very limited extent, V-shaped at their base when viewed from in front (24; 26¾). The Tora Hartebeest (*tora*) (Blue Nile) is pale tawny; Swayne's Hartebeest (*swaynei*) (eastern Ethiopia and Somalia) is deep chocolate brown; both are smaller and their horns are very much expanded, forming a curly bracket or parenthesis sign lying on the side when viewed from the front (18; 20¼). Coke's Hartebeest (*cokii*) (from Kenya to central Tanzania) is also smaller, with a sandy fawn colour; horns rather short (19; 23½) and thick, forming a curly bracket lying on its side.

Habitat: Open country and light bush, particularly in undulating country; sometimes in tall savanna woodland, but never in dense thicket or in the subdesert borders of the Sahara. Map, p. 235.

Habits: Hartebeest are social animals, usually seen in herds of 4 to 15 head, sometimes up to 30. They may congregate into hundreds and in the past, aggregations of thousands were recorded. In East Africa, they often associate with zebras. Old bulls may lead a solitary life; young bulls sometimes form all-male groups. Each herd is under the leadership of a master bull which leads females with their young. The structure of the herd remains the same all the year round. A territory is defended by the male, who often stands on a higher place to watch his herd and the approach of a potential enemy. In some areas, they move great distances according to season; but where water and grazing are adequate, they are the most sedentary of all major antelopes. While a herd is grazing, scouts take up

[1] The typical race (*buselaphus*) from north-west Africa is now extinct.

on some prominent position, such as a termite mound, to give warning of any danger.

Primarily grazers, they are like many antelopes especially partial to young growth on burns. Although they drink regularly when water is available, they can dispense with it for long periods; wallowing points are visited regularly. They are placid, though rival bulls fight with energy. They are fleet of foot and their sense of smell is better developed than their sight.

The alarm call is a nasal snort. They are a favourite prey of Lion.

Some races, particularly Swayne's Hartebeest, survive very precariously due to rinderpest epidemics and uncontrolled hunting.

RED or CAPE HARTEBEEST *Alcelaphus caama* (G. Cuvier)[1] p. 208
F Bubale caama A Rooihartbees G Kaama

Identification: Height at shoulder 49 in.; weight 350–400 lb. A large antelope, with the general features of the Bubal Hartebeest, the frontal pedicle being greatly expanded. General colour light reddish fawn. Face with a median dark blaze, interrupted between the eyes by a fulvous band. Back of neck, chin, and limbs up to shoulders and hips more or less tinged with blackish. A conspicuous broad whitish patch on lower rump, in strong contrast with the darker upperside and the hips. Horns (19; 26¾) heavily ridged, V-shaped at their base when viewed from in front; curved at first slightly forwards and inwards, then sharply backwards.

Female similar to the male, but with more slender horns.

Intraspecific variation: A subspecies *selbornei*, the Transvaal Red Hartebeest, was described on the grounds that it was more richly coloured than the nominate race. If the separation of these two forms is warranted, which is doubtful, then all existing animals must be considered as belonging to the race *selbornei* and the nominate race is extinct.

Habitat: Now found in arid regions of the north-western Cape, Botswana and South-West Africa. Originally also distributed over most of the Cape Province, southern and western Transvaal, Orange Free State, Lesotho and the western part of Natal. Reintroduced into several game reserves and National Parks in South Africa (not the Kruger National Park where it never occurred), and also in western Rhodesia. Grassland and savanna, also mountainous country to the summit of the Drakensberg. Map, p. 243.

Habits: Red Hartebeest live in herds of 10–30 head. Formerly it gathered at some seasons in enormous troops covering the plains. Old bulls are sometimes solitary. It drinks regularly when water is available, but may dispense with water for long periods. It feeds on grass and Karroo vegetation, but seldom browses. It is very fleet of foot.

It is rather silent, but occasionally utters a kind of sneeze or sneezing cough when alarmed.

[1] Probably conspecific with the Bubal Hartebeest (*buselaphus*).

Red Hartebeest, once abundant over a wide range, were on the verge of extinction due to overshooting by 1875. They are now plentiful in the Kalahari Gemsbok National Park in Botswana and South-West Africa, and increase very satisfactorily in the regions into which they have been reintroduced.

LICHTENSTEIN'S HARTEBEEST   *Alcelaphus lichtensteini* (Peters)

p. 208

F Bubale de Lichtenstein   A Mofhartbees
G Konzi, Lichtensteins Kuhantilope

Identification: Height at shoulder 49 in.; weight 260–320 lb. A large antelope, with hartebeest features, but frontal region very wide and not forming a pedicle. Back bright rufous contrasting with the pale fawn flanks and the whitish hindquarters. A dark blaze on the middle of face. A dark stripe down the front of the legs. Horns short (20; 23⅞), flattened, and thick at their base, strongly ringed except near the tips, with a double curvature like the letter Z, curved first outwards, then upwards and inwards, finally backwards, their terminal portions nearly parallel.

Female similar to the male but with less robust horns.

Similar species: Differs from the Bubal Hartebeest (which does not occur in the same areas) by the more contrasted coloration; the line of the back which is less sloping backwards (withers proportionately lower) and the shape of the horns.

Habitat: Guinea savanna and woodland, generally in woodland stands characterized by a ground cover of perennial bunch grasses. Map, p. 243.

Habits: Lichtenstein's Hartebeest usually live in small herds of up to 10 head, temporarily joining roan, wildebeest and zebra. Each herd is a family group with a master bull and a harem of up to 8 or 9 females with attendant calves. The bull occupies a dominant position, but the herd is led by a female in case of danger. Bachelors form groups by themselves and old males often are solitary. Lichtenstein's Hartebeest are territorial in behaviour. Demarcation of territory is by horning of earth: the animal goes down on the 'knees' and digs up earth with its horns; it then rubs the sides of its head in the earth in order to leave a part of the secretion of its well developed pre-orbital glands.

When alarmed, they utter a 'sneeze-snort' through the nostrils; a bellow is sometimes emitted when fighting.

Sight and hearing are very acute, but the sense of smell is apparently not well developed.

Lichtenstein's Hartebeest are grazers and feed during much of the day and night, though lying down during the heat of the day. They drink daily, usually in the early morning. They are generally sedentary.

Fighting between males occurs during the rutting season. The gestation period is 240 days and most of the calves are dropped in July and August,

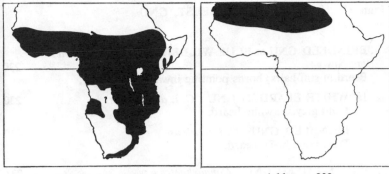

Bushbuck, p. 198

Addax, p. 200

Scimitar-horned Oryx, p. 201

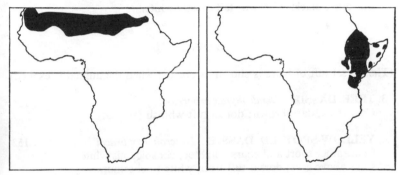

Beisa Oryx, p. 201

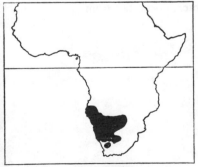

Gemsbok, p. 202

Roan Antelope, p. 204

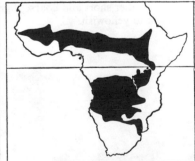

Plate 37   WILDEBEEST, GNU

1. **BRINDLED GNU or BLUE WILDEBEEST** *Connochaetes taurinus*   230
   Beard of stiff hairs; horns pointing inwards; tail black.

   1a. **WHITE BEARDED GNU** *C. t. albojubatus*   230
       Light greyish; white beard.

   1b. **BRINDLED GNU** *C. t. taurinus*   230
       Dark grey; black beard.

2. **WHITE-TAILED GNU** *Connochaetes gnu*   231
   Tuft of stiff hairs on face; tuft on chest; horns pointing
   upwards; blackish brown; tail mostly white.

DASSIE

(The dorsal tuft of hairs is shown as erected when the animal is excited)

3. **TREE DASSIE** *Dendrohyrax arboreus*   154
   Coat thick, dark brown; dorsal tuft whitish (erected).

4. **YELLOW-SPOTTED DASSIE** *Heterohyrax brucei*   153
   Coat rather short and coarse, lighter; conspicuous white
   spots above eyes; dorsal tuft from white to chestnut.

5. **ROCK DASSIE** *Procavia capensis*   152
   Coat rather short and coarse, lighter; dorsal tuft from
   black to yellowish.

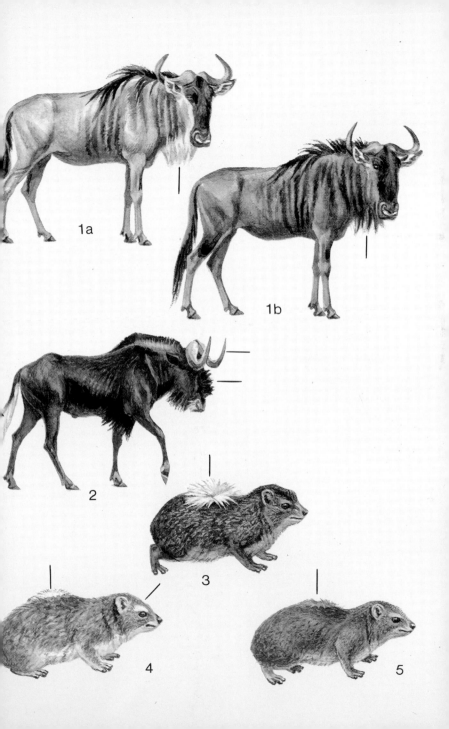

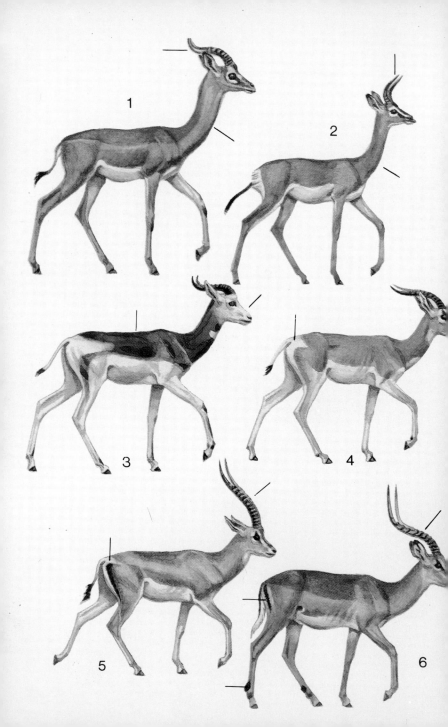

LARGER GAZELLE

Plate 38

1. **GERENUK** *Litocranius walleri*   *page* 232
   Very long neck; long limbs; ruddy brown; tail rather
   short; horns recurved backwards.

2. **DIBATAG** *Ammodorcas clarkei*   233
   Long neck; long limbs; purplish grey; tail very long;
   horns recurved forwards.

3. **DAMA GAZELLE** *Gazella dama*   236
   Head white; neck and back rufous, hindquarters white.

4. **SOEMMERING'S GAZELLE** *G. soemmeringi*   237
   Rufous fawn; head with dark blaze; white patch on
   hindquarters.

5. **GRANT'S GAZELLE** *G. granti*   238
   Fawn; white patch bordered with black on hindquarters;
   horns long.

6. **IMPALA** *Aepyceros melampus*   234
   Glossy rufous; buttocks white; black stripe on back of
   thigh; tufts of black hairs above heels of hind legs; horns
   very long and lyrate.

Lichtenstein's Hartebeest are mainly preyed on by Lion, half of the animals killed being young, and to some extent by Wild Dog, Cheetah and Leopard.

TIANG, TOPI and KORRIGUM   *Damaliscus korrigum* (Ogilby)   p. 209
F Damalisque, Topi, Tiang   K Nyamera   G Leierantilope, Topi, Tiang
Identification: Height at shoulder 39–51 in.; weight 200–300 lb. A large antelope with a fairly long head, but frontal region not drawn upwards; shoulder noticeably higher than the rump, giving the back an ungainly slope (body shape similar to that of true Hartebeests, but less exaggerated in length of the head and obliqueness of the back). General colour reddish brown to purplish red, very glossy (in bright sunlight, an iridescent sheen is clearly visible), with distinct dark patches on face, upper part of forelegs, hips and thighs, without any white marking. Lower part of legs orange-fawn. Horns thick, deeply ridged, lyrate, rising vertically and curving evenly backwards as they diverge, their tips slightly recurved upwards.

Female similar to the male, but usually lighter in colour, with horns shorter and less deeply ridged.
Intraspecific variation: Several races are recognised according to size, development of the horns and colour of the coat. The Korrigum (*korrigum*) (from Senegal to western Sudan) is the largest, with a very bright reddish orange colour; horns well developed (24; 28½). The Tiang (*tiang*) (Sudan, south-west Ethiopia and Lake Albert) is smaller, redder in colour with a purplish tinge; horns slenderer on the average (21; 26½). The Topi (*jimela, topi* and allies) (from Uganda and south Somalia through Kenya to south-west Tanzania) is darker, rich rufous brown with a strong purplish hue; a mixture of long and short hairs, disposed in patches producing a brindled appearance; horns decidedly smaller (19; 24⅞).
Habitat: Open savanna and park woodland, sometimes found in very dry country. Map, p. 243.
Habits: These antelopes probably have the greatest population of any African species. Highly gregarious, they live in herds of 15 to 30, sometimes up to several hundreds. At certain seasons, they gather in enormous assemblages of up to 12,000 individuals. This coincides with a mass migration in search of fresh pastures (in West Africa they move from north to south in the early rains). Often they mingle with herds of Hartebeest, Wildebeest and Zebra, sometimes of Buffalo and Kob. Topi willingly crowd together in a dense mass, especially if alarmed. During the mating season, males settle on well marked stamping grounds, where the grass is kept short. Each male has its own territory, defended against the intruders, while females and young wander freely around. Mating takes place within the territory. After reproduction, the herds split, males and females forming parties by themselves.

Although they drink and are especially fond of extensive flood plains, they can go without water for long periods, as long as lush pastures are available. They are purely grazers and particularly appreciate the short grass lawns, in some semi-desert areas. They often thrive on dry grasses not eaten by other antelopes. Due to some unknown factor, they show a discontinuous distribution over the vast range which they now inhabit, being unaccountably absent from regions which appear to be favourable (soil or vegetation factors?). They can run very fast with a bounding gait, less exaggerated than true hartebeest.

The voice is a snort and grunts. They are preyed on by Lion.

SASSABY or TSESSEBE *Damaliscus lunatus* (Burchell)[1]   p. 209
F Sassaby   A Basterhartbees   G Halbmondantilope
Identification: Height at shoulder 47 in.; weight 300–350 lb. A large antelope with the general features of the Topi. General colour rich dark reddish chestnut, with a purplish gloss. Front of face black. Lower part of shoulders, hips and legs to the knees and hocks blackish, below yellowish brown. Belly rufous. Horns (16; 18½) ringed except at the tips, evenly curved, bending outwards, then turning backwards and inwards; crescent shaped when viewed from in front.

Female similar, but smaller, with thinner horns.
Habitat: Formerly from the Zambezi River to northern Botswana, northern Transvaal and northern Natal (Zululand). Grassland, swampy flood plains and open country with scattered patches of bush; will enter thickets on occasion. Map, p. 243.
Habits: Not so highly gregarious as other members of the group, Sassaby live in family parties or small herds of 8–10 head, which may join together into larger herds, up to 200 head during the dry season. They are exclusively grazers.

Sassaby have the reputation of being one of the fastest of all African antelopes, but probably no speedier than Topi.

The call is a snort.

BONTEBOK and BLESBOK *Damaliscus dorcas* (Pallas)   p. 209
F Bontebok-Blesbok   A Bontbok-Blesbok   G Bunt- and Blessbock
Identification: Height at shoulder 33–39 in.; weight 130–220 lb. Fairly large antelopes but definitely smaller than the Topi, with a striking pattern of white markings on the head, rump and legs. General colour rich brown, with a purplish gloss, turning to silvery rufous fawn on shoulders and back. A conspicuous white area from the base of the horns to the nose, the part above the eyes narrower. Hinder part of the rump pale or pure white like the underparts. Legs partly white, with a blackish stripe in front of the forelegs and a mark on the hind legs. Horns rather small (15; 20), heavily ringed, evenly curved backwards and outwards, their tips recurved upwards, in a simple lyrate form.

[1] Probably conspecific with the Korrigum.

Female similar, but smaller and with thinner horns.

Intraspecific variation: These antelopes have generally been considered as two distinct species: the Bontebok and the Blesbok. But they are so closely allied that their relationship among Hartebeest is better expressed by their reduction to races of one species, formerly widely distributed over South Africa. They differ as follows:

BONTEBOK (*D. dorcas=pygargus*) Larger, darker and more richly coloured. Facial white band usually continuous from base of horns to the nose, narrower between the eyes. Pure white patch on rump large. Lower parts of legs mostly white.

BLESBOK (*D. phillipsi=albifrons*) Smaller and lighter. Facial white band usually interrupted by a dark narrow band between the eyes. An inconspicuous, pale brown patch on rump; only base of tail pure white. Lower parts of legs mostly dark.

The Bontebok was never very numerous within its restricted range in the south-western Cape Province. Nevertheless hunting reduced its numbers considerably and it was only saved from complete extinction by the protection extended by a few private farmers. Now preserved in the Bontebok National Park and on some private farms. Total population estimated at about 600 in 1962 and increasing satisfactorily.

The Blesbok was formerly distributed over the northern Cape Province, Orange Free State, southern and western Transvaal and western Natal, and occurred in very large numbers. When all the wild land of its original range had been settled, numbers had decreased considerably. However, there has since been an upsurge as farmers have restocked their properties and populations have been established in many reserves. Now again quite numerous and utilised as a meat animal on a large scale.

Both Bontebok and Blesbok are grazers which inhabit open grassland. They live in herds of from 6 to 30 head, sometimes hundreds strong, and drink regularly. When disturbed, a herd will usually form a single file and run upwind. Map, p. 243.

HUNTER'S HARTEBEEST or HIROLA *Damaliscus hunteri*
(Sclater)   p. 209
F Damalisque de Hunter, Hirola G Hunters Leierantilope

Identification: Height at shoulder 39 in.; weight 160 lb. A fairly large antelope, with general features of Hartebeest, but more lightly built and more graceful. General colour uniform rufous tawny, somewhat darker on the legs. On the head a well defined white chevron between the eyes. A long hairy tail reaching to the hocks, white for its greater distal section, except for a blackish tip surrounded by a whitish area. Horns not rising from an elevated pedicle, long (24; 28½) and rather thin, curving outwards and upwards and becoming parallel for the greater portion of their length, very sharp at the tip (they show some similarities with those of the Kob or Impala).

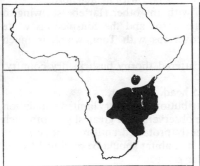

Sable Antelope, p. 205

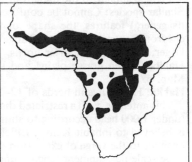

Defassa Waterbuck, p. 206

Common Waterbuck, p. 210

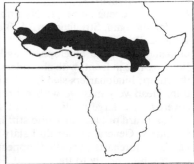

Kob, p. 210

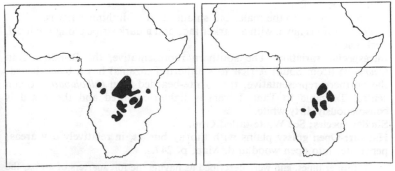

Puku, p. 212

Lechwe, p. 212

Female similar to the male, but smaller and with lighter horns.

Similar species: Cannot be confused with any other Hartebeest owing to its general features, the shape of the horns and the conspicuous white chevron between the eyes. Range overlaps with Topi, which is much larger, darker, with shorter horns.

Habitat: Open grassy plains and scattered thorny bush in dry country. Map, p. 243.

Habits: Hirola live in herds of 12–25 head. A grazer.

This antelope, with a restricted distribution, has a very limited population (under 1,000 head according to some observers), the greatest part of which is believed to inhabit Kenya. Efficiently protected until now, it could be brought to the verge of extinction if its habitat should be modified by the large scale development scheme under project.

BRINDLED GNU or WILDEBEEST *Connochaetes* (*Gorgon*) *taurinus* (Burchell)   p. 224

F   Gnou à queue noire   K Nyumbu ya montu
G Weissbartgnu, Streifengnu   A Blouwildebees

Identification: Height at shoulder 51–55 in.; weight 350–600 lb. An unmistakable large antelope, heavily built and of clumsy appearance;[1] Body ox-like in front, with shoulders massive but only slightly higher than the rump; hindquarters slenderly built and quite disproportionate. Limbs thin. Head very massive with a broad flattened, bristly muzzle and face covered by a large median tuft of thick black hairs. Under throat and neck, a beard of black or white stiff hairs. A long black mane on neck and shoulders. General colour dull slaty grey, more or less crossed by darker bands on foreparts ('brindled' appearance). Tail black, long and hairy, its tuft reaching nearly to the ground. Horns (21; 25⅝) present in both sexes, with a low, rather small palm at their base, curving downwards and then upwards, forwards and inwards transversely to the head (not unlike those of the Cape Buffalo).

Female similar to the male, but smaller and with thinner horns.

Young rufous fawn, with a darker face and a dark stripe along the head, neck and back.

Intraspecific variation: The southern representative, the Brindled Gnu (*taurinus*) (from South Africa to southern Tanzania) has a black beard; the northern representative, the White-bearded Gnu (*albojubatus*) (from central Tanzania to Tana River) is lighter-coloured and the beard is conspicuously dirty white.

Similar species: See White-tailed Gnu.

Habitat: Open grassy plains with thorny bushes, in relatively dry areas; penetrates into open woodland. Map, p. 247.

---

[1] In former times, gnu were described as having the forequarters of an ox, the hindquarters of an antelope and the tail of a horse. This description gives a good idea of an animal which has been described as 'the old fool of the veld'.

Habits: Very gregarious, Wildebeest are mostly seen in large herds. During their wanderings, herds numbering up to tens of thousands head may be seen together. During the mating season, breeding groups of from 2 or 3 to more than 150 females and young are herded by from 1 to 3 bulls; the males apparently share the herd without any hierarchy among themselves. They trot around in a head-high rocking gait, forcing the herd into a tighter mass. Males defend a zone around their herd, even when on the move. At the end of the mating season, the breeding herds are absorbed into the larger herds and there is no observable social structure. Wildebeest may be found in close association with Zebra and Thomson's Gazelle, sometimes with other herbivores of the plains.

On the move, they follow favourable conditions of food and water, their extensive movements (sometimes the distance covered by the animals is well over 1,000 miles) being in some areas apparently annual migrations. They often walk and run in a single file. Like many plains animals, they scatter during the rains and concentrate during the dry season around water holes or streams, seeking palatable grass. They tend to graze in a scattered formation. Active at all hours of the day and night, except in the middle of hot days, they feed on grass (up to 98 per cent. of their diet) and appear to have a strong preference for certain species when sprouting (in parts of East Africa, oat grass, *Themeda triandra*, is by far the most important, followed by *Pennisetum*). Wildebeest drink every day if water is available, but can live for 5 days without drinking. During the dry season they may move over 30 miles a day to drink. Sometimes water may be supplemented with succulents and wild melons. Wildebeest show more rigid water requirements than other animals living in the same area, particularly Oryx and Grant's Gazelle.

They are preyed on by Lion (providing half of their diet in some cases), Cheetah and Wild Dog; in east Africa, hyaenas take a heavy toll of newly born calves. In a plains environment, especially in Masailand, East Africa, Wildebeest can be the principal herbivorous species.

The voice is a loud explosive snort and a low moaning grunt. Wildebeest are very noisy. Scent is an important form of communication.

WHITE-TAILED GNU   *Connochaetes gnou* (Zimmermann)   p. 224
(Black Wildebeest)
F Gnou à queue blanche   A Swartwildebees   G Weissschwanzgnu
Identification: Height at shoulder 45 in.; weight 350 lb. An unmistakable, large antelope, heavily built and of peculiarly grotesque aspect, with shoulders massive, higher than the rump; hindquarters slenderly built. Head very massive with the face covered by a large brush-like tuft of stiff hairs pointing upwards. A beard under the throat and a tuft of hairs on the chest between the fore legs. A mane on neck and shoulders, buffish white at the base, dark at the tip. A long tail, reaching nearly to the ground, black at its base then pure white. General colour dark brown, jet black in

old males freshly moulted. Horns (21; 29) present in both sexes, very wide and nearly in contact at their base, bent downwards and forwards then turning upwards, pointing nearly vertically.

Female similar to the male, but somewhat smaller, with thinner horns.
Similar species: Could possibly be confused with the Brindled Gnu; but the brush-like tuft on the muzzle, the tufts on the throat and between the legs, the colour of the tail and the shape of the horns are, with a smaller size, excellent characteristics for identification.
Habitat: Formerly distributed over the central plateau of South Africa—Cape Province, Orange Free State, southern Transvaal and Natal. Now found only on a few private farms and a number of parks and game reserves. Open grass veld and subdesert steppes. Map, p. 247.
Habits: White-tailed Gnu live in herds of up to 20 or 30. Formerly in large aggregations, in association with Quagga and Ostriches. Males have a territory at least for part of the year. They feed mainly on grasses, but take some succulents, karoo-bushes, and other shrubs. They often kneel as they graze. They drink regularly. They can run at a good speed; extraordinary capers are characteristic. (It is often referred to as the clown of the animal kingdom.) Aggressive; bulls fight fiercely during the mating season.

The call is a loud bellowing snort (hence their name, from the Hottentot 't'gnu'), sometimes a whistling sound.

Formerly very numerous, White-tailed Gnu have been nearly exterminated by the Boer farmers for meat and hide. They are now well preserved in reserves and on private farms, where they increase very satisfactorily. Total population may be estimated at about 2,000, as against 1,000 in 1947.

GAZELLE, IMPALA and allies: Antilopinae

Small to medium-sized, slender and graceful antelopes, with thin, long limbs (often with tufts of hair on the 'knees') giving them great speed. Muzzle hairy. The horns, carried by both sexes (except in Gerenuk, Dibatag and Impala), are often lyrate and heavily ringed. Most live in open dry country, never in closed habitat (except Impala), and some even in true desert to which they are highly adapted, owing to their ability to exist without water. This group of antelope is also spread over Arabia, northwest and central Asia to India.

GERENUK *Litocranius walleri* (Brooke)   p. 225
(Giraffe-Gazelle)
F Gazelle de Waller, Gazelle-Giraffe   K Swala twiga   G Giraffengazelle
Identification: Height at shoulder 35–41 in.; weight 80–115 lb. A large gazelle, with an exceptionally long neck (hence its common names), and very elongated limbs; eyes very large. General colour ruddy brown with

the upper back distinctly darker, contrasting with lighter sides. No lateral band; line separating the rufous flank from the white underparts clearly defined. Median part of face more rufous; no facial stripes, a white ring around the eye, extending as a streak towards the muzzle. Tufts of long hairs on the 'knees'. Tail rather short, broadened and flattened at the base, then tapering to the terminal black tuft, never held straight upright, but curled round the body or put between the legs. Horns (14; 17⅔) very stout, heavily ringed, widely separated at their base, sublyrate, curved at first outwards and upwards, then backwards and inwards, their tips recurved upwards or forwards.

Female similar to the male, but without horns and with a dark patch on the crown.

Similar species: The Gerenuk may be confused with the Dibatag which is also long-necked. But the Dibatag has a more slender neck and a longer tail, held differently; the shape of the horns is quite different in the adult. Nevertheless an immature buck may have almost exactly the same shape of horns. Facial markings may help to avoid misidentification.

Habitat: Dry thorn-bush country and even desert. One of the very few African antelopes which seems to have extended its range during the past 50 years (like Hunter's Hartebeest which lives in the same area). Map, p. 247.

Habits: Gerenuk live singly or in small groups up to 7 head.

They very seldom graze, but browse on prickly bushes and trees (*Commiphora*, acacias), mainly eating the tender leaves and shoots. Their long neck ('Gerenuk' means Giraffe-necked in Somali) and their long limbs enable them to browse on tall bushes, as they stand erect on their hind legs, neck extended and fore legs against the trunk, using one of these to pull down higher branches. They do not require water at all. When running, they stretch their long neck down in a line with the body, and the legs are so extended that the animal loses a good deal of its standing height.

DIBATAG *Ammodorcas clarkei* (Thomas)[1]   p. 225
(Clarke's Gazelle)
F Dibatag, Gazelle de Clarke   G Dibatag, **Lamagazelle**
Identification: Height at shoulder 31–35 in.; weight 65–70 lb. A medium-sized gazelle-like antelope, gracefully built, with a long, slender neck (not so long as in the Gerenuk) and long limbs. General colour uniform dark purplish grey tinged with rufous, with no lateral band. Underparts and buttocks white. Head with a rich chestnut median blaze; on each side, a white stripe from base of the horn to the muzzle; area around the eye white; from the eye to the muzzle, a dark facial streak. Tail very long, thin,

---

[1] The Dibatag is sometimes classified near the Reedbucks with which it shares the horn formation and certain anatomical features. For practical reasons we prefer to treat it with the Gerenuk with which it may be confused.

entirely black; held straight upright or thrown forward when the animal is alarmed or running with the head lifted high.[1] Horns moderately long (10; 12⅝), strongly ridged at their base, evenly divergent, 'sickle-like', curved upwards and backwards, then forwards.

Female similar to the male, but without horns.

Similar species: See Gerenuk.

Habitat: Low thorn bush (not dense big bushes; in this respect differing from the Gerenuk), alternating with patches of grass; sometimes grassy plains. Map, p. 247.

Habits: Dibatag live singly, but usually in pairs or in groups of 3 to 5; sometimes in small family parties up to 9 head.

Browsers, they feed for preference on small bushes, acacias and *Commiphora* trees, their long neck enabling them to reach the young shoots. Like the Gerenuk, they are able to stand on their hind legs, fore feet against a branch. They also feed on berries (*Solanum*) and to some extent graze when grass is green.

Very shy and alert, Dibatag move around a great deal; home range structure is very flexible. They are rare, although may be common locally. Though protected, they are commonly poached for their hides. Destruction of the habitat through overgrazing by domestic livestock is also a serious threat to their survival.

IMPALA   *Aepyceros melampus* (Lichtenstein)[2]   p. 225
F Impala   K Swala pala   G Impala, Schwarzfersenantilope   A Rooibok
Identification: Height at shoulder 33–37 in.; weight 100–180 lb. A medium-sized lightly built and very graceful antelope with a glossy coat. General colour bright rufous fawn, paler on the flanks. Face with no contrasted pattern, except a white line over the eye and a blackish blaze in some races. Chin and upper throat white. A narrow black line along the middle of the rump to the tail. Underparts and buttocks white. A vertical black stripe on back of thighs, but not bordering the white buttocks. A brush-like tuft of long and coarse black hairs above the heels of the hind legs (a unique feature among antelopes). Tail fairly long, white with a dark median line, terminated by a white tuft. Horns long (20; 36⅝), slender and very graceful, lyrate, S-shaped, convex for their basal half, then curving upwards as they spread.

Female similar to the male, but smaller and without horns.

Intraspecific variation: The Southern Impala (*melampus*) (from south-east Congo, Zambia and southern Tanzania to the Orange River) is smaller and duller with shorter horns; the East African Impala (*rendilis*) (from northern Kenya and Uganda southwards) is brighter with larger horns.

---

[1] 'Dibatag' is derived from the Somali words *dabu*=tail and *tag*=erect.

[2] Actually, the Impala is not a true gazelle, and is considered by some as forming a subfamily (Aepycerotinae) by itself. It is more like the Kob than any gazelle.

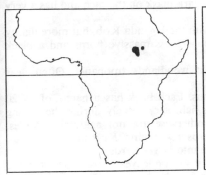

Nile Lechwe, p. 214

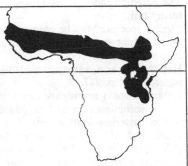

Bohor Reedbuck, p. 215

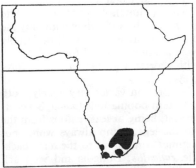

Southern Reedbuck, p. 216

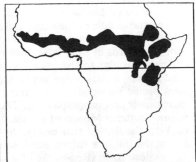

Mountain Reedbuck, p. 216

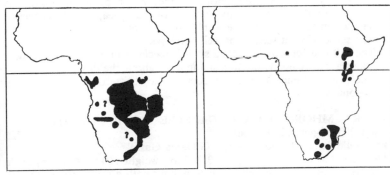

Vaal Rhebuck, p. 217

Bubal Hartebeest, p. 218

The Angolan race (*petersi*) shows a dark mask on the face and has a very bushy tail.

Similar species: May be confused with the Uganda Kob, but more lightly built, lighter coloured and with longer, less massive horns and a black stripe on the rump.

Habitat: Acacia savanna and light woodlands (mopane). Often near water. Map, p. 247.

Habits: Impala are highly gregarious. Each buck has a harem of 15–20 'ewes', sometimes up to 100. Males fight very fiercely during the rutting season, uttering loud grunts, but otherwise are not aggressive. Males, young and old, form bachelor herds resembling Kob in this respect. During the dry months, Impala join into larger herds.

Active both night and day, they browse on leaves of trees (acacias) and bushes, and also feed on grasses (preferably short grass) and fruits. They are very dependent upon water, but can survive on dew for long periods.

Their movements are very fast and they are capable of prodigious jumps, even when there are no obstacles to clear; leaps of thirty feet in length or ten feet in height are within their powers.

The sense of sight seems not well developed.

The call is a loud high-pitched snort, especially uttered when alarmed. Impalas are very noisy, often grunting throughout the day.

The principal enemies are the leopard, the cheetah and the wild dog, occasionally the lion.

ADDRA, MHORR or DAMA GAZELLE   *Gazella* (*Nanger*) *dama*
(Pallas) (Red-necked Gazelle)   p. 225
F Gazelle dama, 'Biche Robert'   G Dama-Gazelle

Identification: Height at shoulder 35–43 in.; weight 160 lb. A large gazelle (the largest of all true gazelle), slenderly built with a proportionately long neck and legs. Neck and upperparts uniform rufous or chestnut brown, sharply contrasting with the white rump and lower parts of body. No lateral band on the flank. Head pure white (adults). A conspicuous white spot on the middle of the neck. Tail short, well haired, white with only the very tip black. Horns short (13; 17) and thick, strongly ringed, noticeably bent backwards at their base, then recurved upwards and forwards.

Female similar to the male, but with shorter and thinner horns; forehead rufous; a dark stripe across the eye.

Intraspecific variation: The pattern of coloration varies very widely, both individually and geographically. The western populations (*dama*, Senegal; *mhorr*, southern Morocco) are the darkest, being at least rufous from the back to the flanks with extensions to the legs; rump always white, but across the thigh, a rufous band, sometimes contiguous to the dark back. The eastern form (Red-necked Gazelle, *ruficollis*; Dongola and Sennaar), is the lightest, only the neck and a saddle on the shoulder being rufous. Intermediate forms *permista* exist in the central part of the range. The

1   2   3

13. Pattern of coloration of Dama Gazelle (*Gazella dama*)
1 Western Dama (*mhorr*)   2 Central African Dama (*permista*)   3 Red-necked Gazelle (*ruficollis*)

amount of chestnut rufous differs according to seasonal changes, age, and individual variation.

Habitat: Desert and outer edge in the Sahelian zone. Map, p. 247.
Habits: Dama Gazelle live singly or in small herds, up to 10–15 head. Sometimes they may be observed in larger herds, of up to 600 head or more, especially during their seasonal movements, which look like large-scale migrations from the Sahara to the Sahelian zone, during the driest season of the year. They often live side by side with Dorcas Gazelle.

They mainly browse on various desert shrubs and acacias, rearing up on their hind legs to reach young shoots, but also feed on the rough desert grasses. They can resist long periods of drought without drinking, but their water requirements are much higher than those of the Dorcas.

SOEMMERING'S GAZELLE   *Gazella (Nanger) soemmeringi*
(Cretzschmar)   p. 225
F Gazelle de Soemmering   G Sömmering-Gazelle
Identification: Height at shoulder 33–35 in.; weight 100 lb. A large gazelle, with an elongated head and a relatively short neck. General colour uniformly pale rufous fawn. No lateral band, or only a faint one, the colour of the flanks passing abruptly to the white underparts. Head with a very contrasted pattern. A dark blackish brown median band on the blaze, down to the muzzle which is entirely dark. A pure white ring around the eye, extending forwards as a stripe to the side of the muzzle; interrupted across the eye by a lateral black stripe, from the base of the horn to the muzzle. A broad white patch on the hindquarters, encroaching angularly forwards on the fawn rump, never bordered with black. Horns rather long (15; 23), strongly ringed, noticeably bent backwards, little divergent for

their basal half, then curving widely outwards, their tips being abruptly hooked inwards.

Female similar to the male, but with thinner horns.

Intraspecific variation: The Borani Soemmering's Gazelle (*butteri*) (Dana Valley, Boran, Gallaland) is smaller, and has an ill-defined band along the flanks and a dark band bordering the white patch on the rump.

Habitat: Bush and acacia scrub in hilly country, but also open grassy plains. Map, p. 251.

Habits: Soemmering's Gazelle live in small family parties, but sometimes congregate into larger herds, up to 100 or more, the sexes being mixed with a preponderance of females. Old bucks are often solitary. They feed on grasses, but may also browse on leaves of shrubs. Although they drink when water is available, they may very well dispense with this element. In certain parts of their range they migrate seeking the best pasture according to the seasons.

GRANT'S GAZELLE *Gazella (Nanger) granti* Brooke p. 225
F Gazelle de Grant K Swala granti G Grant-Gazelle

Identification: Height at shoulder 31–35 in.; weight 100–175 lb. A large gazelle, rather massive and heavily built. General colour fawn, with lateral band generally not conspicuous (adults). On the head, a median rufous chestnut facial band; a blackish spot on the muzzle; lateral facial stripes white, sharply defined, from the base of the horn over the eye to the muzzle. A broad white patch on the rump, encroaching upwards, bordered on the thigh by a black pygal band. Underparts white. Tail with the proximal half white, then with a black tuft. Horns long (22; 31¾) and very stout at their base, strongly ringed, evenly curved backwards, then forwards terminally; diverging very variably according to the races.

Female similar to the male, with a dark band along the flank and smaller horns.

Intraspecific variation: Many races of Grant's Gazelle (*lacuum*, Ethiopia; *brighti*, Uganda; *raineyi*, Somalia, northern Kenya) have been described according to size, shape of horns, and coloration; some are not recognisable in the field. Peters's Gazelle (*petersi*) (coast districts of Kenya near Tana River) has narrow and short horns, nearly straight, and the rump patch is divided into two by a wide fawn band. Roberts's Gazelle (*robertsi*) (from Speke Gulf to Loita plains) has widely diverging horns, with the tip directed downwards.

Similar species: See Thomson's Gazelle.

Habitat: Open plains with a certain amount of bush; also in thick bush country, but never in long grasses. In northern Kenya, barren semi-desert country. Map, p. 251.

Habits: Grant's Gazelle usually live in small herds of 6 to 30 head. A male usually has up to a dozen females.

Mixed feeders, they feed on grass and browse also on bushes. They can

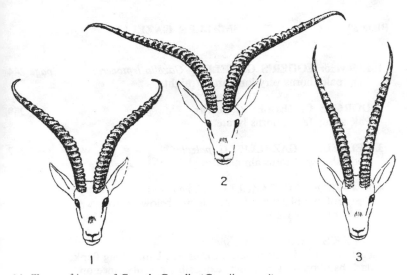

14. Shape of horns of Grant's Gazelle (*Gazella granti*)
    1 Grant's Gazelle (*granti*)   2 Roberts's Gazelle (*robertsi*)   3 Rainey's
    Gazelle (*raineyi*)

go without water for long periods, and commonly remain in the open during the heat of the day, which supposes an astonishing economy of water.

The alarm call is a grunt or a bleat.

DORCAS GAZELLE   *Gazella dorcas* (L.)   p. 240
F Gazelle dorcas   G Dorcas-Gazelle
Identification: Height at shoulder 22–26 in.; weight 45–50 lb. A small gazelle with no sharply contrasted pattern on the body. General colour pale sandy fawn, with a faint rufous fawn band along the lower flank, never black or blackish, contrasting with the white belly. A median rufous fawn band on the blaze and a brownish fawn stripe from eye to mouth, both separated by a white band from the base of the horn to the upper lip. Long tufts of rufous brown hairs on the 'knees' of the forelegs. A white patch on the rump. Horns of medium length (10; 15⅝), lyrate, strongly ringed, curved backwards and evenly divergent, then converging inwards with their tips bent upwards in a well marked curve.

Female similar to the male, but with horns shorter, slighter and less curved.
Intraspecific variation: The Isabelline Gazelle (*isabella*) (Ethiopia, eastern

Plate 39   SMALLER GAZELLE

1. **RHIM or LODER'S GAZELLE** *Gazella leptoceros*   *page* 244
Very pale; horns very long and straight.

2. **DORCAS GAZELLE** *G. dorcas*   239
Pale sandy fawn; horns lyrate.

3. **PELZELN'S GAZELLE** *G. pelzelni*   242
Reddish fawn; horns almost straight.

4. **RED-FRONTED GAZELLE** *G. rufifrons*   245
Deep rufous; black band along flank, below narrow
streak of sandy rufous.

5. **SPEKE'S GAZELLE** *G. spekei*   245
Pale brownish fawn; broad dark brown band along flank;
dark band on back of thigh; extensible protuberance on
nose.

6. **THOMSON'S GAZELLE** *G. thomsoni*   246
Very small; rufous fawn; broad black band along flank.

7. **SPRINGBUCK** *Antidorcas marsupialis*   248
Rufous fawn; broad dark brown band along flank;
head white; lower rump white; when excited, crest of
long white hairs on back.

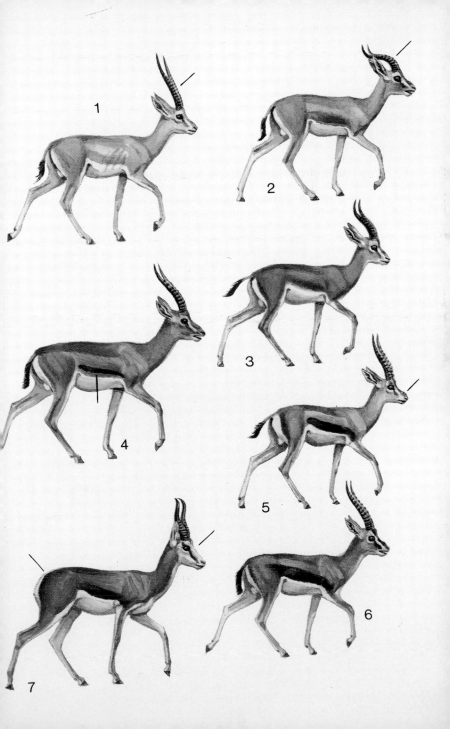

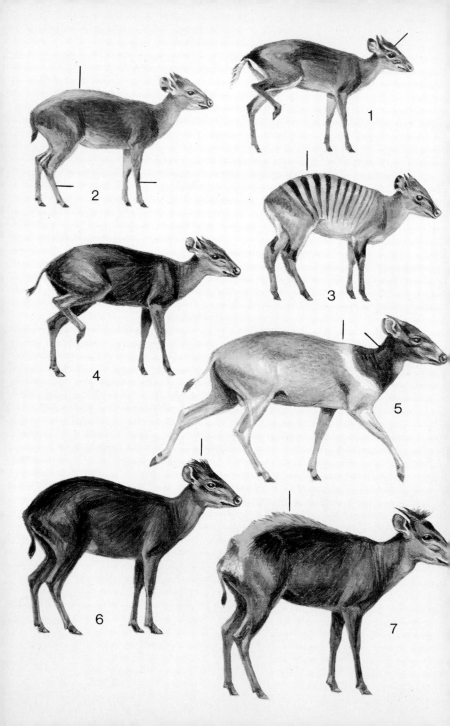

DUIKER i

Plate 40

1. **BLUE DUIKER** *Cephalophus monticola* *page* 254
Small; slaty grey to dark brown; light superciliary stripe.

2. **RED-FLANKED DUIKER** *Cephalophus rufilatus* 252
Bright orange rufous; bluish grey band from nose to
tail; bluish legs.

3. **BANDED DUIKER** *Cephalophus zebra* 252
Transverse brownish bands alternating with pale rufous.

4. **BLACK DUIKER** *Cephalophus niger* 250
Uniform dark smoky brown, except chestnut forehead.

5. **JENTINK'S DUIKER** *Cephalophus jentinki* 250
Large; head and neck blackish; light grey collar; body
grey.

6. **ABBOTT'S DUIKER** *Cephalophus spadix* 250
Large; dark chestnut brown.

7. **YELLOW-BACKED DUIKER** *Cephalophus sylvicultor* 250
Large; broad yellowish buff patch on lower back and rump.

Sudan), sometimes considered a distinct species, is somewhat larger and browner, less sandy in tinge.

Similar species: May be confused with Loder's Gazelle (see this species). Both may be confused in their northern range with the Edmi or Atlas Gazelle (*G. cuvieri*), a rare species confined to the mountains of Morocco, Algeria and Tunisia, up to 7,000 ft., which is considerably larger and heavier, with a rough and thick coat, a darker fawn coloration, the markings on head and flank more pronounced, the horns thick and relatively short.

Easily distinguished from the Red-fronted Gazelle by smaller size, colour of forehead, and absence of conspicuous black lateral band.

Habitat: Also Israel, Syria and Arabia. The most northern representative of the group. A semi-desert-dweller, living on sand dunes and in stony desert, to the border of the Sahelian zone. Flat rather than hilly country. Mainly in rocky areas where severely hunted. Map, p. 251.

Habits: Dorcas Gazelle live in small herds up to 20 head, sometimes up to 60; males are sometimes solitary, and young bucks gather in troops up to 50 head.

They are well adapted to desert conditions. Their colour blends well with the surroundings and exposure to intense sun does not appear to affect them. They wander long distances after nutritious pastures, some of these movements having the appearance of migrations.

They browse and graze on almost any desert vegetation, especially acacias. Succulents (*Aizoon*) provide a good water supply in desert country, but they drink when water is available. They also eat locusts and their larvae.

PELZELN'S GAZELLE *Gazella pelzelni* Kohl[1]   p. 240
F Gazelle de Pelzeln   G Pelzelns-Gazelle

Identification: Height at shoulder 26 in.; weight 40 lb. A small gazelle, with rather uniform coloration. General colour reddish fawn, with a broad, but ill defined dark rufous lateral band (sometimes absent). Underparts white. Head with a dark rufous median band on the blaze; no blackish spot on nose. A whitish stripe over the eye to the muzzle, contrasting with a brown cheek stripe extending below it. Horns rather short (12; 14½) evenly divergent, almost straight and only slightly curved backwards except at the tip.

Female similar to the male, but with slenderer and shorter horns.

Habitat: Maritime desert lowlands, in dry and stony plains covered with low bushes. Map, p. 251.

Habits: Pelzeln's Gazelle live in small parties of 2–12 head; old males are often solitary. They live in the most desolate country, preferring areas covered with stones and not hiding themselves among vegetation. They browse on shoots of acacias and desert bushes. They are able to dispense with water for long periods.

Probably conspecific with Dorcas Gazelle.

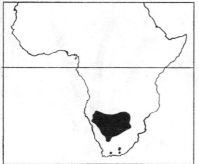

Red Hartebeest, p. 221

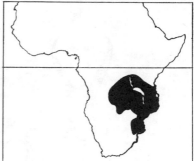

Lichtenstein's Hartebeest, p. 222

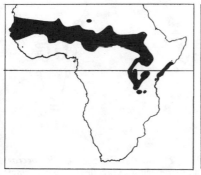

Tiang, Topi, Korrigum, p. 226

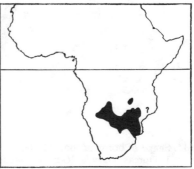

Sassaby p. 227

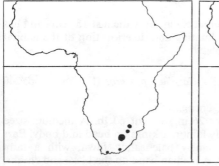

Bontebok and Blesbok, p. 227

Hunter's Hartebeest, p. 228

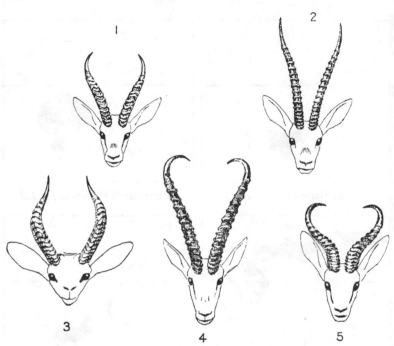

15. Shape of horns of some Gazelle
    1 Dorcas Gazelle (*Gazella dorcas*)   2 Loder's Gazelle (*G. leptoceros*)
    3 Gerenuk (*Litocranius walleri*)   4 Soemmering's Gazelle (*G. soemmeringi*)
    5 Springbuck (*Antidorcas marsupialis*)

This gazelle has declined to a great extent over the last 15 years and has become very rare. Uncontrolled hunting and deterioration of the habitat due to overgrazing are responsible.

RHIM or LODER'S GAZELLE   *Gazella leptoceros* (F. Cuvier) p. 240
(Slender-horned Gazelle)
F Gazelle leptocère, Rhim   G Dünengazelle
Identification: Height at shoulder 26 in.; weight 60 lb. A medium-sized gazelle, the palest of all, with only faint markings on head and body. Ears very large. General colour extremely pale sandy fawn, with a faint brownish band along lower flank. A median band on the blaze and cheeks, darker sandy, with a facial white stripe from above the eye to the muzzle. Hooves somewhat broadened. Horns strongly ringed, long (14; 16½), very

slender, nearly straight, curving but slightly backwards, diverging sometimes very widely.

Female similar to the male, but with more slender and less curved horns.
Similar species: May be confused with the Dorcas, but distinguished by its paler coloration, no conspicuous head markings and different shape of horns.
Habitat: True desert. Mountainous country, but also sandy plains. Also Arabia (*marica*). Map, p. 251.
Habits: Rhim live in small parties, feed on desert plants and drink only occasionally. Strongly nomadic, their broad hooves enable them to traverse deep sand dunes, as in the Addax.

This gazelle is reduced to a precarious level through overshooting.

RED-FRONTED GAZELLE   *Gazella rufifrons* Gray   p. 240
F Gazelle à front roux, G. corinne   G Rotstirn-Gazelle
Identification: Height at shoulder 27 in.; weight 55–65 lb. A medium-sized gazelle, rather stockily built. General colour deep reddish sandy fawn, with a narrow, but well defined and strongly contrasted, black band along the lower flank, leaving below it a narrow streak of sandy rufous ('shadow band'), contrasting with the pure white underparts. Forehead and muzzle rich rufous, with a whitish facial stripe running from the eye to the mouth. 'Knee'-tufts absent. Back of hindquarters white. Horns rather short (12; 13¾), but stout and strongly ringed, evenly divergent, curving slightly backwards, then forwards.

Female similar to the male, but horns straighter and slenderer.
Intraspecific variation: This species has been divided into a number of races, difficult to recognise in the field. Heuglin's Gazelle (*tilonura*) (Ethiopia, Sennaar, Bahr-el-Ghazal), considered by some as a full species, is the eastern representative of the Red-fronted Gazelle, only distinguished by the shape of horns, their tips turning inwards and being sharply hooked.
Similar species: See Dorcas Gazelle.
Habitat: Subdesert steppe, and also northern Sudan zone. Open arid country with thorn bushes; avoids thick cover. Map, p. 255.
Habits: Red-fronted Gazelle live singly, in pairs or in small herds averaging 5–6 head, never exceeding 15. They feed on grasses and also browse on acacias and various other shrubs (*Calotropis, Balanites, Zizyphus, Leptadenia, Boscia, Salvadora, Euphorbia*).

SPEKE'S GAZELLE   *Gazella spekei* Blyth   p. 240
F Gazelle de Speke   G Spekes Gazelle
Identification: Height at shoulder 24 in.; weight 40 lb. A small gazelle, with a swollen and extensible protuberance on the nose, which can be inflated in situations of excitement or alarm ('Flabby-nosed Gazelle'). General colour pale brownish fawn, with a broad dark brown band separating the white underparts. On the head, a dark brownish median

band on the blaze, with a blackish patch on the nose. A dark cheek band contrasting with the whitish sides of face. Buttocks pure white, bordered by a vertical dark band on the back of the thighs. Horns (11; 12½) slightly divergent, evenly and strongly curved backwards, with their tips recurved upwards.

Female similar to the male, but horns slenderer and less curved.

Habitat: Interior plateaux of Somalia, mostly at altitudes from 3,000 to 6,000 ft.; bare areas covered with stones and coarse grass. Map, p. 251.

Habits: Speke's Gazelle, a very rare species, live in small herds up to 20 head, usually of 5–12. Their habits are almost unknown.

THOMSON'S GAZELLE *Gazella thomsoni* Günther   p. 240
F Gazelle de Thomson   K Swala tomi, lala
G Thomson-Gazelle, Zwerggazelle

Identification: Height at shoulder 26 in.; weight 40–60 lb. A small gazelle, very gracefully built, with a distinctive pattern. General colour deep sandy fawn. A very broad and sharply defined black lateral band, in direct contrast with the white underparts. Head rufous with a median chestnut band on the blaze from the base of the horns to the muzzle, sometimes ending in a blackish spot on the nose; a white ring around the eye, extending as a stripe to the muzzle; a blackish stripe across the cheek. Underparts white. Hindquarters white, bordered by a narrow black stripe. Tail entirely covered with long black hairs. Horns (12; 17) strongly ridged, little divergent, slightly curved backwards, their tips recurved forwards.

Female similar to the male, but crown of same colour as the back (chestnut stripe on the blaze less extended backwards) and horns smaller, sometimes very small.

Intraspecific variation: Thomson's Gazelle varies to a great extent in colour and in the size of the horns. However, the differences on which about 15 races have been described seem superficial. Only the Mongalla Gazelle (*albonotata*) (eastern Ethiopia to southern Sudan and northern Kenya) is recognisable by the white ring around the eye continued upwards, the existence of a white patch on the forehead and the horns turned slightly inwards at their tips.

Similar species: Grant's Gazelle is much larger, with longer and heavier horns, and usually with no conspicuous band on flank (when this band exists there is a 'shadow band' below); it has a distinct dark stripe down the front of the rump patch.

Habitat: Grasslands and open plains, avoiding long grass and dense bush. Map, p. 255.

Habits: The 'Tommies' are definitely the commonest gazelles in East Africa. They live in herds of from 5 to 60 or more with a single adult male; these harem herds are, however, loosely organised and their size may vary from hour to hour. The leader of such a herd is usually an old female

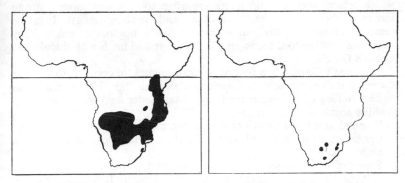

Wildebeest, p. 230

White-tailed Gnu, p. 231

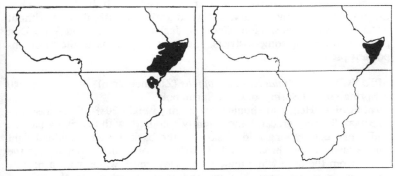

Gerenuk, p. 232

Dibatag, p. 233

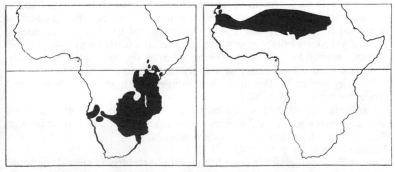

Impala, p. 234

Addra or Dama Gazelle, p. 236

which acts as sentinel. Old males are often solitary and show a strong territorial behaviour (defecating sites and 'rubbing' spots). In some seasons 'Tommies' gather in enormous herds, up to thousands. They migrate according to the seasons. They form mixed herds with Impala and Grant's Gazelle.

Thomson's Gazelle is a relatively silent animal (in contrast to Grant's Gazelle). It does not seem to have any alarm call; the alarm signal seems to be a ruffling or flicking of the flanks. Males utter a succession of barely audible grunts during courtship.

When alarmed, it adopts a characteristic gait referred to as 'stotting' or 'spronking'; with head and legs stiff, they spring up and down in a 'wooden' manner.

Senses of sight and smell are acute and hearing is good.

It is most active in the early morning and evening. It is almost entirely a grazer; short grasses (*Themeda*, *Pennisetum*, etc.) form 90 per cent. of the diet and twigs and leaves of various trees 10 per cent. It drinks daily when the grazing conditions are dry, but when grazing is lush, they do without water for long periods. Lion, Cheetah, Jackals, Leopard and Wild Dog prey on them. In some districts, the Spotted Hyaena is the most important predator.

SPRINGBUCK   *Antidorcas marsupialis* (Zimmermann)   p. 240
F Springbok   G Springbock   A Springbok
Identification: Height at shoulder 30–33 in.; weight 70–80 lb. A medium-sized gazelle, very graceful and brightly coloured, with a striking pattern and a particularly long fold of skin on the back. General colour bright rufous fawn, with a broad band of dark chocolate brown separating the flanks from the pure white underparts. Head pure white, with a narrow dark brown stripe across the eye and from the cheek to the muzzle. Buttocks and a wide triangular patch on the lower rump pure white, bordered with dark brown. In repose, the fold of skin is closed and only a narrow dark line is visible on the back and upper rump. When the animal is excited (fright, play) this fold is widely everted to form a conspicuous crest of very long bristly pure white hairs. Horns fairly short (14; 19½) but strong, heavily ridged, lyrate, rising slightly upwards and backwards, diverging outwards and curving sharply inwards in a hook at their tips.

Female similar to the male, but smaller, with shorter, thinner and straighter horns.
Intraspecific variation: The southern race, *marsupialis*, is smaller and has shorter horns than the subspecies *angolensis* which occurs in Botswana, South-West Africa and south-western Angola.
Habitat: Open dry plains. Map, p. 255.
Habits: The Springbuck is one of the most characteristic animals of South Africa (where it is a national and sporting emblem). It is the only gazelle found south of the Zambezi. Highly gregarious, it used to swarm in

enormous herds which covered the plains as far as the eye could see. Many males are solitary; all-male bachelor herds are commonly found, harem herds are characteristic of the mating season and mixed herds are found during most of the year. In their search for fresh pastures, Springbuck migrated in hundreds of thousands according to the rhythm of drought and rainfall over their range (hence their name 'trekbokken'). They moved in such densely packed masses that any animal met on their way was either trampled or forced along with them. The country was left completely devastated behind them. These huge migrations often ended with enormous losses from starvation, disease, drowning, and predators or through drinking salt water if they reached the sea—a natural method of controlling over-population. These periodical movements, described in much detail by the older observers, still occur in parts of South-West Africa and Botswana where there are large tracts of wild country. In South Africa, the development of farming and overshooting led to a great reduction in numbers. However, they are still quite common on many fenced ranches and the overall population is probably increasing.

When pressed, they bound into the air ('pronking'); the leaps may reach up to 10 ft. in height and be repeated 5–6 times in succession. During this stiff-looking action, the back is arched, the 'fan' expanded and the legs fully extended with the hooves almost bunched together.

They feed on grasses (*Aristida, Schmidtia*) and browse a good deal on leaves of various bushes; in sandy areas they may dig out bulbs and roots. They are able to go without water for a considerable time, but drink regularly when it is available.

The voice of the Springbuck, an almost silent animal, is a feeble bleat and a kind of whistle.

DUIKERS: Cephalophinae

Small antelopes, sometimes very small, which can be divided into two different groups:

FOREST DUIKERS (*Cephalophus*). Squat features, with a hunched back. Legs short, proportionately thin; forelegs often slightly shorter than the hind ones. Head bent to the ground. A well developed frontal crest of long hairs between the horns, often concealing them. On sides of head, a line of pores (glands) forming a long naked line. Horns (both sexes) straight, triangularly flattened in section, very short (always shorter than the head, often much shorter), directed backwards, continuing the line of the nasal profile, coat never grizzled, sleek and glossy.

BUSH DUIKERS (*Sylvicapra*). Back rather straight. Legs long. A well developed crest between the horns. Horns (generally males only), long, slender, circular in section, standing upright. Coat grizzled.

Forest Duikers are confined to forest or very dense bush, while the Bush

Duikers live in scrub country. Not gregarious and with retiring habits, they are often very common, but seldom seen.

YELLOW-BACKED DUIKER   *Cephalophus silvicultor* (Afzelius)

p. 241

F Céphalophe à dos jaune   G Riesenducker, Gelbrückenducker
Identification: Height at shoulder 33 in.; weight 100–140 lb. The largest of all duikers. General features very heavy. Ears proportionately broad. General colour dark velvety brown. Sides of face very light greyish. Crest well developed, orange or rufous, sometimes blackish. A broad triangular yellowish-buff patch broadening from the middle of the back to the rump, duller in young animals; hairs erectile often raised in a brush-like crest. Lower rump silvery grey. Tail short, thin, with a small black tuft. Horns smooth at the base, rather long (5; 8⅜) bowed downwards terminally.
Habitat: Mainly primary high forest, but also clearings. Map, p. 255.

JENTINK'S DUIKER   *Cephalophus jentinki* Thomas

p. 241

F Céphalophe de Jentink   G Jentinks Ducker
Identification: Height at shoulder 31 in.; weight 140 lb. A large duiker almost equal in size to the Yellow-backed, stockily built. Head, except for a whitish muzzle, neck and sternal band brownish black, contrasting with a light grey collar on the shoulders. Back and rump coarsely grizzled grey (the grey coloured skin appearing under the sparse hairs). Legs paler, light grey, tinged with rufous. Horns rather long, bowed downwards terminally.
Habitat: Dense forest. Nothing is apparently known on the habits of this rare antelope. The range probably extends to the Ivory Coast where it is said to be known by the local tribesmen. Map, p. 255.

ABBOTT'S DUIKER   *Cephalophus spadix* True

p. 241

F Céphalophe spadix   K Minde   G Abbots Ducker
Identification: Height at shoulder 26 in.; weight 115–130 lb. A large duiker, rather heavily built. General colour uniform dark chestnut brown, somewhat lighter on the flanks. Forehead tinged with dusky brown; chin and throat greyish. Crest chestnut red, tipped with black. A small grey patch on rump above tail. Tail tipped with white. Horns rather thin, long (3½; 4⅜) and slender, not thickened at base.
Similar species: Distinguished from Red Duiker by larger size and uniform colour, and absence of head markings.
Habitat: Montane forest, up to 12,000 ft. Map, p. 255.

BLACK DUIKER   *Cephalophus niger* Gray

p. 241

F Céphalophe noir   G Schwarz Ducker
Identification: Height at shoulder 20 in.; weight 20–35 lb. A fairly small duiker with a rather thick coat, very dark all over. General colour almost

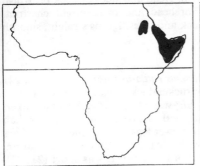

Soemmering's Gazelle, p. 237

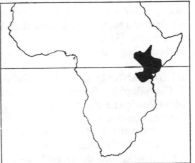

Grant's Gazelle, p. 238

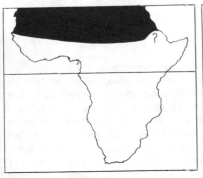

Dorcas Gazelle, p. 240

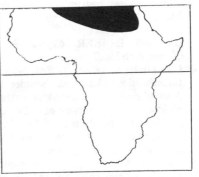

Rhim or Loder's Gazelle, p. 244

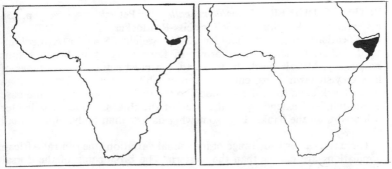

Pelzeln's Gazelle, p. 242

Speke's Gazelle, p. 245

uniform dark smoky brown or blackish. Head and sides of neck brownish fawn, paler on throat and neck. Forehead and crest bright chestnut. Underparts somewhat lighter than back and sides. Horns straight, smooth at the base (3; 6⅞).
Habitat: High forest. Map, p. 261.

RED-FLANKED DUIKER   *Cephalophus rufilatus* Gray   p. 241
F Céphalophe à flancs roux   G Blaurückenducker, Rotflankenducker
Identification: Height at shoulder 14 in.; weight 25–30 lb. A small duiker. General colour bright orange rufous, with a broad bluish grey median band from the nose to the root of tail. Lower legs of the same colour. Ears rather broad, blackish on the back, with a black spot on the lower margin. Crest black, well developed. Tail with a black tip. Horns short (2½; 3¾), conical, straight, ringed at the base.
Habitat: Forest, forest edges and patches through the Guinea savanna, decidedly less restricted to the dense forest than most of the duikers. Map, p. 261.

BANDED DUIKER   *Cephalophus zebra* (Gray)   p. 241
(Zebra Antelope)
F Céphalophe zèbré   G Zebra-Ducker, Streifenducker
Identification: Height at shoulder 16 in.; weight 20–35 lb. Unmistakable. A small duiker with a striking pattern. Ground colour pale rufous, darker, almost chestnut on neck and shoulder. Head with a slaty grey muzzle and a rufous forehead and cheeks. Crest very short. Across back and rump, about 12 conspicuous transverse brownish black bands gradually broadening towards the rump. Underparts lighter. Legs rufous fawn, with broad black markings. Tail longish, well haired, mostly white. Horns tiny (1½; 1⅞), almost concealed by the hairs of the crest, straight, smooth at the base.
Habitat: Mountain forest. Map, p. 261.

PETERS'S DUIKER   *Cephalophus callipygus* Peters[1]   p. 256
F Céphalophe de Peters   G Schönsteiss-Rotducker
Identification: Height at shoulder 22 in.; weight 35–45 lb. A medium-sized duiker. General colour brownish fawn merging to bright rufous posteriorly. Muzzle blackish; forehead and crest rufous brown. Sides of face greyish fawn. Lips, chin and throat white. On the back, a median broad black band from the shoulders to the rump, broadening at the base of the tail, and extending on the back of the thighs. Underparts lighter coloured than the flanks. Legs somewhat darker than body. Horns small (3½; 5 6/16).
    There is a rather wide range of individual variation; the central African populations are darker than the western. The broadening of the dorsal

[1] This duiker is closely related to the next, some authors considering them conspecific. The Congolese subspecies *weynsi* apparently forms a link.

black band towards the tail is always clearly visible in spite of its variable extent.
Habitat: Dense forest, particularly secondary growth. Map, p. 261.

RED DUIKER *Cephalophus natalensis* A. Smith p. 256
F Céphalophe du Natal   K Funo   G Rotducker, Natalducker
A Rooiduiker
Identification: Height 20 in.; weight 30 lb. A rather small duiker. General colour almost uniform bright rufous chestnut all over, somewhat paler on the underparts. Crest long, mixed chestnut and black, sometimes pure chestnut. Chin and upper throat whitish. Tail short, rufous at its base, with a well developed tuft of mixed black and white hairs. Horns short (3; 5), but much thickened and ridged at their base, directed backwards.
Intraspecific variation: A number of races have been described according to coloration. The best defined is Harvey's Duiker (*harveyi*) (from Kilimanjaro to eastern Ruwenzori and the Juba River), sometimes considered as a full species, characterised by its bright bay colour and a blackish blaze. The Zanzibar Duiker (*adersi*) has whitish underparts, a broad whitish band across the upper thigh and white markings on the lower legs.
Habitat: Dense bush and woodlands. Also montane forest. Map, p. 261.

BAY DUIKER *Cephalophus dorsalis* Gray p. 256
(Black-striped Duiker)
F Céphalophe à bande dorsale noire, Céphalophe bai   G Schwarzrückenducker
Identification: Height at shoulder 22 in.; weight 45 lb. A medium-sized duiker. General colour bright chestnut rufous. Head with a much reduced crest, dark brown with a light rufous superciliary band; a spot above the eye, upper lips and chin white. A black median stripe from the head to the tail, spreading out on the lower back and rump, then narrowing again on the lower rump. A blackish band along the middle of the underparts. Legs blackish brown, sometimes darkening to black; in some individuals the dark colour spreads over the shoulders and meets the dorsal band. Tail with a tuft of mixed white and black hairs. Horns parallel, nearly straight, rather long (2; 3¾), smooth at the base.
Habitat: Dense forest. Map, p. 261.

GABON DUIKER *Cephalophus leucogaster* Gray p. 256
(White-bellied Duiker)
F Céphalophe à ventre blanc, C. du Gabon
G Gabun-Ducker, Weissbauchducker
Identification: Height at shoulder 20 in.; weight 40 lb. A medium-sized duiker. General colour lighter than the other species. Head with a dark blackish brown forehead and blaze, contrasting with the lighter sides. Crest mainly rufous mixed with black. A blackish median band from the

nape or the shoulder (sometimes more posteriorly), broadening on the middle of back, then narrowing progressively on the rump, where it is sharply defined. Neck, shoulder and flanks warm brownish, blending gradually with the dorsal band on the back and with the whitish underparts. Rump and thighs decidedly tinged with rufous. Buttocks white. Limbs brownish, darkening on lower half. Tail rather longish, with a conspicuous black and white tuft. Horns short (3; 5), tapering, heavily ringed at the base.

Similar species: Distinguished from the Bay Duiker by the shape of the black median band, the white belly and buttocks.

Habitat: Forests, mainly secondary growth, and even at the edges of savanna. Map, p. 265.

OGILBY'S DUIKER *Cephalophus ogilbyi* (Waterhouse)[1]   p. 256
F Céphalophe d'Ogilby   G Ogilby-Ducker

Identification: Height at shoulder 22 in.; weight 45 lb. A medium-sized duiker. General colour bright orange rufous. Face browner, darker on nose. A rather narrow black central band on the back, running to the base of the tail. Legs darker. Horns rather long (4; 4¾) conical, strongly ringed at the base.

Habitat: High forest. Map, p. 265.

BLACK-FRONTED DUIKER *Cephalophus nigrifrons* Gray   p. 256
F Céphalophe à front noir, Céphalophe rouge   G Schwarzstirnducker

Identification: Height at shoulder 20 in.; weight 40 lb. A rather small duiker. General colour almost uniform rich chestnut. A broad band along the blaze to the forehead deep black, in strong contrast with the rufous sides of the face; crest mostly black, sparingly mixed with rufous hairs. Back of neck darkening somewhat to blackish. No dorsal band. Underparts of the same colour or only slightly lighter than the back. Lower legs blackish. Hooves somewhat elongated. Tail moderately long, with a conspicuous tuft, black with a white tip. Horns short (2; 4¾).

Habitat: Dense forests, particularly inundated and marshy forests (the elongated hooves seem to be an adaptation for walking on soft soil), also in montane forests. Map, p. 265.

BLUE DUIKER *Cephalophus (Philantomba) monticola* (Thünberg)
(including *caeruleus* and *maxwelli*)   p. 241
F Céphalophe bleu   K Paa   G Blauducker; Rotfussducker
A Bloubokkie

Identification: Height at shoulder 14–16 in.; weight 10–20 lb. The smallest of all duikers. General colour varying from slaty grey to dark brown, darker on the back with a bluish gloss. Head sparsely covered with hairs, of the same colour as the body; a lighter superciliary streak extending to

[1] The status of this species is uncertain. It may be conspecific with *C. dorsalis*.

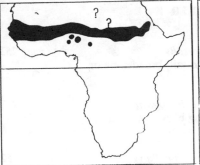

Red-fronted Gazelle, p. 245

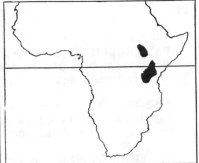

Thomson's Gazelle, p. 246

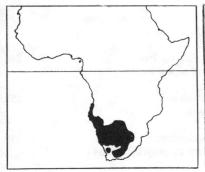

Springbuck, p. 248

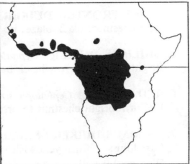

Yellow-backed Duiker, p. 250

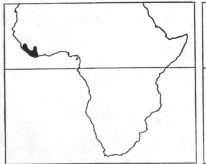

Jentink's Duiker, p. 250

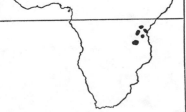

Abbott's Duiker, p. 250

Plate 41   **DUIKER ii**

1. **BAY DUIKER** *Cephalophus dorsalis*   *page* 253
   Black median band from head to tail, broadening on
   lower back and rump.

2. **GABON DUIKER** *Cephalophus leucogaster*   253
   Lightly coloured; brownish along back, blending
   gradually towards whitish underparts.

3. **PETERS'S DUIKER** *Cephalophus callipygus*   252
   Black median band from shoulder to rump, broadening
   at base of tail and extending to thigh.

4. **BLACK-FRONTED DUIKER** *Cephalophus nigrifrons*   254
   Rich chestnut; black blaze; no dorsal band.

5. **OGILBY'S DUIKER** *Cephalophus ogilbyi*   254
   Bright rufous; narrow black band along back.

6. **RED DUIKER** *Cephalophus natalensis*   253
   Uniform bright chestnut to brown.

7. **GRIMM'S DUIKER** *Sylvicapra grimmia*   259
   Ears long; uniform yellowish fawn to greyish; horns
   standing upright.

PYGMY ANTELOPE, CHEVROTAIN, DIK-DIK

Plate 42

1. **ROYAL ANTELOPE** *Neotragus pygmaeus*   *page* 260
Tiny; rufous brown above, white below; rufous collar
across throat; tail rufous above, white below.

2. **BATES'S PYGMY ANTELOPE** *Neotragus batesi*   260
Tiny; dark chestnut above; white below; tail uniform
brownish.

3. **SUNI** *Nesotragus moschatus*   262
Very small; fawn grey to rich chestnut, slightly speckled
above, whitish below; horns relatively long; tail brown
except white tip.

4. **CHEVROTAIN** *Hyemoschus aquaticus*   179
Dark rufous brown above, with whitish spots and stripes;
white below; no horns, but long canines (ad. male).

5. **PHILLIPS'S DIK-DIK** *Madoqua saltiana*   268
Nose only slightly elongated; upperparts grey; underparts
rufous to a variable extent.

   5a. **PHILLIPS'S DIK-DIK** *M. s. phillipsi*   270
   Sides bright rufous, sharply contrasting with grey
   back.

   5b. **SWAYNE'S DIK-DIK** *M. s. swaynei*   270
   Almost uniform greyish fawn; legs pale rufous.

6. **KIRK'S LONG-SNOUTED DIK-DIK** *Rhynchotragus*
kirki   268
Nose elongated; greyish fawn above, pale fawn and
whitish below.

7. **GUENTHER'S LONG-SNOUTED DIK-DIK**
Rhynchotragus guentheri   267
Nose much elongated; greyish fawn above, whitish
below; no ring around eye.

Note. Phillips's, Swayne's and Kirk's Dik-Dik are represented with the
crest erected, and Guenther's Dik-dik with the crest not erected.

the base of the horns, more or less conspicuous, contrasting with the forehead, which is always tinged with brown. Opening of facial glands curved, and not straight as in other duikers. Crest very short. Underparts and buttocks whitish. Legs of the same colour as the body or more or less tinged with rufous, sometimes bright rufous fawn contrasting with the body. Tail rather long, bushy, black, bordered with white, constantly wagged in a characteristic manner. Horns very small (generally present in both sexes, sometimes absent in females) (2; 3⅞), strongly ringed, set up at a slight angle above the nasal profile, slightly curved towards each other at tip.

Intraspecific variation: A large number of local races have been described among the 'Blue' Duikers and some authors consider that they must be split into several species. They vary mainly in size and in the extent of the brown hue. The western representative, Maxwell's Duiker (*maxwelli*) (from Senegal to Nigeria), sometimes considered as a full species, is mouse grey, with the legs not contrasting with the body. The populations from the Cameroons and Gabon (*caeruleus* and allies) are characterised by a darker coloration and the sharp contrast between the dark brown rump and whitish buttocks.

Habitat: Densely wooded country. Map, p. 265.

Habits of Forest Duikers: Most of the Forest Duikers (*Cephalophus*) share the same habits in spite of some ecological differences. They are usually solitary, though sometimes found in pairs or even in groups of a few individuals when attracted by food (particularly the Red Duiker which lives in a more open habitat and may gather in woodland clearings). They move very easily through the dense vegetation, the head carried low, using regular runs, and when disturbed plunge into thick cover (hence their name 'duiker'—from the Dutch 'diver'). Mostly nocturnal (some, like the Black-fronted Duiker, are also partly diurnal), they spend the day concealed in the deepest recesses of the forest, sometimes making nests under fallen trees or in thick bush.

Primarily browsers, they feed on leaves, young shoots, bark, buds and seeds; also to a much greater degree than other antelopes, they eat fruits of various trees (*Scyphocephalium, Staudtia, Irvingia, Pentaclethra, Pachylobus, Elaeis, Ricinodendron, Antrocaryon, Klainedowa, Anthostema* etc.), which are an important part of their diet. They graze only to a very limited extent. Like the Chevrotain, some, particularly the Black-fronted Duiker, also eat fishes and crabs (which has been proved in captivity), even killing young chickens.

They utter a sharp or sniffling whistle when surprised.

They are preyed on by Crowned Eagles, pythons, wild cats and leopards.

Owing to their secluded life, much has still to be learned about their habits.

GRIMM'S DUIKER   *Sylvicapra grimmia* (L.)   p. 256
(Grey Duiker or Bush Duiker)
F Céphalophe de Grimm, C. couronné   K Nsya   G Kronenducker
A Gewone Duiker, Duikerbok

Identification: Height at shoulder 20–26 in.; weight 23–30 lb. Medium sized to fairly large, very different from the other duikers in colour, general features and shape of horns. Back not conspicuously hunched, often nearly straight. Legs longer than in any other species of duiker. Ears long and broad. General colour uniformly grizzled, from yellowish ochraceous to bright fawn mixed with grey, especially on hindquarters. Head sometimes with an extensive black band on the blaze and forehead, sometimes with only a black stripe on the nose, the forehead being then bright rufous. Crest well developed, black to rufous. Underparts pure white or tinged with fulvous or greyish. Legs of the same colour as the body, sometimes with black markings in front; a black ring above the hooves. Tail fairly short, black above, white below. Horns standing upright, raised well above the line of the nasal profile, straight, rather long (4; 7½), slender and tapering.

Female similar to the male, normally without horns.

Intraspecific variation: This widespread duiker varies considerably in different parts of its range which justifies the recognition of a number of local races. These differences concern body size, size of horns, intensity of coloration and thickness of coat (becoming shaggy in mountain populations). Most of these differences are not visible in the field.

Similar species: See Oribi. The Klipspringer has different features, a shorter and more conic head and broader ears.

Habitat: The only duiker regularly found in open habitat. A large range of habitats, from the edge of desert to the summit of high mountains, almost to the snow line (but not in bamboo forest), except dense forest. Scrub country, savanna densely covered with bushes, even open plains if shelter is available in patches of bush or tall grass. Wanders often in cultivated lands and even vegetable gardens. It is a most adaptable animal, able to survive where other species have been exterminated. Map, p. 265.

Habits: Normally sedentary, Grimm's Duiker live singly or in pairs. At breeding season, small parties may be seen. Mainly nocturnal, they are active and feed mostly during the early morning and evening and spend the heat of day in thick cover. They are almost entirely browsers, feeding on leaves, twigs, bark, young shoots, pods and fruits (mainly during the dry season) of a great variety of plants, and do not usually graze. A part of their diet seems to be made of animal matter; insects and guineafowl chicks have been found in their stomach. They are sometimes harmful to crops. They drink when water is available but are able to dispense with it for long periods.

The voice is a 'sniffy' sort of snort.

There is no definite season of reproduction. The period of gestation is 120 days. The newly born lamb is hidden under thick grass.

A very adaptable animal, Grimm's Duiker is able to survive in areas of dense settlement.

PYGMY ANTELOPES, ORIBI, KLIPSPRINGER, GRYSBOK: Neotraginae

Small antelopes with delicate features (except Klipspringer) and straight pointed horns (males only). Muzzle naked. No crest on crown of the head. This is not a satisfactory group of antelopes, as it includes a variety of very different animals, the only common character being apparently the diminutive size.[1] They also differ greatly in their habits.

ROYAL ANTELOPE *Neotragus pygmaeus* (L.) p. 257
F Antilope royale G Kleinstböckchen
Identification: Height at shoulder 10 in.; weight 7–9 lb. A tiny, delicate antelope (the smallest of all the African ungulates), the size of a rabbit. Head and neck dark brown, becoming lighter on upper back. Sides of face and neck, flanks and limbs bright rufous fawn. Underparts pure white, sharply contrasting; a rufous collar across the throat. Tail rather long, well haired, rufous above except the tip which is white like the underside. Horns minute (1; 1¼), smooth throughout their length, very sharply pointed, inclined backwards in the plane of the face.

Female similar to the male, but without horns.
Similar species: See Bates's Pygmy Antelope.
Habitat: Dense high forest. Map, p. 265.

BATES'S PYGMY ANTELOPE *Neotragus batesi* De Winton p. 257
F Antilope de Bates G Bates-Böckchen
Identification: Height at shoulder 12 in.; weight 12 lb. A tiny antelope (after the Royal Antelope, the smallest of all African ungulates), the size of a rabbit. General colour glossy dark chestnut, darkening on the back, and lighter on the flanks. Throat and belly white, sometimes tinged with buff; a fulvous collar. Lower legs lighter. Tail uniform dark brownish. Horns minute (1; 1½), stout and ringed at their base, then smooth, inclined backwards in the plane of the face.

Female similar to the male, but without horns.
Similar species: May be confused with the Royal Antelope, its ecological representative in West Africa. But, apart from some anatomical characters, its somewhat larger size, the different colour of the tail, the presence of rings at the base of the horns and of side hooves (not visible in the field) help to distinguish it.

May be confused with duikers, especially the Blue Duiker. The smaller

[1] It has been split into several subfamilies by some recent authors.

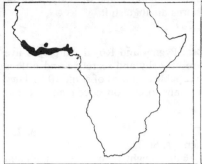

Black Duiker, p. 250

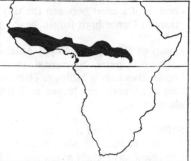

Red-flanked Duiker, p. 252

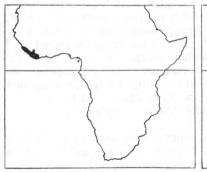

Banded Duiker, p. 252

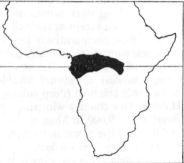

Peters's Duiker, p. 252

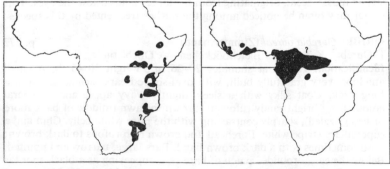

Red Duiker, p. 253

Bay Duiker, p. 253

size, the straight profile of the head, the general shape of body, and the absence of a crest between the tiny horns distinguish it.
Habitat: Dense high forest. Map, p. 269.

Habits of Pygmy and Royal Antelopes: Pygmy and Royal Antelopes live singly or in pairs. Nocturnal, they are very shy and secretive and little is known about their biology. They are capable of jumps of some 10 ft. They feed apparently on leaves and fruits, and occur on cocoa and peanut plantations.

SUNI *Nesotragus moschatus* Von Dueben   p. 257
F Suni   K Paa   G Moschusböckchen   A Soenie
Identification: Height at shoulder 12–16 in.; weight 18 lb. A very small and slender antelope. General colour dull fawn grey to rich chestnut on back, with a slight speckled appearance. Sides of face and body paler. Throat white. Neck pale rufous, not forming a distinct collar. Underparts whitish. Tail rather long, dark brown with a white tip. Horns thick and flattened, strongly ridged except at their tips; straight and sloping backwards in the plane of face, comparatively long ($2\frac{1}{2}$; $4\frac{7}{8}$) for the size of the animal.
  Female similar to the male, but without horns.
Intraspecific variation: The southern representative, Livingstone's Suni (*livingstonianus*), sometimes considered as a distinct species, is larger and more richly coloured (deep rufous, nearing chestnut on the back).
Habitat: Dry country with thick bush. Also reed scrub along rivers and forest above 9,000 ft. Map, p. 269.
Habits: Suni live alone, in pairs, sometimes in small family parties. Mainly browsers, they feed on leaves, young shoots of shrubs and roots, to a limited extent on grass, mostly in the early morning and late afternoon. They are almost independent of water. Suni run like hares, with considerable speed when flushed. The name '*moschatus*' comes from their strong musky scent, originating from the large glands below the eyes. This odour may often be noticed among the bushes frequented by this species.

ORIBI *Ourebia ourebi* (Zimmermann)   p. 272
F Ourébi   K Taya   G Bleichböckchen   A Oorbietjie
Identification: Height at shoulder 20–26 in.; weight 20–45 lb. A small antelope, very gracefully built, with oval-shaped ears, slender legs and a long neck. Coat silky with a sleek slightly wavy appearance. General colour from bright sandy rufous to brownish fawn (middle of back more or less grizzled), sharply contrasting with the pure white belly. Chin and a superciliary stripe white. Forehead and crown rich rufous to dark brown; nose sometimes with a dark brown band. Ears large, narrow and pointed. Below the ear, a rounded patch of bare skin appearing as a black spot (as the Reedbuck). Legs of same colour as the body, with a tuft of long hairs on the 'knees'. Tail short, bushy, rufous brown with a black tip, or black,

displayed conspicuously when running. Horns fairly short (6; 7½), straight, slender, more or less ringed at their base, evenly tapering, almost upright and parallel to each other.

Female similar to the male, sometimes larger, without horns.

Intraspecific variation: Some authors recognise several species of Oribi, particularly in East Africa, according to size, shape of horns, or coloration. They are, however, better considered as subspecies.

Similar species: May perhaps be confused with the Grey Duiker, but distinguished by colour, short head, long neck, absence of crest between the horns, naked patch below the eye and tufts of long hairs on the 'knees'. Steenbok and Grysbok are more lightly built; they have broader ears, a shorter tail and no bare patch below the ear.

Cannot be confused with the Reedbuck, which has quite different horns, larger size, and is heavier.

Habitat: Grassy plains, very thinly bushed country, never far from water. Map, p. 269.

Habits: Oribi live in pairs or in small parties, up to 5 individuals or more. It is almost entirely a grazer. It usually spends the heat of the day concealed in a 'form' in long grass or light bush, but may be seen occasionally in the middle of the day lying in open plains.

When alarmed, it utters a loud, shrill whistle or a sneeze. It begins also a curious 'stotting' action, springing into the air with all four legs straight and stiff. It has a characteristic bounding gait interspersed with occasional high leaps.

It is a grazer.

KLIPSPRINGER *Oreotragus oreotragus* (Zimmermann) p. 272
F Oréotrague K Mbuzi mawe, ngurunguru G Klipspringer
A Klipbokkie, Klipspringer

Identification: Height at shoulder 22 in.; weight 30–40 lb. A rather small antelope, with compact features and a short muzzle, giving to the head a triangular and conic shape. Legs strong, appearing longer than they are because the animal walks on the blunt hoof tips. Thick coat of fairly long, pithy, stiff hairs of brittle texture, unlike the coat of any other African antelope. General colour olive yellow largely speckled with grey (large range of variation). Muzzle brownish; crown sometimes blackish. Ears rounded and broad, conspicuously bordered with black. Chin and upper lips white. Throat grizzled brownish yellow. Underparts white, sometimes washed with yellowish. Legs speckled yellow and grey, lighter than the body, with a broad black ring above the hooves. Tail very short, reduced to a mere stump hardly projecting beyond the contour of the body. Horns short (4; 6½), nearly vertical, slightly curved forwards, ringed at their base.

Female similar to the male, a little heavier, without horns (except in some East African races, like *schillingsi*, Tanzania).

Habitat: The habitat explains the patchy distribution of this species, found only on rocky hills, 'kopjes' and mountains up to 13,000 ft. in Ethiopia, among which it scrambles on most precarious footholds, the structure of its hooves being of the consistency of hard rubber (like the Chamois or the Ibex). It fills a similar niche to the Chamois. Map, p. 269.

Habits: Klipspringer live in small parties though they are not truly gregarious. They are often seen as they stand on the top of a large boulder, from which they can observe the approach of a potential enemy. When they run away, they have a stilted appearance, apparently bouncing along on the tips of the hooves. The gait is a series of stilted hops. They are capable of phenomenal jumps, and make rapid progress on rocks without apparent suitable footholds (the thick coat constitutes a natural cushion against contusions and bumps). Klipspringer feed on grass (very little), herbs and shrubs growing among rocky boulders. They drink when water is available, but may obtain their liquid requirements from succulents. They spend the heat of the day in the shade of bushes or rocks.

The call is an abrupt little snort, which resembles the sound of a toy trumpet.

STEENBOK[1]   *Raphicerus campestris* (Thunberg)   p. 272
F Steenbok   K Dondoro   G Steinantilope   A Vlakbok, Steenbok
Identification: Height at shoulder 22 in.; weight 30 lb. A small antelope, slim and slender, with a short, conical head, a thick, sleek coat, and long legs. General colour uniform bright rufous fawn, sometimes turning to greyish with a light silvery sheen, but not speckled with white, more vivid on the head. Ears long and broad. A lighter stripe in front of the eye, sometimes white and conspicuous, forming a ring around the eye. A small blackish patch on nose and another, crescentic, between the horns. Underparts and buttocks pure white. Tail very short, a mere stump. Horns (5; 7½) straight and very sharp, smooth, slightly curved forwards.

Female similar to the male, sometimes heavier, without horns.
Similar species: See Cape Grysbok.
Habitat: Open plains, with bush and very light woodland; range includes arid country, particularly in dunes. Map, p. 269.
Habits: Steenbok live alone, in pairs only in the breeding season. They can be seen at any time of the day, feeding even during the day time. They are both grazers and browsers, eating grass, leaves, young shoots and even roots and tubers, especially during the dry season. They appear to be completely independent of water.

Steenbok do not frequent hilly country like Grysbok, but generally live on flat plains. They run at a good pace, carrying their head high, and not very low like Grysbok, from which they differ in gait and carriage.

Steenbok often take refuge underground, particularly in old Aardvark burrows, and such cavities are reputed to serve as 'nurseries' for the young.

[1] Sometimes spelled 'Steinbok'.

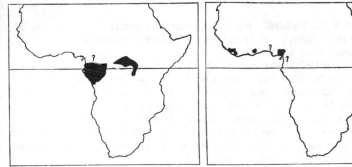

Gabon Duiker, p. 253

Ogilby's Duiker, p. 254

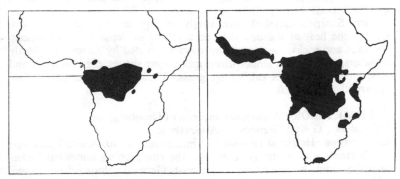

Black-fronted Duiker, p. 254

Blue Duiker, p. 254

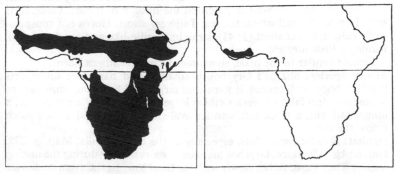

Grimm's Duiker, p. 259

Royal Antelope, p. 260

The call is a sniffy little snort.

SHARPE'S GRYSBOK *Raphicerus sharpei* Thomas p. 272

F Grysbok de Sharpe K Dondoro G Sharpes Greisbock
A Tropiese Grysbok

Identification: Height at shoulder 20 in.; weight 16–25 lb. A small antelope, smaller than the Steenbok, with a wiry coat. General colour rich rufous brown speckled with white, imparting a grizzled appearance, especially along the flanks (in some individuals even patches of white hairs are visible). Muzzle brown. A narrow white superciliary stripe. Ears large (but smaller than in Cape Grysbok and Steenbok), with short hairs. Underparts white. Horns very short (1½; 4⅛), conical, rising vertically from forehead.

Female similar to the male, without horns.

Similar species: See Cape Grysbok.

Habitat: Mostly hilly country near stony kopjes with dense thorny scrub and thick grass. Map, p. 269.

Habits: Sharpe's Grysbok live singly, except during mating season. During the heat of the day they take refuge in dense cover or among boulders and rocks, even in old burrows excavated by Aardvark. Mostly browsers, they feed on tender leaves and young shoots, even on fruits and roots; they sometimes eat young grass. Their water requirements are apparently substantial.

CAPE GRYSBOK *Raphicerus melanotis* (Thunberg) p. 272

F Grysbok G Kap-Greisbock A Grysbok

Identification: Height at shoulder 22 in.; weight 25 lb. A small antelope rather stout, with relatively short legs, the rump being somewhat higher than the shoulder, and a long coarse coat. General colour rufous brown, with numerous white hairs imparting a grizzled appearance. Ears very broad and pointed with long buffy white hairs inside. A dark patch on the crown of the head. A whitish patch on the middle of throat. Underparts buff. Legs with small lateral hooves. Tail very short. Horns not conspicuously ridged, rather short (3; 4⅞), straight, needle-like and nearly vertical, leaning a little forwards.

Female similar to the male, sometimes heavier, without horns.

Similar species: Sharpe's Grysbok is smaller, and has white underparts (no false hooves). Steenbok is somewhat larger and lacks the admixture of white hairs (no false hooves). Oribi is larger and has a different colour, a longer tail with a black tuft, smaller oval-shaped ears, and a bare patch below the ear.

Habitat: Scrub-covered flats, especially at the base of hills. Map, p. 275.

Habits: Usually alone, Grysbok are seen in pairs mainly during the mating season. They move rather slowly with the head low. In the event of danger they often prefer to hide in the grass, lying flat on the ground. They are nocturnal, spending the heat of the day concealed in thick cover. Mainly grazers, they feed also to some extent on leaves and fruits. They may dispense with water for long periods.

BEIRA, DIK-DIK: Madoquinae

This group of antelopes is made up of two different types. The Beira is a rather aberrant member owing to its larger size and gazelline features.

The Dik-dik are tiny antelopes of dainty appearance, with a more or less elongated snout, which in some species resembles a little proboscis. Legs thin and long, the hind legs longer than the forelegs; typically the hind legs are bent, giving the back a characteristic sloping appearance. The horns (males only) are minute, straight and ringed at least basally, level with the profile of the face. A crest of long hairs on the forehead, sometimes partially concealing the horns. Coat soft. Tail short, inconspicuous. They are peculiar to dense bush country.

BEIRA *Dorcatragus megalotis* (Menges)   p. 272
F Beira   G Beira
Identification: Height at shoulder 22 in.; weight 60 lb. A small antelope with a gazelline silhouette, considerably larger than the Dik-dik, with enormous ears, long legs, and the rump higher than the shoulder; coat thick and coarse. General colour grey, finely grizzled, with a pinkish hue. A white ring around the eye contrasting with the yellowish fawn ground colour of the head. No crest between horns. On the flanks, a distinct darkish band from the lower shoulder. Underparts yellowish fawn, except white axillae and groins. Legs fawn. Hooves very short, with a broad and thick internal pad. Tail short and bushy. Horns widely separated, short (4; 5½), straight or faintly curved forwards.

Female similar to the male, but somewhat larger, without horns.
Habitat: Stony barren hills and mountains. Map, p. 275.
Habits: A rare animal, frequently mistaken for Klipspringer, Beira live in pairs or in small herds of up to 7 head, with one or two males. Sedentary, they are highly adapted to live in very dry stony hills, their specialised hooves with their elastic pads obtaining a grip on the rock. They feed on leaves of mimosas and coarse grass. They do not seem to need water. Almost nothing is known about their habits.

GUENTHER'S LONG SNOUTED DIK-DIK *Rhynchotragus*
guentheri (Thomas)   p. 257
F Dik-dik de Günther   G Günther Dik-dik, Rüsselantilope
Identification: Height at shoulder 14 in.; weight 8 lb. A tiny antelope, with the nose much elongated, forming a very distinct proboscis, somewhat 'tapir-like'. General colour greyish fawn, coarsely grizzled above, gradually intergrading, but without any intermediate flank colour into the whitish underparts. Forehead and nose rufous fawn; cheeks light grey. Legs dull rufous. Horns very small (2½; 3¾), spike-like.

Female similar to the male, slightly larger, without horns.
Habitat: Bush and thickets. Map, p. 275.

KIRK'S/DAMARALAND LONG SNOUTED DIK-DIK

Rhynchotragus kirki (Günther)   p. 257

F Dik-dik de Kirk, D. du Damaraland   K Dikidiki, Suguya
G Zwerg-Rüsselantilope   A Damaralandse Bloubokkie

Identification: Height at shoulder 14–16 in.; weight 10–12 lb. A very
small antelope, with the nose moderately elongated, forming a proboscis
of medium size. General colour from grizzled grey to brown above (hairs
pale at their base, then black and finally rufous). Head, neck and shoulder
washed with pale rufous. A whitish ring around the eye. Flanks and limbs
pale fawn. Underparts whitish. Legs rufous fawn. Horns small (2¾; 4).

Female similar to the male, slightly larger, without horns.

Intraspecific variation: The intensity of coloration depends largely on the
humidity of the habitat. Paler coloured races are to be found in desert or
semi-desert areas (e.g. *minor* in northern Kenya), and darker in more
humid country (e.g. *hindei* and *cavendishi*, central Kenya, Tanzania). The
Damaraland Dik-dik (*damarensis*) (Damaraland and Kaokoveld to the
Cunene River, South-West Africa, south-western Angola) sometimes considered as a full species, is separated by a broad gap in the distribution
from the other forms. It is larger than the northern representatives, and
has the flanks pale rufous.

Habitat: Bush and thickets. Map, p. 275.

SALT'S/PHILLIPS'S DIK-DIK   *Madoqua saltiana* (Desmarest)

(and allies)   p. 257

F Dik-dik de Phillips   G Windspielantilope, Rotbauchdikdik

Identification: Height at shoulder 14–16 in.; weight 6–8 lb. A tiny, graceful
antelope, with the nose only slightly elongated, large eyes, and very thin
legs, the hindlegs being much longer than the forelegs. Blaze, forehead
(generally), and back of ears bright rufous; on the forehead, a brush-like
crest of erectile hairs. Around the eye, a conspicuous white ring; in front
of the eye, a black bare patch (glandular area). Neck and back often
grizzled grey, the coat rather thick and harsh; flanks bright cinnamon
rufous, the coat less thick, soft and more sleek. The extent of this colour
varies very much, encroaching more or less on the flanks, the neck and
even the back. Underparts white, sometimes washed with fulvous. Limbs
rich rufous to fulvous. Tail minute, of the same colour as the back. Horns
very small (2; 3½), spike-like.

Female similar to the male, slightly larger, without horns.

Intraspecific variation: A number of races have been described according
to the extent of the rufous coloration, particularly on the sides of body;
some of them are often ranked as full species, but at the present stage, it
seems better to consider them as belonging to one species. *Gubanensis*

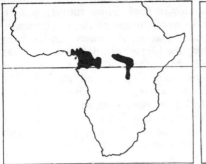

Bates's Pygmy Antelope, p. 260

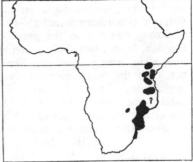

Suni, p. 262

Oribi, p. 262

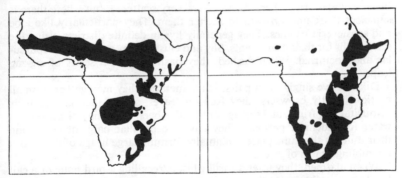

Klipspringer, p. 263

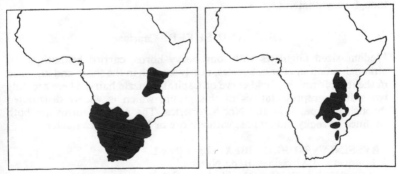

Steenbok, p. 264

Sharpe's Grysbok, p. 266

(coastal lowlands of northern Somalia to French Somaliland)—largely grey, only a narrow band on the lower flank being rufous; *phillipsi* (interior of northern Somalia)—flanks widely bright rufous or cinnamon, in strong contrast to the grey back; *piacentinii* (coastal lowlands of Somalia, from Mogadiscio to Obbia) the greyest of all, the neck, flanks and thighs being grizzled grey like the back; forehead grey, only a rufous patch on the nose; no conspicuous white ring around the eye. The populations of the Ethiopian highlands among which several forms (? valid species) have been described (*erlangeri, hararensis, saltiana, swaynei*) are characterised by having the upperparts suffused with rufous to a variable extent; some are mostly rufous; the back has a very slight greyish hue which darkens the colour; neck often more distinctly grey.

Habitat: Bush and thickets. Map, p. 275.

Habits of Dik-diks: Dik-dik live in bush country, particularly in acacia bush, dry and arid, where the trees are very scattered, but where there is sufficient thick undergrowth to shelter them. They particularly like aloe and sansieveria patches. They generally live in definite districts, using the same paths for their movements. Shy and elusive, they are mostly crepuscular and nocturnal. When flushed, they dash away in a series of zig-zag leaps.

Dik-dik live singly or in pairs, but sometimes they may gather in small parties. Mostly browsers, they feed on leaves, shoots (acacias are their favourite) and fruits, and dig up roots and tubers. They may dispense with water for indefinite periods. They have the peculiar habit of depositing their dung at the same place, eventually forming large heaps of droppings resembling grains of rice.

When alarmed, they utter a shrill whistle, recalling a bird note, or a call like 'zik . . . zik', hence their common name.

Owing to their secretive life, dik-dik are often difficult to observe, though very numerous.

IBEX AND SHEEP: Caprinae

Medium-sized ungulates with long heavy horns, carried by both sexes, although much smaller in females, nearly smooth in the sheep and knobbed in the ibex, forming a bold curve or a spiral. Muzzle hairy. There are only two African representatives of this group, which is widely distributed through Europe, Asia and North America. The African forms are both confined to rocky mountains, with a more or less desert character.

ABYSSINIAN/NUBIAN IBEX *Capra ibex* L.   p. 273
F Bouquetin d'Abyssinie, B. de Nubie
G Abessinischer Steinbok, Nubischer Steinbok
Identification: Height at shoulder 27–43 in.; weight 180–260 lb. A wild goat,

easily recognised by its general features, more lightly built that the related Palaearctic species. General colour brownish or yellowish fawn, with a blackish stripe along the back and a darker band across the shoulders. A long blackish beard. Chin and underparts whitish. Limbs conspicuously blackish and white. Tail short with a brush-like tuft of stiff black hairs. Horns very long, flattened sideways, forming a semi-circle, curving upwards, backwards, then downwards, with transverse knobs throughout their length except at their tip.

Female similar to the male, but paler, without beard, and with horns very short.

Intraspecific variation: Two subspecies, both representatives of the Palaearctic Ibex, are found in Africa: the Abyssinian Ibex (*walie*) (Ethiopia) is larger and heavier, darker chestnut brown in colour, with a shorter beard and shorter, thicker, more massive horns (40; 45). The Nubian Ibex (*nubiana* and allies) (Red Sea hills of the Sudan and Eritrea, Upper Egypt, Nubia; Sinai, Arabia) is smaller, lighter coloured with a longer beard and horns longer and less massive (43; 47½).

Habitat: Also south-west Asia, from Sinai to Hadhramaut. The Nubian Ibex lives at rather low altitude, between 600 and 6,000 feet, in very dry desert mountains, deep valleys and steep cliffs. The Abyssinian Ibex lives in high mountains, at altitudes between 7,500 and 13,500 feet, chiefly below 9,500 feet, in a more humid habitat, and takes refuge among bush, forest and upland vegetation. Map, p. 275.

Habits: The African representatives of the ibex live in small herds; males are often solitary. They feed until the sun grows warm, then take refuge in a cave or under an overhang, where females drop their young.

The Nubian Ibex feeds on various desert bushes and grasses. The Abyssinian Ibex, which lives side by side with Klipspringer, often in company with them, disposes of a larger amount of vegetable matter and particularly browses on giant heath, standing like a goat on its hind legs.

Both are badly threatened as a result of uncontrolled hunting. Probably no more than 300 Nubian Ibex, and 150 Abyssinian Ibex are left. If well protected, their populations could increase, for breeding seems satisfactory.

BARBARY SHEEP *Ammotragus lervia* (Pallas) p. 273
(Arui or Audad)
F Moufflon à manchettes G Mähnenschaf

Identification: Height at shoulder 40 in.; weight up to 250 lb. The only African Wild Sheep, peculiar in having some relationship with the goats; recognised by a short upright mane from neck to middle of back, and a well developed fringe of long soft hairs on the throat, chest and forelegs, enveloping the forequarters and hanging like an apron in front of the animal. A well developed beard under the throat. General colour uniform warm sandy brown, lighter on the underparts. Tail very long, reaching to the hocks, thickly haired. Horns (28; 34⅝) very thick, circular in section,

Plate 43　　　　　　　**GRYSBOK, ORIBI and allies**

1. **BEIRA** *Dorcatragus megalotis*　　　　　　*page* 267
   Grey, with pinkish hue; dark band along flank; tail
   short and bushy.

2. **STEENBOK** *Raphicerus campestris*　　　　　264
   Uniform bright rufous fawn.

3. **CAPE GRYSBOK** *R. melanotis*　　　　　266
   Rufous brown, strongly grizzled with white above;
   buffy below.

4. **SHARPE'S GRYSBOK** *R. sharpei*　　　　266
   Rich rufous fawn, speckled with white, above; white
   below.

5. **ORIBI** *Ourebia ourebi*　　　　　262
   Bright fawn, sharply contrasting with white belly;
   rounded patch of dark naked skin below ear.

6. **KLIPSPRINGER** *Oreotragus oreotragus*　　　263
   Short, conique head; olive yellow, largely speckled with
   grey; ears conspicuously bordered with black; blunt hoof
   tips.

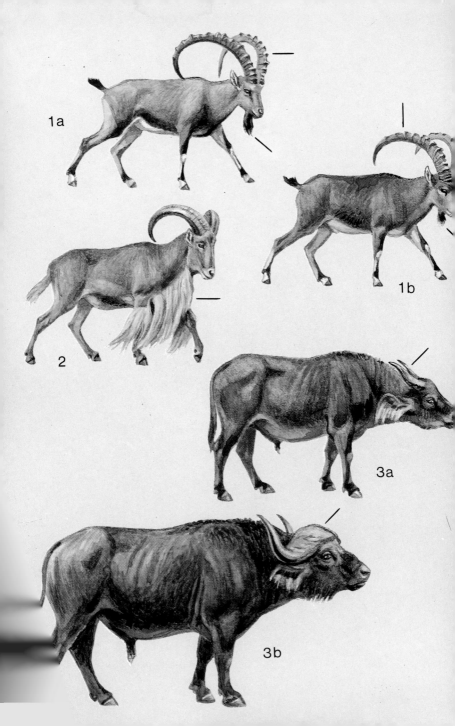

273

IBEX, SHEEP, BUFFALO **Plate 44**

1. **IBEX** *Capra ibex* *page* 270
Horns very long, semi-circular, with transverse knobs.

1a. **NUBIAN IBEX** *C. i. nubiana* 271
Light brown; beard long.

1b. **ABYSSINIAN IBEX** *C. i. walie* 271
Dark chestnut brown; beard short.

2. **BARBARY SHEEP** *Ammotragus lervia* 271
Fringe of long hairs on foreparts, apron-like.

3. **AFRICAN BUFFALO** *Syncerus caffer* 274
Massive, ox-like.

3a. **DWARF FOREST BUFFALO** *S. c. nanus* 274
Smaller; reddish; horns less massive, set apart at
base, curving backwards, not downwards.

3b. **CAPE BUFFALO** *S. c. caffer* 276
Larger; blackish; horns heavy, in close contact at
base, curving at first downwards, with tip upwards.

close at their base, curving evenly upwards, backwards, outwards and then downwards and inwards in a semi-circle over the neck; marked with many strong transverse wrinkles in younger individuals, but with a tendency to disappear through wear with age until they are almost smooth.

Female smaller and lighter with a reduced fringe of hairs, and horns less developed.

Habitat: Rocky dry mountains and broken country of the Saharan zone. Map, p. 276.

Habits: Barbary Sheep live in family parties with an adult ram, several ewes and the youngsters. Herds of 3–6 head are the average, but may be larger, up to 20 at the end of the dry season. Old males are often solitary and so are pregnant females.

They are very agile climbers and jumpers, and are almost invisible against the rocks when they remain motionless, owing to the similarity of the colour of their coat. Their hearing is very acute.

They spend the warmest part of the day in shelters among the rocks and cliffs and come down to the valley to graze at night. They feed on the same desert plants as gazelle, and like a goat stand on their hind legs to browse or collect fruits (*Acacia, Calotropis*). They are able to resist drought by feeding on some plants (*Rumex*), but come to drink at water holes when possible.

BUFFALO: Bovinae

Very large, heavy animals, with cattle-like features, massive body and stout limbs. Muzzle large, broad, bare and moist. Horns very massive. Only one African representative; others in Asia and North America.

AFRICAN BUFFALO *Syncerus caffer* (Sparrman) p. 273
F Buffle d'Afrique   K Nyati, Mbogo   G Afrikanischer Büffel   A Buffel
Identification: Height at shoulder 40–67 in.; weight up to 700 lb. (forest) and 1,800 lb. (savanna). The only African mammal with the features of an ox. Heavily built, with stout strong limbs, a rather short neck, a broad naked muzzle, large ears. Body sparsely covered with hairs in adults (well haired in young individuals). Tail long with a terminal tuft. Horns heavy, with massive base, carried by both sexes, less well developed in females than in males. Size, general coloration, and shape of horns very variable.

Young generally browner or redder.

Intraspecific variation: The systematics of buffalo have given rise to much discussion owing to the great variability of the animals. For practical reasons it is best to consider them as monospecific, though they probably derive from two different types which intergrade on a large scale. These types are as follows:

DWARF FOREST BUFFALO (*nanus*) (West and Central African forests); lightly built and smaller (height at shoulder 40–47 in.); hair fairly thick;

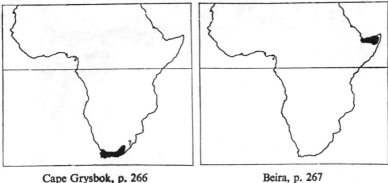

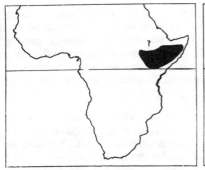

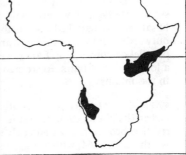

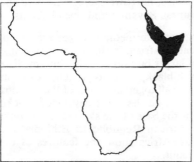

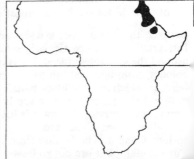

Cape Grysbok, p. 266

Beira, p. 267

Guenther's Dik-dik, p. 267

Damaraland & Kirk's Dik-dik, p. 268

Salt's & Phillips's Dik-dik, p. 268

Abyssinian & Nubian Ibex, p. 270

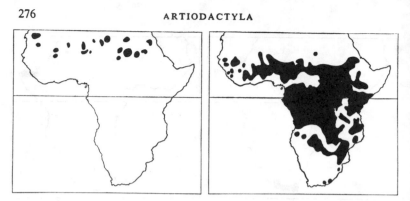

Barbary Sheep, p. 271   African Buffalo, p. 274

colour reddish or even bright red, darker in old bulls. Horns relatively small (20; 29¼), set widely apart at their base, lacking the frontal bosses; basal section flattened and in the same plane as the forehead, curving outwards, backwards and upwards, never downwards; terminal section parallel or converging. Ears never partly hidden behind the horns, with a long fringe of hairs. Restricted to dense forests, in lowlands as well as in mountains.

CAPE BUFFALO (*caffer*). (Southern Africa). Heavily built and much larger (height at shoulder up to 67 in.). General colour blackish (more reddish brown in cows and calves). Horns very heavy (36; 53; greatest width outside, 64) with a rugged surface for the basal third, and in close contact at their base; spreading outwards and curving downwards, well below the base of the skull, then narrowing as they curve upwards and inwards (in cows, horns are less massive, narrower across the base and not so wide across the outermost curve). Savanna and open habitats.

Between these two types a wide range of intermediate stages are found. Intergrading occurs particularly in Central Africa. In the forested savanna, around the Congolese forest, herds of larger buffalo showing intermediate colours, from light reddish to brownish black, are to be found, as well as herds in which red and black buffalo live all together. Most of the savanna buffalo have horns like the Cape Buffalo, but less well developed, not so heavy, never curving downwards below the base of the skull (*aequinoctialis* and allies, from Chad and Central African Republic to Ethiopia and eastern Congo). The buffalo from East Africa show the features of the Cape Buffalo, but are not so heavily built.

Habitat: Buffalo show a wide range of ecological adaptation, living from the dense forest (seldom in high forest, and more frequently in secondary growth and clearings) to open plains, interspersed with bushes and patches of forest; also in mountains, up to 13,000 feet. Never found in the driest areas nor far from water. Map, p. 276.

Habits: In forest, buffalo live in small herds, mostly of 3–4, sometimes up to 10 head, even more where clearings occur. In open habitat they become very gregarious and may be found in herds of several hundreds, up to 2,000. Herds are dominated by a master bull, and generally led by an old female. When the herd is grazing, scouts give warning of any danger. Old bulls may live by themselves or associate in small groups, as do wounded animals.

Sight is poor and hearing rather poor, but scent is much developed. Buffalo are silent animals, except during the mating season when they utter grunts and hoarse bellows. They have a bad reputation of deliberate savagery among hunters all over the world. Indeed, they can be very dangerous when cornered or wounded, but if unmolested they are placid animals. Bulls fight fiercely at rutting season.

Buffalo are mostly nocturnal, except in protected areas. They remain hidden among dense vegetation during the heat of the day, preferably near water; they come out to drink and feed at dusk and during the night, then come back to ruminate. They are sedentary.

Primarily grazers, they feed on grasses, even the coarsest; they may also browse on leaves, small twigs and young shoots, particularly in forested areas. They are very voracious. Water is essential to them and, like cattle, they must drink each day, a strict limitation of their distribution. They are also very fond of wallowing in muddy shallow pools.

The gestation period is 330–345 days.

Their principal natural enemy is the lion, but crocodiles occasionally prey on them when they are crossing rivers.

Buffalo are still numerous and the vitality of the populations is great almost all over their range. They were severely struck by the various outbreaks of rinderpest in the 1890s, and in some places never recovered their former status. But in some East African districts, they are commoner now than in former times.

BIBLIOGRAPHY

There is no room here to list all the publications dealing with African mammals. We here list a few of the more important books arranged according to the geographical area covered by them.

General

ALLEN, G. M. 1939. A Checklist of African Mammals, *Bull. Mus. Comp. Zool.* 83, Cambridge, USA.

BEST, G. A., F. EDMOND-BLANC and R. COURTENAY WITTING (Editors) 1962. Rowland Ward's *Records of Big Game*. XIth edn. Africa. With two addendum lists. London (Rowland Ward).

HALTENORTH, TH. and W. TRENSE. 1956. *Das Grosswild der Erde und seine Trophäen*. Bonn (Bayerischer Landwirtschaftsverlag).

LYDEKKER, R. 1926. *The Game Animals of Africa*. 2nd ed. London (Rowland Ward).

SCLATER, P. L. and O. THOMAS. 1894–1900. *The Book of Antelopes*. 4 vols. London (R. H. Porter).

SIDNEY, J. 1965. *The Past and Present Distribution of some African Ungulates*. London (Zoological Society of London).

West Africa

BIGOURDAN, J. and R. PRUNIER. 1937. *Les Mammifères sauvages de l'Ouest africain et leur Milieu*. Montrouge.

DEKEYSER, P. L. 1955. *Les Mammifères de l'Afrique noire française*. 2nd ed. Dakar (IFAN).

MALBRANT, R. and A. MACLATCHY. 1949. *Faune de l'Equateur africain français. II. Mammifères*. Paris (Lechevalier).

ROSEVEAR, D. R. 1953. *Checklist and Atlas of Nigerian Mammals*. Lagos (Nigerian Government).

Central Africa

MALBRANT, R. 1952. *Faune du Centre africain français (Mammifères et Oiseaux)*. 2nd ed. Paris (Lechevalier).

Publications de l'Institut des Parcs Nationaux du Congo belge et du Ruanda-Urundi. Brussels.

SCHOUTEDEN, H. 1944. De Zoogdieren van Belgisch-Congo en van Ruanda-Urundi. Tervuren. (*Ann. Mus. Belg. Congo.*)

SCHOUTEDEN, H. 1948. Faune du Congo belge et du Ruanda-Urundi. I. Mammifères. Tervuren. (*Ann. Mus. Belg. Congo.*)

East Africa

BERE, R. M. 1962. *The Wild Mammals of Uganda*. London (Longmans).

BROCKLEHURST, H. C. 1931. *Game Animals of the Sudan*. London (Gurney and Jackson).

DRAKE-BROCKMAN, R. E. 1910. *The Mammals of Somaliland*. London (Hurst and Blackett).

FUNAIOLI, U. 1957. *Fauna e Caccia in Somalia*. Mogadiscio (Gov. della Somalia).

MABERLY, C. T. A. 1962. *Animals of East Africa*. Cape Town (Howard Timmins).

278

ROOSEVELT, TH. and E. HELLER. 1915. *Life-histories of African Game Animals.* 2 vols. London (J. Murray).

SWYNNERTON, G. H. and R. W. HAYMAN. 1951. A Checklist of the Land Mammals of the Tanganyika territory and the Zanzibar Protectorate. *J.E. Afr. N.H. Soc.* 20.

WILLIAMS, JOHN G. 1967. *A Field Guide to the National Parks of East Africa.* London (Collins).

ZAMMARANO, V. T. 1930. Le Colonie italiane di diretto dominio. *Fauna e Caccia.* Rome (Min. delle Colonie).

Southern Africa

ANSELL, W. F. H. 1960. *Mammals of Northern Rhodesia.* Lusaka (Government Printer).

ELLERMAN, J. R., T. C. S. MORRISON-SCOTT and R. W. HAYMAN. 1953. *Southern African Mammals. 1758 to 1951: a reclassification.* London (Brit. Mus. Nat. Hist.).

HILL, J. E. and T. D. CARTER. 1941. The Mammals of Angola, Africa. New York. *(Bull. Am. Mus. Nat. Hist.* 78.)

MABERLY, C. T. A. 1963. *The Game Animals of Southern Africa.* Johannesburg (Nelson).

ROBERTS, A. 1951. *The Mammals of South Africa.* Cape Town (Central News Agency).

SHORTRIDGE, G. C. 1934. *The Mammals of South West Africa.* London (Heinemann).

SMITHERS, R. H. N. 1966. *The Mammals of Rhodesia. Zambia and Malawi.* London (Collins).

INDEX

The figures in italics refer to the pages opposite which the illustrations appear. The other figures refer to the description in the text. The pages on which the corresponding maps of distribution appear are indicated in the text under the heading "Habitat".

Aardvark, 150
Aardwolf, 135, *113*
Acinonyx jubatus, 145, *140*
Addax, 200, *188*
Addax nasomaculatus, 200, *188*
Aepyceros melampus, 234, *225*
Alcelaphus buselaphus, 218, *208*
   caama, 221, *208*
   lichtensteini, 222, *208*
Allenopithecus nigroviridis, 56, *64*
Ammodorcas clarkei, 233, *225*
Ammotragus lervia, 271, *273*
Angwantibo, 40, *52*
Anomalurops beecrofti, 28, *48*
Anomalurus derbianus, 28, *48*
   erythronotus, 28, *48*
   fulgens, 28, *48*
   peli, 28, *48*
   pusillus, 28, *48*
Antbear, 150
Antelope, Bates's Pygmy, 260, *257*
   Giant Sable, 206
   Roan, 204, *188*
   Royal, 260, *257*
   Sable, 205, *188*
Antidorcas marsupialis, 248, *240*
Aonyx capensis, 108, *85*
   congica, 106, *85*
Arctocebus calabarensis, 40, *52*
Arui, 271
Ass, Wild, 159, *141*
Atelerix albiventris, 17, *32*
Atherurus, 34, *49*
Atilax paludinosus, 120, *96*
Audad, 271

Baboon, Anubis, 44, *53*
   Chacma, 44, *53*
   Gelada, 47, *53*
   Western, 43, *53*

Yellow, 44, *53*
Badger, Honey, 105
Bdeogale crassicauda, 118, *97*
   nigripes, 117, *96*
Beira, 267, *272*
Blesbok, 227, *209*
Boar, Wild, 173, *161*
Bongo, 190, *177*
Bontebok, 227, *209*
Boocercus euryceros, 190, *177*
Buffalo, African, 274, *273*
   Cape, 276, *273*
   Dwarf Forest, 274, *273*
Bunolagus monticularis, 21
Bushbuck, 198, *181*
Bush-pig, 178, *161*

Callitrix, 72
Canis adustus, 91, *81*
   aureus, 91, *81*
   mesomelas, 94, *81*
   simensis, 94, *81*
Capra ibex, 270, *273*
Caracal, 138, *132*
Cat, African Wild, 136, *132*
   Black-footed, 137, *132*
   Golden, 138, *133*
   Sand, 136, *132*
   Swamp, 136, *132*
Cephalophus caeruleus, 254
   callipygus, 252, *256*
   dorsalis, 253, *256*
   jentinki, 250, *241*
   leucogaster, 253, *256*
   maxwelli, 254
   monticola, 254, *241*
   natalensis, 253, *256*
   niger, 250, *241*
   nigrifrons, 254, *256*
   ogilbyi, 254, *256*

Cephalophus (*contd.*)
  rufilatus 252, *241*
  silvicultor 250, *241*
  spadix, 250, *241*
  zebra, 252, *241*
Cercocebus albigena, 56, *60*
  aterrimus, 54, *60*
  galeritus, 54, *60*
  torquatus, 54, *60*
Cercopithecus aethiops, 71, *64*
  ascanius, 62, *61*
  cephus, 57, *61*
  diana, 67, *64*
  erythrogaster, 58, *61*
  erythrotis, 58, *61*
  hamlyni, 68, *64*
  l'hoesti, 68, *64*
  mitis, 63, *64*
  mona, 66, *64*
  neglectus, 67, *64*
  nictitans, 63, *61*
  petaurista, 62, *61*
Ceratotherium simum, 169, *160*
Cheetah, 145, *140*
Chevrotain, Water, 179, *257*
Chimpanzee, 88, *80*
  Pygmy, 89, *80*
Choeropsis liberiensis, 172, *160*
Civet, African, 109, *85*
  Aquatic, 117, *92*
  Tree, 110
  Two-spotted Palm, 110, *92*
Colobus abyssinicus, 77, *65*
  angolensis, 76, *65*
  badius, 78, *65*
  pennanti, 78, *65*
  polykomos, 76, *65*
  satanas, 78, *65*
  verus, 82, *65*
Colobus, Abyssinian Black-and-white,
    77, *65*
  Angolan Black-and-white, 76, *65*
  Black, 78, *65*
  Olive, 82, *65*
  Red, 78, *65*
  Western Black-and-white, 76, *65*
  Western Red, 78, *65*
Connochaetes gnou, 231, *224*
  taurinus, 230, *224*
Cricetomys spp., 30, *49*

Crocuta crocuta, 129, *113*
Crossarchus alexandri, 124
  ansorgei, 124
  obscurus, 123, *97*
Cusimanse, 123
Cynictis penicillata, 126, *97*

Damaliscus dorcas, 227, *209*
  hunteri, 228, *209*
  korrigum, 226, *209*
  lunatus, 227, *209*
Dassie, Rock, 152, *224*
  Tree, 154, *224*
  Yellow-spotted, 153, *224*
Dendrohyrax arboreus, 154, *224*
Dibatag, 233, *225*
Diceros bicornis, 166, *160*
Dik-dik, Damaraland, 268
  Guenther's Long Snouted, 267, *257*
  Kirk's Long Snouted, 268, *257*
  Phillips's, 268, *257*
  Salt's, 268
Dog, Hunting, 101
  Wild, 101, *113*
Dologale dybowskii, 122, *112*
Dorcatragus megalotis, 267, *272*
Drill, 50, *53*
Dugong, 147
Dugong dugon, 147
Duiker, Abbott's, 250, *241*
  Banded, 252, *241*
  Bay, 253, *256*
  Black, 250, *241*
  Black-fronted, 254, *256*
  Black-striped, 253
  Blue, 254, *241*
  Bush, 259
  Gabon, 253, *256*
  Grey, 259
  Grimm's, 259, *256*
  Harvey's, 253
  Jentink's, 250, *241*
  Ogilby's, 254, *256*
  Peters's, 252, *256*
  Red, 253, *256*
  Red-flanked, 252, *241*
  White-bellied, 253
  Yellow-backed, 250, *241*
  Zanzibar, 253

Edmi, 242
Eland, Cape, 187, *177*
  Giant, 186, *177*
  Livingstone's, 187
Elephant, African, 155
Elephant-shrew, Chequered, 18, *32*
  Four-toed, 18, *32*
Epixerus ebii, 24, *33*
Equus asinus, 159, *141*
  burchelli, 162, *141*
  grevyi, 159, *141*
  zebra, 165, *141*
Erinaceus frontalis, 17, *32*
Erythrocebus patas, 73, *60*
Euoticus elegantulus, 41, *52*

Felis aurata, 138, *133*
  caracal, 138, *132*
  chaus, 136, *132*
  libyca, 136, *132*
  margarita, 136, *132*
  nigripes, 137, *132*
  serval, 137, *133*
Fennec, 100, *84*
Fennecus zerda, 100, *84*
Fox, Bat-eared, 101, *84*
  Cape, 100, *84*
  Pale, 98, *84*
  Red, 95, *81*
  Rüppell's, 95, *84*
  Sand, 98, *84*
  Semien, 94, *81*
Funisciurus lemniscatus, 24, *33*
  pyrrhopus, 24, *33*

Galago, Allen's, 41, *52*
  Dwarf, 42, *52*
  Lesser, 40, *52*
  Needle-clawed, 41, *52*
  Thick-tailed, 40, *52*
Galago alleni, 41, *52*
  crassicaudatus, 40, *52*
  senegalensis, 40, *52*
Galagoides demidovi, 42, *52*
Gazella cuvieri, 242
  dama, 236, *225*
  dorcas, 239, *240*
  granti, 238, *225*
  leptoceros, 244, *240*

  pelzelni, 242, *240*
  rufifrons, 245, *240*
  soemmeringi, 237, *225*
  spekei, 245, *240*
  thomsoni, 246, *240*
  tilonura, 245
Gazelle, Addra, 236
  Atlas, 242
  Clarke's, 233
  Dama, 236, *225*
  Dorcas, 239, *240*
  Flabby-nosed, 245
  Giraffe, 232
  Grant's, 238, *225*
  Heuglin's, 245
  Isabelline, 239
  Loder's, 244, *240*
  Mhorr, 236
  Mongalla, 246
  Pelzeln's, 242, *240*
  Peters's, 238
  Red-fronted, 245, *240*
  Red-necked, 236
  Rhim, 244, *240*
  Soemmering's, 237, *225*
  Speke's, 245, *240*
  Thomson's, 246, *240*
Genet, Abyssinian, 115, *92*
  Common, 114, *93*
  Forest, 115, *93*
  Giant, 115, *93*
  Large-spotted, 114, *93*
  Small-spotted, 114, *93*
  Villiers', 115, *92*
Genetta abyssinica, 115, *92*
  genetta, 114, *93*
  pardina, 115, *93*
  servalina, 114, *93*
  tigrina, 114, *93*
  victoriae, 115, *93*
  villiersi, 115, *92*
Gemsbok, 202, *188*
Gerenuk, 232, *225*
Giraffa camelopardalis, 182, *176*
Giraffe, 182, *176*
  Baringo, 183, *176*
  Reticulated, 183, *176*
Gnu, Brindled, 230, *224*
  White-bearded, 230, *224*
  White-tailed, 231, *224*

Gorilla, 83, *80*
Gorilla gorilla, 83, *80*
Grysbok, Cape, 266, *272*
  Sharpe's, 266, *272*
Guereza, 77

Hamadryas, 43, *53*
Hare, Abyssinian, 21
  Bushman, 21
  Cape, 20
  Crawshay's, 20, *49*
  Red Rock, 21
  Southern Bush, 21
  Southern Scrub, 21
  Spring, 29, *49*
Hartebeest, Bubal, 218, *208*
  Coke's 220, *208*
  Hunter's, 228, *209*
  Jackson's 220, *208*
  Lelwel, 220
  Lichtenstein's, 222, *208*
  Red, 221, *208*
  Swayne's, 220, *208*
  Tora, 220
Hedgehog, Desert, 17
  Long-eared, 17
  Southern African, 17, *32*
  Tropical African, 17, *32*
Helioscirus gambianus, 24, *33*
  rufobrachium, 26, *33*
Helogale parvula, 123, *112*
Hemiechinus auritus, 17
Herpestes ichneumon, 121, *96*
  naso, 120, *97*
  pulverulentus, 121, *112*
  sanguineus, 122, *112*
Heterohyrax brucei, 153, *224*
Hippopotamus, 171, *160*
  Pigmy, 172, *160*
Hippopotamus amphibius, 171, *160*
Hippotragus, equinus, 204, *188*
  niger, 205, *188*
Hirola, 228
Hog, Giant Forest, 179, *161*
  Red River, 178
Hyaena, Brown, 134, *113*
  Spotted, 129, *113*
  Striped, 134, *113*
Hyaena brunnea, 134, *113*
  hyaena, 134, *113*

Hyemoschus aquaticus, 179, *257*
Hylochoerus meinertzhageni, 179, *161*
Hystrix, 34, *49*

Ibex, Abyssinian, 270, *273*
  Nubian, 270, *273*
Ichneumia albicauda, 117, *96*
Ichneumon, 121
Ictonyx striatus, 104, *112*
Idiurus zenkeri, 28, *48*
Impala, 234, *225*

Jackal, Black-backed, 94, *81*
  Common, 91, *81*
  Side-striped, 91, *81*

Klipspringer, 263, *272*
Kob, 210, *189*
  Buffon's, 211
  Thomas's, 211, *189*
  White-eared, 211, *189*
Kobus defassa, 206, *189*
  ellipsiprymnus, 210, *189*
  kob, 210, *189*
  leche, 212, *192*
  megaceros, 214, *192*
  vardoni, 212, *189*
Korrigum, 226
Kudu, Greater, 191, *180*
  Lesser, 194, *180*

Lechwe, 212, *192*
  Black, 212, *192*
  Kafue, 212, *192*
  Nile, 214, *192*
  Red, 212, *192*
Leopard, 144, *140*
Lepus capensis, 20
  crawshayi, 20, *49*
  habessinicus, 21
  saxatilis, 21
Linsang, African, 116, *92*
Lion, 142, *140*
Litocranius walleri, 232, *225*
Lophiomys imhausi, 30, *49*
Loxodonta africana, 155
Lutra maculicollis, 108, *85*
Lycaon pictus, 101, *113*

Lynx, African, 138

Madoqua saltiana, 268, 257
Malbrouck, 72
Manatee, African, 148
Mandrill, 50, 53
Mangabey, Agile Crested, 60
  Black, 54, 60
  Crested, 54, 60
  Golden Bellied Crested, 60
  Grey-cheeked, 56, 60
  White-collared, 54, 60
Manis gigantea, 35, 32
  temmincki, 36
  tetradactyla, 36, 32
  tricuspis, 36, 32
Meerkat, Bushy-tailed, 126
  Grey, 128, 97
  Red, 126, 97
Mellivora capensis, 105, 85
Miopithecus talapoin, 57, 61
Mongoose, Alexander's, 124
  Angolan, 124
  Banded, 124, 97
  Black-legged, 117, 96
  Bushy-tailed, 118, 97
  Grey Cape, 121, 112
  Dark, 123, 97
  Dwarf, 123, 112
  Egyptian, 121, 96
  Gambian, 125, 112
  Greater Grey, 121
  Lesser, 122
  Long-snouted, 120, 97
  Marsh, 120, 96
  Meller's, 118, 96
  Pousargues', 122, 112
  Pygmy, 123
  Selous', 126, 97
  Slender, 122, 112
  Water, 120
  White-tailed, 117, 96
  Yellow, 126
Monkey, Allen's, 56, 64
  Black Cheeked White-nosed, 62, 61
  Blue, 63, 64
  Brazza's, 67, 64
  Diademed, 63
  Diana, 67, 64
  Greater White-nosed, 63, 61

Green, 71, 64
Grivet, 71
Lesser White-nosed, 62, 61
L'Hoest's, 68, 64
Mona, 66, 64
Moustached, 57, 61
Owl-faced, 68, 64
Putty-nosed, 63
Red, 73
Red-bellied, 58, 61
Red-eared Nose-spotted, 58, 61
Samango, 66
Sykes, 66
Tantalus, 72
Vervet, 71
Mungos gambianus, 125, 112
  mungo, 124, 97
Myosciurus pumilio, 26, 33

Nandinia binotata, 110, 92
Neotragus batesi, 260, 257
  pygmaeus, 260, 257
Nesotragus moschatus, 262, 257
Nisnas, 74
Nyala, 195, 180
  Mountain, 195, 180

Okapi, 184, 176
Okapia johnstoni, 184, 176
Oreotragus oreotragus, 263, 272
Oribi, 262, 272
Orycteropus afer, 150
Oryx beisa, 201, 188
  dammah, 201, 188
  gazella, 202, 188
Oryx, Beisa, 201, 188
  Fringe-eared, 202
  Scimitar-horned, 201, 188
  Tufted, 202
Osbornictis piscivora, 117, 92
Otocyon megalotis, 101, 84
Otter, Cape Clawless, 108, 85
  Congo Clawless, 106, 85
  Spotted-necked, 108, 85
Ourebia ourebi, 262, 272

Pan troglodytes, 88, 80
Pangolin, Cape, 36

Pangolin (cont.)
  Giant, 35, 32
  Long-tailed, 36, 32
  Tree, 36, 32
Panthera leo, 142, 140
  pardus, 144, 140
Papio anubis, 44, 53
  cynocephalus, 44, 53
  gelada, 47, 53
  hamadryas, 43, 53
  leucophaeus, 50, 53
  papio, 43, 53
  sphinx, 50, 53
  ursinus, 44, 53
Paracynictis selousi, 126, 97
Paraechinus aethiopicus, 17
Paraxerus palliatus, 33
Patas, 73, 60
Pedetes capensis, 29, 49
Pelea capreolus, 217. 193
Perodicticus potto, 38, 53
Petrodromus tetradactylus, 18, 32
Phacochoerus aethiopicus, 174, 161
Poecilictis libyca, 104, 112
Poecilogale albinucha. 105, 112
Poelagus marjorita, 22, 49
Poiana richardsoni, 116 92
Polecat, Striped 104
Porcupine, Brush-tailed, 34, 49
  Crested, 34, 49
Potamochoerus porcus, 178. 161
Potamogale velox 18, 32
Potto, Bosman's, 38, 52
  Golden, 40, 52
Procavia capensis, 152, 224
Pronolagus crassicaudatus, 21
Proteles cristatus, 135, 113
Protoxerus stangeri, 24, 33
Puku, 212, 189

Rabbit, African, 22, 49
Raphicerus campestris, 264, 272
  melanotis, 266, 272
  sharpei, 266, 272
Rat, Cane, 31, 49
  Giant, 30, 49
  Maned, 30, 49
Ratel, 105, 85
Redunca arundinum, 216. 193
  fulvorufula, 216, 193

  redunca, 215, 193
Reedbuck, Bohor, 215, 193
  Mountain. 216, 193
  Nagor, 215
  Southern, 216, 193
Rhebuck, Vaal, 217, 193
Rhinoceros, Black, 166, 160
  Hook-lipped, 166
  Square-lipped, 169
  White, 169, 160
Rhynchocyon cirnei, 18, 32
Rhynchogale melleri, 118, 96
Rhynchotragus guentheri, 267, 257
  kirki, 268, 257

Sassaby, 227, 209
Serval, 137, 133
  Small-spotted 138
Servaline, 138, 133
Sheep, Barbary, 271, 273
Shrew. Otter, 18, 32
Sitatunga, 196, 181
Springbuck, 248, 240
Squirrel, Beecroft's Flying, 28, 48
  Bush, 26, 33
  Flightless Scaly-tailed, 29, 48
  Four-striped 24, 33
  Fraser's Flying, 28, 48
  Gambian Sun, 24, 33
  Giant Forest, 24, 33
  Green, 26
  Lesser Flying, 28, 48
  Pallid ground, 27, 33
  Palm, 24, 33
  Pel's Flying, 28, 48
  Pygmy, 26, 33
  Pygmy Flying, 28, 48
  Red-backed Flying, 28, 48
  Red Flying, 28, 48
  Red-footed, 24, 33
  Red-legged Sun, 26, 33
  Striped, 24
  Striped Ground, 27, 33
  Sun, 24
Steenbok, 264, 272
Suni, 262 257
  Livingstone's, 262
Suricata suricatta, 128, 97
Suricate, 128, 97
Sus scrofa, 173, 161

Syncerus caffer, 274, *273*
Sylvicapra grimmia, 259, *256*

Talapoin, 57, *61*
Taurotragus derbianus, 186, *177*
  oryx, 187, *177*
Thryonomys spp., 31, *49*
  gregorianus, 31
  swinderianus, 31
Tiang, 226
Topi, 226, *209*
Tragelaphus angasi, 195, *180*
  buxtoni, 195, *180*
  imberbis, 194, *180*
  scriptus, 198, *181*
  spekei, 196, *181*
  strepsiceros, 191, *180*
Trichechus senegalensis, 148
Tsessebe, 227

Viverra civetta, 109, *85*
Vulpes chama, 100, *84*
  pallida, 98, *84*

rüppelli, 95, *84*
vulpes, 95, *81*

Warthog, 174, *161*
Waterbuck, Common, 210, *189*
  Defassa, 206, *189*
Weasel, Libyan Striped, 104, *112*
  White-naped, 105, *112*
Wildebeest, 230, *224*
Wolf, Abyssinian, 94

Xerus erythropus, 27, *33*
  rutilus, 27, *33*

Zebra, Burchell's, 162, *141*
  Chapman's, 164, *141*
  Grant's, 162, *141*
  Grévy's, 159, *141*
  Hartmann's, 165
  Mountain, 165, *141*
  Selous', 164
Zenkerella insignis, 29, *48*
Zorilla, 104, *112*